Raymund Schwager (L) and René Girard (R), Wiesbaden, 1994 (Photo courtesy of Herlinde Koelbl)

Violence, Desire, and the Sacred

Series Editors:
Scott Cowdell, Chris Fleming, and Joel Hodge

Volumes in the series:
Vol. 1. *Girard's Mimetic Theory Across the Disciplines*
edited by Scott Cowdell, Chris Fleming, and Joel Hodge

Vol. 2. *René Girard and Sacrifice in Life, Love, and Literature*
edited by Scott Cowdell, Chris Fleming, and Joel Hodge

Vol. 3. *Mimesis, Movies, and Media*
edited by Scott Cowdell, Chris Fleming, and Joel Hodge

Vol. 4. *René Girard and Raymund Schwager: Correspondence 1974–1991*
edited by Scott Cowdell, Chris Fleming,
Joel Hodge, and Mathias Moosbrugger

Vol. 5. *Mimesis and Atonement: René Girard and
the Doctrine of Salvation* (forthcoming)
edited by Michael Kirwan SJ and Sheelah Treflé Hidden

René Girard and Raymund Schwager

Correspondence 1974–1991

Edited by

Scott Cowdell, Chris Fleming, Joel Hodge,
and Mathias Moosbrugger

Translated by

Chris Fleming and Sheelah Treflé Hidden

BLOOMSBURY ACADEMIC
NEW YORK • LONDON • OXFORD • NEW DELHI • SYDNEY

BLOOMSBURY ACADEMIC
Bloomsbury Publishing Inc
1385 Broadway, New York, NY 10018, USA

BLOOMSBURY, BLOOMSBURY ACADEMIC and the Diana logo
are trademarks of Bloomsbury Publishing Plc

First published in the United States of America 2016
Paperback edition published 2018

© Scott Cowdell, Chris Fleming, Joel Hodge, Mathias Moosbrugger, and
Contributors, 2016

English translation © Chris Fleming and Sheelah Treflé Hidden

Cover design: Catherine Wood

The translation reproduced in this volume is based on the original French correspondence between Raymund Schwager and René Girard, which is kept in the Raymund-Schwager-Archiv, Innsbruck (Austria). Prof. Józef Niewiadomski, Innsbruck, who manages the estate of Raymund Schwager SJ, which is held by the Swiss Province of the Society of Jesus, gave permission for this correspondence to be translated into English and published in the present volume. All other rights remain reserved.

All rights reserved. No part of this publication may be reproduced or transmitted in any form or by any means, electronic or mechanical, including photocopying, recording, or any information storage or retrieval system, without prior permission in writing from the publishers.

Bloomsbury Publishing Inc does not have any control over, or responsibility for, any third-party websites referred to or in this book. All internet addresses given in this book were correct at the time of going to press. The author and publisher regret any inconvenience caused if addresses have changed or sites have ceased to exist, but can accept no responsibility for any such changes.

No responsibility for loss caused to any individual or organization acting on or refraining from action as a result of the material in this publication can be accepted by Bloomsbury or the author.

Library of Congress Cataloging-in-Publication Data
Names: Girard, René, 1923-2015, author. | Schwager, Raymund, author. | Cowdell, Scott, editor.
Title: René Girard and Raymund Schwager : correspondence 1974-1991 / translated by Chris Fleming and Sheelah Treflâe Hidden ; edited by Scott Cowdell, Chris Fleming, Joel Hodge, and Mathias Moosbrugger.
Description: 1st [edition]. | New York : Bloomsbury Academic, 2016. | Series: Violence, desire, and the sacred | Includes bibliographical references and index. | Description based on print version record and CIP data provided by publisher; resource not viewed.
Identifiers: LCCN 2016031200 (print) | LCCN 2016012094 (ebook) | ISBN 9781501320491 (ePDF) | ISBN 9781501320484 (ePub) | ISBN 9781501320477 (hardcover : alk. paper)
Subjects: LCSH: Girard, René, 1923-2015–Correspondence. | Philosophers--United States--Correspondence. | Schwager, Raymund--Correspondence. | Theologians–Switzerland–Correspondence.
Classification: LCC B2430.G494 (print) | LCC B2430.G494 A4 2016 (ebook) | DDC 194–dc23
LC record available at https://lccn.loc.gov/2016031200

ISBN: HB: 978-1-5013-2047-7
PB: 978-1-5013-4176-2
ePub: 978-1-5013-2048-4
ePDF: 978-1-5013-2049-1

Series: Violence, Desire, and the Sacred

Typeset by Fakenham Prepress Solutions, Fakenham, Norfolk NR21 8NN

To find out more about our authors and books visit
www.bloomsbury.com and sign up for our newsletters.

In Memoriam
René Girard, 1923–2015
Raymund Schwager, SJ, 1935–2004

Contents

List of Contributors — viii

Editors' Introduction — ix

Beautiful Minds in Dialogue — 1
Karin Peter and Nikolaus Wandinger

Notes on the English Translation — 13

The Girard–Schwager Correspondence, 1974–1991 — 15

Publications Cited in the Correspondence — 189

Who's Who in the Correspondence — 199

Index — 201

List of Contributors

Scott Cowdell is Research Professor in Public and Contextual Theology at Charles Sturt University, Canberra, and Canon Theologian of the Canberra-Goulburn Anglican Diocese. His latest book is *René Girard and Secular Modernity: Christ, Culture, and Crisis* (University of Notre Dame Press, 2013).

Chris Fleming is Senior Lecturer in Philosophy and Anthropology at Western Sydney University. He is the author of *René Girard: Violence and Mimesis* (Polity, 2004).

Joel Hodge is Senior Lecturer in Systematic Theology at Australian Catholic University, Melbourne. He is the author of *Resisting Violence and Victimisation: Christian Faith and Solidarity in East Timor* (Ashgate, 2012).

Mathias Moosbrugger is a Postdoctoral Researcher in the Department of Systematic Theology at the University of Innsbruck, Austria, where he serves as Coordinator of the "Raymund Schwager: Dramatic Theology" research project. He is the author of *Die Rehabilitierung des Opfers: Zum Dialog zwischen René Girard und Raymund Schwager über die Angemessenheit der Rede vom Opfer im christlichen Kontext* (Innsbruck: Tyrolia, 2014).

Karin Peter is a Postdoctoral Researcher and Lecturer in Religious Education at the Department of Practical Theology, University of Vienna, Austria.

Sheelah Treflé Hidden is a Research Associate with the Heythrop Institute for Religion and Society at the University of London. She is the editor of *Jewish, Christian, and Islamic Mystical Perspectives on the Love of God* (Palgrave Macmillan, 2014) and co-editor of *Mimesis and Atonement: René Girard and the Doctrine of Salvation* (forthcoming in this series).

Nikolaus Wandinger is Associate Professor for Dogmatic Theology at the Department of Systematic Theology, University of Innsbruck, Austria.

Editors' Introduction

This correspondence provides a window into the formative years of René Girard's mimetic theory and Raymund Schwager's dramatic theology, in the last quarter of the twentieth century. It takes place between two convinced Catholic intellectuals. The older man was a French-American genius whose powerful synthesis of psychology, culture, and religion impressed and shaped the younger man—a Swiss Jesuit theologian, who built a base for developing and commending the mimetic theory at Innsbruck that is still going strong. Not only did Girard influence Schwager's project, which gradually developed into a systematically fully rendered model called dramatic theology,[1] but Schwager was a major influence on Girard as well.

Our volume presents all of the letters that have come to light. The essay "Beautiful Minds in Dialogue" sets out the provenance of these letters and the story of how a critical edition of the French originals was first published, with parallel German translation. We know that this set of extant letters does not represent the complete correspondence, and you will notice gaps in the flow of communication where some letters are missing. However, what we do have represents a sufficient tranche to establish the strong collaboration, mutual influence, and personal friendship that developed between Girard and Schwager.

In one of his deservedly well-known little treatises on the virtues, German philosopher Josef Pieper wrote that friends do not look at each other as lovers do. They hardly talk about their friendship as such, but focus instead on matters of mutual interest.[2] The correspondence between Raymund Schwager and René Girard represents, in this respect, more than the dialogue between a cultural theorist and a theologian, or simply a new resource for scholars of

---

[1] For this see Raymund Schwager, *Jesus in the Drama of Salvation: Toward a Biblical Doctrine of Redemption* (New York: Crossroad, 1999).
[2] Josef Pieper, *Über die Liebe* (München: Kösel, 1972), 171; *About Love* (Chicago: Franciscan Herald, 1974).

mimetic theory and theology. It is, above all, the documenting of a very rare thing: real intellectual friendship. Indeed, we have here a model of high-level intellectual exchange that is respectful but does not minimize differences. That said, the letters are also marked by a genuine expression of deepening mutual affection, from the first meeting at Avignon in 1975, to mountain walks in Austria, to Schwager's travels in the United States. What makes the letters exemplary from a scholarly point of view is the fact that, not only are we able to access (more or less clearly) the results of their dialogue in many articles, essays, and books, but we are able to observe the intellectual process. There are real questions, misunderstandings, controversies, and, from both men, a constant willingness to engage in finding answers to vital questions. It is a privilege to observe their ideas in the process of formation.

This correspondence covers the period in which mimetic theory came to be fully articulated for the first time, as set out in Girard's *Des choses cachées depuis la fondation du monde* (1978),[3] and began to wield its influence. The reception was initially marred by incomprehension, resistance, and various practical problems to do with translation and publishing, all of which make for interesting reading. There is a sense that Girard was relying on Schwager as a support and champion for his work, not least in theological circles. The Innsbruck honorary doctorate awarded to Girard in 1988, which his friend labored to bring off, is an important sign of how Schwager saw himself contributing.

A great deal of personal information is contained in the letters, which adds immensely to the picture that emerges of the times in which they were written. Schwager mentions stressful academic politics and Girard the settled happiness of his family life. They reflect ruefully on the plight of theology in general and, in particular, on postconciliar Catholicism both European and American. Both men regard the development of mimetic theory, in which they see themselves very much as collaborators, as of great potential benefit to theology. Nevertheless, Girard is as clear here, as elsewhere, that his eye is on the world and the future, not on any narrow church agenda. There is also some

---

[3] An English translation of this book, *Things Hidden since the Foundation of the World*, was published in 1987 (Stanford: Stanford University Press).

fun to be had at their expense. Both demonstrate the learned helplessness of a generation of male academics who—in their case, for much if not all of the time—had the luxury of secretarial assistance. We eavesdrop when, in the early 1980s, Girard becomes an initially reluctant but soon enthusiastic convert to word processing:

> Imagine a typewriter without a fixed spatial reference. You can work at any time on any part of the text, in all directions, add, delete, modify, correct as much as you want, add an entire book to the third line of the first, if that appeals to you, and everything is reformatted and organizes itself right before your eyes … .
> (Girard to Schwager, September 12, 1983)

The intellectual dimension being of foremost importance in this correspondence, we note some important aspects.

There is a phase of adjustment as Schwager, who was clearly impressed with Girard's *La violence et le sacré* (1972)[4] and eager to work through its theological implications, pursues various questions with Girard. Does the work of the cross bring not only *knowledge* of the scapegoat mechanism, but also incorporation into a new form of life? St. Paul and the law is another early focus. Questions concerning the precedence of the law are debated: does the law emerge from the sacrificial mechanism, as Girard would have it, or does it provide the seed of rivalry with God from which original sin and then sacrifice emerge?

In one form or another the issue of sin and freedom at the point of human origins resurfaced throughout the whole correspondence, receiving a resolution of sorts only in the important final letters of October 1991. There, we find tantalizing reflections about Henri de Lubac's *desiderium naturale videndi dei* and how such natural yearning for God might underpin Girard's account of "metaphysical desire," focused on the being of a model—albeit a yearning aborted by original sin. Schwager's important essay "Mimesis and Freedom," based on a presentation made in Provo, Utah, provided a focus as this conversation proceeded.[5] Here one sees Girard either finally answering

---

[4] An English translation of this book, *Violence and the Sacred*, was published in 1977 (Baltimore: Johns Hopkins University Press).
[5] Raymund Schwager, "Mimesis and Freedom," *Contagion* 21 (2014): 29–45.

his critics about the ontology of violence in his work, affirming the goodness of creation and the primal innocence of human beings, or else adapting his presentation of mimetic theory to gain acceptance in Catholic theological circles, depending on one's perspective—perhaps both. Schwager's attention to original sin in his own work, and Girard's sustained interest in questions of hominization, with one eye on Darwin and the other eye on theological orthodoxy, might indicate a mutually formative role in this exchange.

Another major issue between the two men concerned the category of sacrifice, and whether Girard ought to view it more positively. The development of their approach to this question, often in agreement, yet often not, is especially interesting for Girardians. Schwager wants to be able to reassure theologians that Girard does not dismiss this important soteriological and sacramental category. And, indeed, Schwager helps convince Girard that there is a difference between texts *structured* by sacrifice and others that *name and reveal* it. Hence a sacrifice of forced immolation is not the same as a sacrifice of voluntary consecration and self-giving. Girard was keen to preserve Christianity's anti-sacrificial distinctiveness against the then-fashionable homogenizing of religion. Schwager helped him achieve this while honoring an important dimension of Christian proclamation that Girard had neglected. A significant turning point for Girard was his admission in a 1993 interview that, in order to maintain his total dismissal of sacrifice, he had scapegoated the Epistle to the Hebrews.[6] In the correspondence we see this issue being pressed on him by Schwager some fifteen years earlier. There are, of course, other issues pursued: the relationship between science and religion, the structure of philosophical inquiry, and the charge brought against mimetic theory that it posits a "mono-causal" explanation of all cultural and religious phenomena.

Our thanks go to Karin Peter and Nikolaus Wandinger for permission to use their essay "Beautiful Minds in Dialogue,"[7] which is reproduced here in modified form. A more extensive German version of this essay, in two

---

[6] René Girard, "Violence, Difference, Sacrifice: A Conversation with René Girard" (with Rebecca Adams), *Religion and Literature* 25(2) (Summer 1993): 11–33. See also Girard's essay, published for the first time in German in a 1995 festschrift for Schwager, "Mimetic Theory and Theology," in *The One by Whom Scandal Comes* (East Lansing: Michigan State University Press, 2014), 33–45.

[7] Karin Peter and Nikolaus Wandinger, "Beautiful Minds in Dialogue," *Contagion* 21 (2014): 23–8.

parts, helped introduce the first publication of these letters in 2014, in the aforementioned version of the French text with a German translation, which was accompanied by expansive notes and critical apparatus. That publication constitutes volume six in the Herder edition of the *Collected Works* of Raymund Schwager (*Raymund Schwager Gesammelte Schriften*), which is being edited by a research group at the Innsbruck Faculty of Catholic Theology, following Fr. Schwager's untimely death in 2004.[8] Dr. Wandinger and Dr. Peter are the editors of that volume, and the critical edition of the correspondence in its original French that it incorporates forms the basis of this English translation. Our volume would simply not have been possible without their meticulous work.

The three editors of this Bloomsbury series, *Violence, Desire, and the Sacred*—Scott Cowdell, Chris Fleming, and Joel Hodge, who cofounded the Australian Girard Seminar—are honored to have the opportunity to publish this correspondence. A great debt of thanks is owed to Fr. Józef Niewiadomski, Schwager's successor as Dean of the Faculty of Catholic Theology at Innsbruck, who is also head of the *Gesammelte Schriften* research group, and Keeper of the Raymund Schwager Archive, in collaboration with Mathias Moosbrugger. Dr. Moosbrugger agreed to join our editorial team in a show of friendship and as a sign of fruitful synergy between our two centers of research in mimetic theory. In Girardian circles, Austria and Australia are close in more than name!

The English translation emerged in two stages. In 2010, Sheelah Treflé Hidden, from Heythrop College in London, produced a first rendering privately for a gathering of Girardian scholars, covering the letters that were in hand at the time. With this publication in view, Dr. Chris Fleming, whose *René Girard: Violence and Mimesis* remains the standard critical introduction first published in English,[9] translated the letters that had come to light subsequently and reworked the earlier translation. He and Sheelah Treflé Hidden have jointly provided "Notes on the English Translation." Mathias

---

[8] Raymund Schwager, *Briefwechsel mit René Girard*, ed. Nikolaus Wandinger and Karin Peter (Freiburg im Breisgau: Herder, 2014).
[9] See Robert Doran, "Editor's Introduction," in *Mimesis and Theory: Essays on Literature and Criticism, 1953–2005*, ed. Robert Doran (Stanford, CA: Stanford University Press, 2008), 294 n.6. See also Chris Fleming, *René Girard: Violence and Mimesis* (Cambridge: Polity, 2004).

Moosbrugger kindly adapted supporting documentation from the German edition, including the "Beautiful Minds" essay. Rosamund Dalziell and Scott Cowdell thoroughly reviewed the translation. For a grant supporting Dr. Dalziell's contribution, we thank the Public and Contextual Theology Research Centre at Charles Sturt University, Canberra, and its Director, Bishop Stephen Pickard. We are grateful to Herlinde Koelbl for her kind permission to reproduce two fine photographs of René Girard and Raymund Schwager that "bookend" the present volume, reminding us of Josef Pieper's aforementioned insight about friendship. Christopher Brennan has once again adorned our Bloomsbury series with his meticulous copyediting and indexing. Thanks, too, to Kim Storry in Fakenham for her project management. Finally, we owe a debt of gratitude to Haaris Naqvi at Bloomsbury in New York for his continuing interest and support.

Last but not least we express profound gratitude to our friends at *Imitatio*, a program of the San Francisco-based Thiel Foundation, for the financial support that made the preparation of this volume possible. To Lindy Fishburne, Jimmy Kaltreider, and to Dr. Trevor Cribben Merrill—who negotiated the arrangements during the 2015 COV&R Conference in St. Louis (involving some memorable sessions in a motorcycle memorabilia-themed bar)—we give a heartfelt thank you, and of course to Peter Thiel. We hope that the efforts, intellectual engagements, and new friendships that this volume represents are a sign that the Schwager–Girard friendship is extending its mimetic influence to the next generation.

As we were preparing the manuscript of this volume for press—indeed, while this Introduction was first being drafted—news came through from California that René Girard had died peacefully in his sleep early on the morning of November 4, 2015. It is a fitting thought for Christians that he and Fr. Schwager can now renew their friendship in that trinitarian embrace where all friendship will be perfected, every injustice will be put right, and every tear will be wiped away.

Scott Cowdell, Chris Fleming, Joel Hodge, and Mathias Moosbrugger
Canberra/Sydney/Melbourne/Innsbruck, April 2016

Beautiful Minds in Dialogue:
The Correspondence between René Girard and Raymund Schwager and the Story of its First Publication (with German Translation) in 2014[1]

Karin Peter and Nikolaus Wandinger

René Girard died in early November 2015, just short of his ninety-second birthday. It seems hard to believe for those of us who knew Raymund Schwager, SJ, the Professor of Dogmatic Theology at the University of Innsbruck and first President of the Colloquium on Violence and Religion (COV&R), that he has been gone now for twelve years. After his sudden and untimely death in 2004, Fr. Schwager's office had to be cleared out and, soon after this sad work had begun, it became clear that there were treasures to be retrieved: letters, typescripts, drafts for a book and several articles, along with other academic material. József Niewiadomski, who was Schwager's successor as Dean of the Faculty of Theology, decided to establish a Raymund Schwager Archive, and Niewiadomski's students Stefan Huber and Mathias Moosbrugger compiled the first inventory.[2]

One discovery was especially interesting: among the material were fifty-four letters from René Girard, dating from 1974 to 1991. It was obvious that they were half of an extensive, sustained dialogue, and the question was whether the other half of the correspondence could be obtained, too. That was not easy. At first, Girard claimed that he had none of this correspondence. Only after some thinking and searching did he find thirty-seven letters from

---

[1] This is an updated and edited version of an article published in *Contagion* 21 (2014): 23–7, based in turn on an essay in the 2014 French-German Herder edition of the Girard–Schwager correspondence.
[2] Cf. http://www.uibk.ac.at/systheol/schwagerdrama/schwager-archiv/ (accessed August 27, 2015).

Schwager in his garage in California—and he entrusted those to Wolfgang Palaver, who brought them to Innsbruck. Later on, Benoît Chantre, who is compiling the personal archive of René Girard at the *Bibliothèque nationale de France* in Paris, discovered more letters and delivered them to us. Finally, in March 2014, another ten letters were found. In the end, we have fifty-five letters that Schwager wrote to Girard, in addition to the fifty-four letters from Girard to Schwager. All of them are published in this volume. It is still evident that this is not their complete correspondence; especially from the years 1982 and 1983, when Girard lived in Paris, several letters are obviously absent. Nevertheless, what we have is a large chunk of the correspondence—and it contains enough material to make it worth examining more closely and presenting to the public.

Background

When we realized the importance of Schwager's academic estate, we set to work to formulate an application for a research grant to the Austrian Science Fund (FWF). This application was drafted by Józef Niewiadomski and Nikolaus Wandinger, with valuable input from the Innsbruck dramatic theology research group; the application was accepted on the first submission. This provided us with the necessary funds for a research project from January 2010 to August 2013. Mathias Moosbrugger was hired as the project's coordinator, assisted by Karin Peter and Simon de Keukelaere. Józef Niewiadomski directed the whole project, and Nikolaus Wandinger played a small part in the editing of the letters. We were happy that negotiations with the German publisher Herder were successful, so that the letters and Schwager's final, unfinished monograph *Dogma und dramatische Geschichte* ("Dogma and Dramatic History") could be published there. These are part of an eight-volume *Collected Works* (*Raymund Schwager Gesammelte Schriften*).[3] In 2014, two books resulting from the research project were published, followed by a

---

[3] Cf. http://www.herder.de/theologie/programm/index_html?par_onl_struktur=704728&onl_struktur=4092753 (accessed August 27, 2015).

separate volume with insightful commentaries from several authors on the correspondence as well as Schwager's last monograph.[4] In 2015 and 2016, four more volumes from the *Collected Works* series have appeared, consisting of critical re-editions of his most important books.[5] The final two volumes of the series, including important essays and yet unpublished material on creation and evolution, original sin, the theology of the Holy Spirit, several smaller pieces of correspondence, and political statements, are due for publication in 2017.[6]

This all comes by way of background to the focus of this essay and volume: the correspondence with René Girard. The first publication of these letters (with their translation into German) posed legal problems. A letter belongs to its recipient; the copyright, however, remains with the author. René Girard kindly granted us the right to publish his letters. For Schwager's letters, we had to negotiate with the beneficiary of his estate, the Swiss province of the Society of Jesus. We were lucky that the collaboration here was very positive. However, we were obliged to make sure that the rights of third parties mentioned in the letters would not be infringed upon. This was especially important when it came to deciding if including the names of such parties—whether living or dead—was advisable. Luckily, neither Girard nor Schwager ever wrote derogatorily about others, so this was, in fact, no problem. Telephone numbers and

---

[4] Raymund Schwager, *Dogma und dramatische Geschichte: Christologie im Kontext von Judentum, Islam und moderner Marktkultur*, ed. Józef Niewiadomski and Mathias Moosbrugger (Freiburg im Breisgau: Herder, 2014); Raymund Schwager, *Briefwechsel mit René Girard*, ed. Nikolaus Wandinger and Karin Peter (Freiburg im Breisgau: Herder, 2014); *Auf dem Weg zur Neubewertung der Tradition: Die Theologie von Raymund Schwager und sein neu erschlossener Nachlass*, ed. Mathias Moosbrugger and Józef Niewiadomski (Freiburg im Breisgau: Herder, 2015).

[5] Raymund Schwager, *Heilsdrama: Systematische und narrative Zugänge*, ed. Józef Niewiadomski (Freiburg im Breisgau: Herder, 2015); both reprinted in this volume are available in English: *Jesus in the Drama of Salvation: Toward a Biblical Doctrine of Redemption* (New York: Crossroad, 1999); *Jesus of Nazareth: How He Understood His Life* (New York: Crossroad, 1998). Raymund Schwager, *Der wunderbare Tausch: Zur Geschichte und Deutung der Erlösungslehre*, ed. Nikolaus Wandinger (Freiburg im Breisgau: Herder, 2015). Raymund Schwager, *Brauchen wir einen Sündenbock? Gewalt und Erlösung in den biblischen Schriften*, ed. Karin Peter and Mathias Moosbrugger (Freiburg im Breisgau: Herder, 2016); this book is available in English: *Must There Be Scapegoats? Violence and Redemption in the Bible* (San Francisco: Harper and Row, 1987). Raymund Schwager, *Frühe Hauptwerke*, ed. Mathias Moosbrugger (Freiburg im Breisgau: Herder, 2016).

[6] Raymund Schwager, *Beiträge zur Schöpfungslehre, Erbsündenlehre und zur Pneumatologie*, ed. Nikolaus Wandinger (Freiburg im Breisgau: Herder, forthcoming); Raymund Schwager, *Kirchliche, politische und theologische Zeitgenossenschaft*, ed. Mathias Moosbrugger (Freiburg im Breisgau: Herder, forthcoming).

addresses that are mentioned in the correspondence have been omitted in the current volume; the omissions are indicated by ellipses.

The correspondence was conducted in French, Girard's mother tongue and Schwager's preferred foreign language. The Herder edition of this correspondence in Schwager's *Collected Works* contains the original French text alongside a German translation.

The letters are diverse in nature. Some are typed, most are handwritten; some are long academic treatises, some short personal notes, while others are more organizational or pragmatic in content. Some letters are clearly dated, some undated, some are incompletely dated, and some are certainly dated incorrectly, because digits have been accidentally switched, or a date that will later be mentioned in the text of the letter occupied the mind of the writer to such an extent that he also placed it at the head of the letter. Thankfully, these mistakes can be detected from the contents of the letters with a high degree of certainty. Not all letters have been completely preserved. Some are missing a page, so that we have only a truncated version.

One might ask why the correspondence ends in 1991. There are probably two main reasons for this. One is the foundation of COV&R. Because of COV&R and its regular annual conferences, Schwager and Girard met personally at least once a year and thus could probably conduct their conversation directly. The other reason might be the rise of email. What they had to write between meetings, they probably sent by email. When Schwager died suddenly in 2004, nobody thought of securing his email account, and the IT division of the University of Innsbruck deleted it promptly and thoroughly. Nevertheless, we are confident that the letters we have cover the most important period of that conversation.

Content of the correspondence

Let us now give you a short overview of topics in the correspondence. One element of the letters that impresses itself upon the reader is being witness to a scholarly relationship turning into a friendship. It was a relationship between two people who had not met before commencing their correspondence.

Table 1 Overview of the correspondence in the current volume (as can presently be determined)

Year	Schwager to Girard	Girard to Schwager
1974	March 18	
		April 8
	December 6	
		December 18
1975	April 7	
		April 12
	September 16	
		November 2
1976	January 25	
		June 13
	June 30	
		August 19
	August/September	
		December 6
1977	January 31	
		February 12
	March 3	
		May 18
	May 26	
		June 2
	July 4	
		September 1
	October 12	
1978	January 1	
		January 14
	January 28	
		February 22
	March 29	
		April 17
	April 22	
		May 19
	May 28	
		July 6
		July 18
	August 9	
	December 20	
1979		February 10
	June 27	
		August 1
	August 19	
	November 27	
		December 10

Year	Schwager to Girard	Girard to Schwager
1980	March 4	
	April 20	
		May 7
		June
	August 3	
		Aug 18
	September 3	
	December 8	
		December 28
	letter missing	
1981		May 13
	May 24	
		Aug 9
	August 30	
		September 29
	October 26	
1982	January 10	
		January 26
	letter missing	
		June 20
	letter missing	
		November 2
		November 13
		December 11
	letter missing	
1983		May 12
	June 27	
		July 16
	August 12	
		September 12
	December 4	
		December 7
	December 21	
		December 28
1984		January 8
	January 28	
	February 26	
		April 13
	April 22	
		May 8
	September 30	
	letter missing	
1985		February 23
		July 2
	September 20	
	December 23	

Year	Schwager to Girard	Girard to Schwager
1986		January 10
	letter missing	
		January–May
	May 18	
	August 1	
		August 21
	October 12	
		October 19
	December 24	
1987		January 2
	February 4	
		February 25
	April 16	
	December 20	
1988		January 6
	February 22	
		June 27
	July 31	
	December 25	
1989	December 19	
1990		January 24
1991	January 4	
		January 24
	October 3	
		October 30
	November 21	
		December 7

Schwager made the first step and initiated the correspondence in March 1974. The letters testify to an academic exchange over a long period of time that was supportive and appreciative, yet always intellectually lively and critical. The respect that both thinkers had for each other's work permeates all the letters—they are characterized by a mood of mutual gratitude, with each sharing the concerns of the other. Still, they used the formal *vous* (you, in French) for ten years, until—in 1984—they eventually settled on the more relaxed alternative *tu*.

The letters also clearly reveal the authors' different starting points. Girard explains several times that he works in a mostly a-religious environment, which leads him to argue anthropologically, even if his final aim is theological insight. Schwager speaks as a full-blooded theologian and Jesuit, bringing the Catholic dogmatic tradition to the table. These differing starting points are evident in several areas—for example, in the question of the meaning of the cross. Initially, Girard sees the cross primarily as a source of *knowledge* about sacrificial thinking. Schwager emphasizes that Christianity also—and more importantly—regards the cross as a source of *life*. Yet, after some explanation, Schwager comes to understand Girard's point of view and his concern—namely, to make the insights of the gospel, and of the cross in particular, acceptable to nonreligious readers of his books. Similarly, Girard could appreciate the point made by Schwager not to yield to the intellectual's temptation to reduce the gospel to gnostic knowledge.

Mimeticism is another important point of discussion, especially in the early 1980s: Girard has to defend himself against accusations that he construes mimeticism as leading to violence with an almost mechanical necessity and that, consequently, he adheres to an ontology of violence. Schwager supports him in the defense. He agrees that mimeticism cannot be understood mechanically. To this end Schwager emphasizes human freedom, probably more than Girard does. Schwager connects Girard's anthropological ideas on mimesis and violence with the theological doctrine of original sin, thereby emphasizing that violence is not ontologically necessary but, rather, comes out of a certain kind of abuse of human freedom. Following this line of thought, Schwager sees freedom essentially as a consequence of faith. Girard later takes up this line of argument himself. All indications are that he found it helpful for defending his theory against the accusation of mechanistic necessity.

The theme occupying most space in the letters is sacrifice. Every so often the letters take up the question of a sacrificial or non-sacrificial interpretation of certain biblical passages. While both thinkers basically agree on the meaning of archaic sacrifice and also on biblical hermeneutics, they profoundly disagree in the beginning over how to interpret the Letter to the Hebrews. Girard views it as a sacrificial text; Schwager concurs that Hebrews' *language* is indeed sacrificial, but subversively so—sacrificial language is used to transform sacrificial thinking. In the context of this discussion, Schwager finally succeeds in convincing Girard that the dogmatic tradition of the church was actually onto something when it used the term *sacrifice* in a very specific way (of self-giving) to refer to the death of Christ on the cross.[7]

Other themes that are touched upon, though not discussed as thoroughly, are the meaning of the Old Testament law and its connection with sacrifice, universalism as a phenomenon in Scripture and in the world, and the importance of philosophy, along with the extent to which philosophy is nourished by sacrificial roots.

In this correspondence, we witness two remarkable intellectuals working out their thinking. They write books, they change jobs, they enjoy their work, they are disheartened, they are encouraged when understood by others (but more often they feel misunderstood), they have new ideas, and they retract old ones. This is fascinating, but for readers unfamiliar with their chronologies and intellectual biographies it can be confusing—for example, when they refer to new appointments or the development of a new book idea without providing any context. We therefore hope that the following overview of the most important stages of their biographies will be helpful.

---

[7] For this see Girard's essay, which was published for the first time in a German version in a 1995 festschrift for Schwager: René Girard, "Mimetic Theory and Theology," in *The One by Whom Scandal Comes* (East Lansing: Michigan State University Press, 2014), 33–45. See also his earlier interview: René Girard, "Violence, Difference, Sacrifice: A Conversation with René Girard" (with Rebecca Adams), *Religion and Literature* 25(2) (1993): 11–33, esp. 28–32. For a comprehensive study of the controversy on this topic, cf. Mathias Moosbrugger, *Die Rehabilitierung des Opfers: Zum Dialog zwischen René Girard und Raymund Schwager über die Angemessenheit der Rede vom Opfer im christlichen Kontext* (Innsbruck: Tyrolia, 2014). See also Mathias Moosbrugger, "René Girard and Raymund Schwager on Religion, Violence, and Sacrifice: New Insights from Their Correspondence," *Journal of Religion and Violence* 1 (2013): 147–66.

Table 2 Comparative life and work time lines of René Girard and Raymund Schwager

René Girard	Raymund Schwager
1923: birth, Dec. 25, Avignon, France	
	1935: birth, Nov. 11, Balterswil, Switzerland
1941: baccalauréat, Avignon	
1943–7: studies of medieval history (PhD), École Nationale des Chartes, Paris	
1947–50: studies of contemporary history (PhD), Indiana University, Bloomington, IN, USA	
1947–52: language teacher (French), Indiana University	
1951: marriage to Martha McCullough	
1952–3: language teacher (French), Duke University, Durham, NC, USA	
1953–7: Assistant Professor of French, Bryn Mawr College, Bryn Mawr, PA, USA	1955: entry into Society of Jesus (SJ)
1957–68: Associate Professor then Professor of French, Johns Hopkins University, Baltimore, MD, USA	1957–60: studies in philosophy, Pullach near Munich, Germany
	1960–3: educator, Stella Matutina Jesuit school, Feldkirch, Austria
1961: *Mensonge romantique et vérité romanesque*	
1963: *Dostoïevski: Du double à l'unité*	1963–7: studies of theology, Lyon-Fourvière, France
	1966: ordained priest
	1967–9: doctoral studies in theology, University of Fribourg, Switzerland
1968–76: Professor of Arts and Letters, State University of New York, Buffalo, NY, USA	1970–7: editorial journalist, journal *Orientierung*, Zurich, Switzerland
	1970: *Das dramatische Kirchenverständnis bei Ignatius von Loyola: Historisch-pastoraltheologische Studie über die Stellung der Kirche in den Exerzitien und im Leben des Ignatius*
1972: *La violence et le sacré*	
	1973: *Jesus-Nachfolge: Woraus lebt der Glaube?*
1974: first contact, initiated by Schwager (very likely on Mar. 18)	1974: first contact, initiated by Schwager (very likely on Mar. 18)
1976: *Critique dans un souterrain*	1976: *Glaube, der die Welt verwandelt*

René Girard	Raymund Schwager
1976–80: James M. Beall Professor of French and Humanities, Johns Hopkins University, Baltimore, MD, USA	1977–2004: Professor of Dogmatic and Ecumenical Theology, University of Innsbruck, Austria
1978: *"To Double Business Bound"*: *Essays on Literature, Mimesis, and Anthropology* and *Des choses cachées depuis la fondation du monde*	1978: *Brauchen wir einen Sündenbock? Gewalt und Erlösung in den biblischen Schriften*
1980–95: Andrew B. Hammond Professor of French Language, Literature, and Civilization, Stanford University, Stanford, CA, USA	
1982: *Le bouc émissaire*	
1985: *La route antique des hommes pervers*	1985–7: Dean of the Theological Faculty, University of Innsbruck
	1986: *Der wunderbare Tausch: Zur Geschichte und Deutung der Erlösungslehre* and *Für Gerechtigkeit und Frieden: Der Glaube als Antwort auf die Anliegen der Gegenwart*
	1990: *Jesus im Heilsdrama: Entwurf einer biblischen Erlösungslehre*
1990: foundation of the Colloquium on Violence & Religion (COV&R)	1990: foundation of the Colloquium on Violence & Religion (COV&R)
1991: *A Theater of Envy: William Shakespeare*	1991–5: first president of COV&R
	1991: *Dem Netz des Jägers entronnen: Das Jesusdrama nacherzählt*
1994: *Quand ces choses commenceront: Entretiens avec Michel Treguer*	1994: *Evolution: Eine Kontroverse*, ed. with Gerhard Haszprunar
1995: retirement; Professor Emeritus, Stanford University	
1996: *The Girard Reader*	1996: *Christus allein? Der Streit um die pluralistische Religionstheorie*, ed.

René Girard	Raymund Schwager
	1997: *Erbsünde und Heilsdrama: Im Kontext von Evolution, Gentechnologie und Apokalyptik*
	1998: *Relativierung der Wahrheit? Kontextuelle Christologie auf dem Prüfstand*, ed.
1999: *Je vois Satan tomber comme l'éclair*	1999–2003: Dean of the Theological Faculty, University of Innsbruck
2001: *Celui par qui le scandale arrive*	
2002: *La voix méconnue du réel: Une théorie des mythes archaïque et modernes*	
2003: *Le sacrifice*	2003: *Religion erzeugt Gewalt—Einspruch! Innsbrucker Forschungsprojekt "Religion—Gewalt—Kommunikation—Weltordnung,"* ed. with Józef Niewiadomski
2004: *Oedipus Unbound: Selected Writings on Rivalry and Desire* and *Les origins de la culture: Entretiens avec Pierpaolo Antonello et João Cezar de Castro Rocha*	2004: death, Feb. 27, Innsbruck, Austria
2005: membership of l'Académie Française	
2007: *Achever Clausewitz: Entretiens avec Benoît Chantre*	
2008: *Mimesis and Theory: Essays on Literature and Criticism, 1953-2005*, ed. Robert Doran	
2015: death, Nov. 4, Stanford, CA, USA	2014–17: publication of the German eight-volume edition of Schwager's *Gesammelte Schriften (Collected Works)*

Notes on the English Translation

This text presented some unique challenges, many of which were the result of its specific context and genre. Although perhaps obvious, it is still worth drawing attention to the fact that the correspondence translated here was not written for an audience larger than one other person—the intended recipient. As such, the original text has all the features one might expect of (originally, mostly handwritten) correspondence: allusions to previous letters and real-world discussions (for some of which we have no record); grammatical variations, abbreviations, and misspellings; idiosyncratic typography and formatting, and so on.

Translating this remarkable correspondence between two good friends frequently felt akin to eavesdropping. And we were regularly amused by the long, expansive, rambling sentences of René Girard, the Mediterranean Frenchman, alongside the beautifully crafted, very precise ones of Raymund Schwager, the Swiss Jesuit.

Where we were able—that is, where no alteration of mood or meaning was involved—we tidied up formal elements of the writing (syntax, spelling, and so on) to facilitate its reading. Otherwise, we have rendered the text as close to the original as possible. In cases where a series of complicated and/or subtle ideas are advanced, where the claim being made is tightly bound to the French language, or where more than one possible translation presented itself, we have quoted the original French in square brackets after the English translation. Other occasional interpolations, added for the sake of clarity, are also in square brackets. We have not attempted to "inclusivize" many references to "man" etc., because such usage was not the custom of our correspondents. Finally, note that Fr. Schwager's first name is sometimes spelled in its German form (Raymund) and sometimes in its French form (Raymond)—this variation is not an error!

Chris Fleming and Sheelah Treflé Hidden, February 2016

The Girard–Schwager Correspondence, 1974–1991

[Schwager] March 18, 1974[1]

Dear Sir,

I discovered your book *La violence et le sacré*[2] from reading the journal *Esprit*.[3] I bought it immediately, and what I've read I've found to be admirable. I am certainly incapable of making a competent judgment on all passages, but I was greatly impressed overall and am very inclined to accept your theory.

As I am one of the editors of the revue *Orientierung*,[4] I have introduced your book to our readers (18,000 subscribers in Switzerland, Germany, and

---

[1] In the French original, this letter is clearly dated April 18, 1974. Girard's handwritten reply, however, is *also* clearly dated—as April 8. Obviously, either Schwager or Girard must have made a mistake. It is very likely that the mistake is Schwager's and that he sent his initial letter on March 18, mistaking the month. The reason for this is that Schwager's text in the Swiss journal *Orientierung*, which he mentions here, was published on February 28, while his translation of Girard's text, also mentioned here, was published on March 15. Knowing his way of corresponding with authors of books he had read and written about (preserved in many letters in the Raymund Schwager Archive in Innsbruck), it seems very likely that he sent his letter to Girard right after this second text was published. In addition, Girard writes in his letter of reply that he would be sending a list to Schwager at the end of April. This means Girard cannot have responded to a letter of April 18—also consider his mention of having received Schwager's letter very late. The most probable scenario is, therefore, that Girard wrote in the first half of April (just as his letter actually says), whereas Schwager wrote earlier, but not before the middle of March. March 18 seems to be a plausible date.
[2] Girard, *La violence et le sacré*. This appeared later in English as *Violence and the Sacred*. The full bibliographical details of this work and indeed of all the works cited in the footnotes to the correspondence may be found in "Publications Cited in the Correspondence," below.
[3] Girard, "Discussion avec René Girard."
[4] The Swiss Jesuit journal *Orientierung* was published from 1936 to 2009. Schwager was an editor from May 1970 to December 1977. After becoming Professor of Dogmatic Theology in Innsbruck in 1977, he served as permanent member of the editorial team from January 1978 to December 1985.

Austria)⁵ and with the agreement of the journal *Esprit*, I have translated your reflections on Christianity.⁶ I am sending these two issues by separate mail.

Your reflections on the efficacy of Christianity are very much in line with my own thinking. This is perhaps why I was so well disposed to liking your book. If you have any other writings on Christianity, I would be most grateful if you would send them to me, including any reviews of your book. I have not found anything here.

I would be delighted if we could translate your book into German and I have already taken steps to find a publisher. But this is not easy, given that ethnology plays almost no current role in German thought. Marxism has triumphed for the moment. But I will do what I can.

With heartfelt thanks for what you have given me through your book.

Raymond Schwager

STANFORD UNIVERSITY⁷

April 8, 1974⁸

Dear Sir,

Your letter found me here after quite some delay and gave me great pleasure. I am planning a book on the Old and the New Testaments,⁹ but for the moment, I am concentrating on a tighter reworking in English of the ethnological theory that underlies my work. By doing this, I hope to attract a larger audience and one that is less methodologically biased than French-speaking ethnologists. Perhaps I am wrong, but I have the impression that advancing a theory of ethnology is necessary for understanding my thesis concerning

---

⁵ Schwager, "Gewalt und Opfer."
⁶ Girard, "Das Evangelium legt die Gewalt bloß."
⁷ Girard, then professor at the State University of New York, Buffalo, probably used Stanford letterhead here because, at this time, he was a visiting professor there for one year. Throughout this correspondence, whenever the name of an institution appears in upper case at the head of a letter, it signifies the use of official letterhead.
⁸ See the relevant editorial footnote to the dating of Schwager's first letter.
⁹ Girard, *Des choses cachées*.

Christianity. Given, moreover, the prejudice and resistance that the whole thesis cannot but fail to provoke, in *La v. et le s*[10] I wanted to present—and I am still looking for the right way to do it—the ethnological system as such. I think it should be possible to present it in so logical a fashion that it becomes impossible to deny.

I have no texts on Christianity that are really finished and presentable. I'll be sure to send you those that I manage to finish.

As to reviews, there haven't been a lot—although there are some. They are either very good or very bad. I haven't got to hand the list—probably incomplete—that I collected. I'll send it to you at the end of April, when I am back home for the weekend of [Saturday] the twenty-seventh.

I look forward to your translation of the text in *Esprit*.[11] As I feel quite isolated, especially here in California, the interest that you are showing in my work is precious to me. I am very grateful for anything that you can do with *La v. et le s*.

With my thanks, and the hope of future contacts,
René Girard

Zürich, December 6, 1974

Dear Sir,

Months have passed since I received your letter from California. In the meantime, I have been trying to find a publisher for the translation of your book,[12] but so far without success. Two publishers showed an interest, but eventually withdrew for financial reasons. Nevertheless, I continue to try, given that I am finding your book more and more important. If I have no success with the French text, the reformulation in English of your theory of ethnology may be more attractive. The German public is not used to the issues and theories of ethnology; that's why the publishers don't think that the book will sell.

---

[10] Girard, *La violence et le sacré*.
[11] Girard, "Das Evangelium legt die Gewalt bloß."
[12] Girard, *La violence et le sacré*.

I would be delighted to stay in contact with you. Academic output is enormous today, but books that bring something substantial to the great problems of our time are nevertheless rare. I consider yours to be among these rare works. I hope therefore that your thesis will one day be the subject of a great intellectual debate, both religious and political. Perhaps the groundwork for this has not yet been laid, but for my part, I will do my utmost to work toward this, with my very limited means.

If I have any success I will let you know; if in the meantime you finish a text, I would be very grateful if you would send me a copy.

With my very best wishes,
Raymond Schwager

State University of New York at Buffalo

December 18, 1974

Dear Sir,

Thank you very much for your letter, and for your efforts to find a publisher who'd be interested in a German translation of my book. The current economic situation is making these things so much more difficult.

In the event of your finding an opportunity somewhere, it may be possible to get some funding here from the university, which would not, of course, be sufficient to cover everything, but which could, however, be useful all the same—something in the order of a thousand dollars. I am not certain of this, but I think the chances would be good.

I will not be far from Zürich on January 24 and 25, as I will be speaking at the Centre Protestant d' Etudes in Geneva, at no. 7 Rue Tabaran. If, by chance, you happen to be passing through Geneva, we could meet.

In any event, I will be back next summer in June and July in Paris and Avignon, and perhaps it will be possible to meet then.

Please accept, dear Sir, the assurance of my warmest regards.
René Girard

Zürich, April 7, 1975

Dear Sir,

My friend Josef Hug spoke to me of the paper that you read in Geneva, which he said made a strong impression on him. At the same time he told me that you will be in Avignon from June 15 until July 15. I would like to take this opportunity to meet and to discuss several issues. If nothing unexpected happens I can arrange to travel to Avignon in the first half of July, but I don't yet know the exact day. Could you send me a word to let me know if you are more or less free at the beginning of July?

I am looking forward to meeting you in person.

All the best to you,
    Raymond Schwager

State University of New York at Buffalo

April 12, 1975

Dear Sir,

I will actually be in Avignon in early July and would be very happy to make your acquaintance. As yet I have no address for this period, but I will be teaching at Bryn Mawr College, Avignon, which is to be found at the Palais du Roure (very close to the Place de l'Horloge, in the middle of town). You will be able to get details of my activities there if I'm not here when you arrive.

In anticipation of our meeting, I send my very best wishes.
    René Girard

Zürich, September 16, 1975

Dear Sir,

I continue to think of our meeting in Avignon with delight. I would very much like to thank you for the way that you welcomed me. A book stays with one when a personal memory is associated with it, and its contents are livelier when one has been able to discuss them.

I have thought a lot about what you said to me in Avignon, and the result of all this thinking is a question that I'd now like to put to you. The question concerns *the law* and its role in how violence plays out. First of all, I would like to mention several points that have attracted my attention.

1. In the Old Testament, it is not sacrifice but the law that has the most important function.
2. Saint Paul almost never speaks of sacrifice; rather, his theology is dominated by a confrontation with the law. And this law has, according to him—among other things—a very precise function: *it awakens desire*. "I would not have known what it meant to covet if the law had not said: You are not to covet." (Rom. 7:7)
3. The same idea is found already in Genesis. Before the story of Cain and Abel and the playing out [*avec le jeu*] of violence,[13] is the story of paradise, where it is shown that the *prohibition* to eat arouses Eve's desire.[14]

If I have understood your thinking correctly, you situate the law as emerging after the transfer of collective violence onto a single victim. You write in "Les malédictions contre les pharisiens":[15] "surrounding the sacrificial victim, and in its name, (is) an elaboration of prohibitions and rituals which function to prevent the return of the crisis" (p. 5).

And now my question: Is the law to be situated only after the crisis? Does it not already have a function in the unleashing of uncontrolled violence?

---

[13] Cf. Gen. 4:1-16.
[14] Cf. Gen. 2:4b–3:24.
[15] Girard, "Les malédictions."

Animals also have their rivalries, but these conflicts almost never lead to collective violence. The strongest animal dominates, and the others submit; it's different with humans, where those who feel inferior do not back down, but continue the struggle until an outbreak of widespread violence is unleashed. Whence this difference? The tragedies demonstrate that conflicts begin with verbal insults. One person does not merely covet the object of the other's desire—he also says "no" to him in a more general sense. In so doing he negates the status—and even the very being—of the other. And this "no" unleashes violence without limit.

Hence my idea: should we not distinguish between *the content of the prohibitions* that proliferate around the victim, and the essence or basis of the law as a general "no" against desire and even the being of the other? The law, as this fundamental "no," precedes the collective transfer (of violence). The law awakens violence.

I have another question—whether a distinction of this kind is necessary to describe a state of generalized violence. You describe this state as "undifferentiation" (e.g., "one can speak of undifferentiation because of the rapidity of the reprisals; the feedback of the violence excludes all 'difference' stable enough to be perceived" [*Esprit*, p. 537][16]). In this situation, one could not observe, of course, any precise content that would correspond to any particular difference. But it is certainly still possible to observe difference itself. In the rapidity of the violence, difference loses its content, but does not disappear; if anything, it "hypostatizes" itself [*elle "s'hypostasie" plutôt*]. The difference is no longer anything other than difference (itself).

Therefore it seems to me that we can speak of undifferentiation when we observe *the content of difference*. But, at the same time, we must assert that *difference feeds on itself*. Difference appears in collective violence as nothing other than difference itself; it presents as absolute difference.

Given this, it seems to me that we can explain the divinization of the victim in a more convincing manner. If violence, under the impulse of the "law," engenders "hypostatic difference," absolute difference; and if this difference is projected—together with violence—onto the victim, then this victim must

---

[16] Girard, "Discussion avec René Girard."

appear to the community to be absolutely different, like a hypostatic, i.e., divine, force. Without postulating a hypostatic, absolute difference that is projected onto the scapegoat, it seems to me difficult to adequately explain the divine character of the victim.

Therefore, underlying this are two aspects of the same idea: to distinguish between concrete law and concrete, practical difference on the one hand, and *the law* and *hypostatic difference* on the other.

I would be very happy if you are able in the days or weeks to come, to find a little time to reply to my twofold question.

In the meantime I send my gratitude and very best wishes.
Raymund Schwager

State University of New York at Buffalo

November 2, 1975

My dear Father,

Thank you very much for your letter and please excuse the tardiness of my reply. I had somehow mislaid your letter and, given that it is quite complex, did not want to reply before I found it—which I did, in my extremely untidy office, and here it is.

The heart of the problem for me now [*A l'intérieur de ma problématique actuelle*] is that I am obliged to emphasize the law of the victim, and not the victim of the law, which is already abstract and symbolic, while the victimage mechanism is concrete and can serve quite literally to map the transition between animality and humanity.

The whole question is whether this response is valid with respect to the way you conceive these things. Personally, I think it is. It seems to me that there is a difference here between the gospel perspective and certain passages in Paul—or at least the interpretations that we are obliged to give these. Paul is writing during a time of conflict and his attitude toward the law echoes a negativity tied to certain pre-exilic problems. In the gospels, love both transcends and fulfills the law, because love does everything that the law demands, but much better. The law is blind, in that it seeks to avoid violence, beginning with that which it sees in itself, by prescribing rules that eventually become atrophied and lose all contact with reality. Consequently, I believe that, as history unfolds, the law can become a source of sin, whereupon the time comes for it to be replaced, and above all replaced by love. The law is necessarily negative when it says: don't do that. But it says it essentially because the thing prohibited truly is dangerous.

What you have to say about the law and the language of violence seems to me to be true in a relative sense, in the framework of a well-established culture, but not true in an absolute sense.

On this point, it seems to me that Paul, with his anti-legal side (or at least in the "hard" reading that we give him), is a harbinger of a Freud or a Nietzsche, who see the law as responsible for a struggle, which, in fact, is always with a double. It is Wagner who irritates Nietzsche, not the law. But, at a certain point, the law becomes a sort of final scapegoat, which results in its being able to provide protection. It seems to me that people who condemn the law often do so only to find themselves falling into an inverse version of it. This would certainly be true of the inverted philosophies of Freud and Nietzsche, but perhaps, also, of certain aspects of historical and legal Christianity that would make it a double of Judaism.

What seems to me to be essential in the gospel is the possibility of bypassing the law if we are to be reconciled with our brother. This is where the emphasis is placed—not in some sort of magical effacement of the law.

This is obviously the basic problem. In incriminating the law, we run the risk of deluding ourselves into thinking that we can easily do without it, when, in reality, without it, men are threatened with falling into absolute violence. In incriminating the law, do we not run the risk of minimizing the formidable revolution that the gospels represent? Does the indication of violence not mean that man risks doing away with the law, to claim the freedom that the gospels bring, but without truly taking on the responsibility of love? The apocalyptic theme is introduced into the breach of this failure, which is certainly not a sign of despair, but a sign that man, deprived of the law, is constantly threatened with the possibility of falling into a much worse predicament than any that could be produced by the rejected legalities. If eventually things do improve, it is thanks to a mysterious savior, from whom, it appears to me, we have not understood a word.

I understand how you see hypostatic difference projected onto the victim, but I am not sure that I understand your distinction between concrete law and concrete difference, on the one hand, and the law and hypostatic difference, on the other.

I believe that we always have to deal with a mixture [*mélange*] here; the law is halting and fallible, always linked to a transcendence provided by the sacralized victim, and historically unstable. But the law possesses no absolute "no." In pre-state societies [*les sociétés primitives*], sexual prohibitions are not valid outside the community, because they have a purely utilitarian function, inhibiting disorder within the community.

I would say that the quintessentially modern error involves resentment toward the law, which results merely in its inversion. (We see this with Freud, Nietzsche, etc.) That is to say, we see an ultra-sacrificial crisis [*super-crise sacrificielle*]. It seems to me that modernism is coming to an end, and that the gospel perspective will reappear with formidable power when we rightly recognize that in this resentment toward the law we see the last relic of the law—paradoxically, the last protection it provides.

I don't know if what I am saying here amounts to a response to your questions.

From the moment that resentment toward the law ceases, we will see that historical Christianity, like Judaism, cannot be judged by us as it constitutes a step—the same in many respects—toward an authentically Christian awareness, the end of all sacrificial protection, including the idea that all of man's misfortunes come from the law.

What I am saying here does not refer, of course, to any individual resentment toward the law, but to a cultural attitude, which makes such resentment inevitable.

I don't know if I am making myself understood, but as this is a subject that is very close to my heart, I will come back to it in another letter.

It was also a great pleasure for me to meet you in Avignon after the "Orientierung" lectures. I hope that we will have the opportunity to chat again in the very near future.

With my very best wishes,
René Girard

Institut für weltanschauliche Fragen—ORIENTIERUNG—Redaktion und Verlag—Zürich

January 25, 1976

Dear Sir,

Thank you for your letter of November 2, 1975, which I read with a great deal of interest. What you have written convinces me. Your way of seeing the Law seems to me to be in accord with the New Testament. Paul, for his part, puts the negative aspect of the law before everything, whereas according to Matthew, Christ perfects the law with his love, which is at the same time unlimited forgiveness and nonviolence.

Nevertheless, I still have several problems related to this that I would like to put to you:

1. If, with the coming of Christ, the law does not disappear in the same way as sacrifice, is this not a sign that the law does not originate in the same way as does sacrifice [of victims]?
2. With animals, there is rivalry and mimesis, but there is no fight to the death. Where does this difference come from? How can we describe human rivalry so as to understand our tendency to murder?

These two problems were behind the questions I put to you last time, but perhaps I will manage to clarify my aim better this time.

How do we know that triangular desire is without limits? Should we not say that *human* desire is motivated by the search for recognition (Suche nach Anerkennung[17])? (Human consciousness only finds its identity through the recognition of another consciousness. It is perhaps interesting to note here that, in Hegel's logic, the decisive step from "Bewusstein" to "*Selbstbewusstein*"[18] is engendered by a fight to the death, and what is at stake in this struggle is mutual recognition.)

This quest for recognition is of prime importance on the emotional plane as well as the logical (whence the constitution of meaning). So it seems to me that this quest for recognition could well describe human violence as human, and so make humanity's tendency toward murder comprehensible.

If rivalry is driven by the quest for recognition, the *no* of a protagonist against the other takes on an "absolute" dimension. It is not the content of this "no" that is important, but the concrete fact that the quest for recognition is not answered in the affirmative. This is a "no" to a consciousness that is looking for its identity, so it is a "no" that feels like a "no" to its very existence. From this "no" springs the violence that leads to death.

I am not going to say, as I did last time, that this "no" is the basis of the law, but [merely] that this "no" can seize the law and turn it into a law that kills [*et le détourner vers une loi qui tue*] (as Paul puts it, unsparingly).

And the positive basis of the law? We locate it in the history of the Jewish people in the Old Testament, the people who, in the final analysis, shatter the mechanism of violence, starting with the elections (of Abraham, of Moses, and then of the entire people). And this election translates into a covenant between God and his people. And what is a covenant?—A positive response to the quest for recognition! (The beginning of the Kingdom of God, of perfect reciprocity.)

In the Old Testament the law appears in the context of a covenant. So, can we not then say:

1. Concrete formulations of the law come from the victim. (*This is forbidden, that is forbidden*).
2. The tendency in the law toward death comes from the fact that this mysterious "no," which gives a negative response to the quest for recognition, takes hold of the law [*se saisit de la loi*].

---

[17] German in the original French text.
[18] German in the original French text.

3. The ultimate positive basis of the law is covenant; this is perfect reciprocity.

From the beginning, the law would have been "worked" by two contradictory tendencies: the tendency toward death, and the announcement of the Kingdom of God—of itself it can't account for [*découvrir le fondement de*] these two tendencies.

In friendship,
   Raymond Schwager

Some days ago, the publisher Fischer in Frankfurt replied to me that, in the end, they had to pass on translating your book[19] [into German]. However, I received an indication that there is another publisher who is interested.

State University of New York at Buffalo

June 13, 1976

Dear Sir,

I received your *Glaube, der die Welt verwandelt*[20] and I started from the end! Obviously to read the passages where you spoke of my book. I did this with great pleasure, but not without difficulty and hesitation, as my handling of the German language has nothing in common with your handling of French.

I will answer the two questions you sent in January, with apologies also for my tardiness.

Your question concerning rivalry among animals interests me, as I am currently working on just this topic.

I believe that, scientifically, we have to acknowledge that human mimetic rivalry becomes so intense that the "dominance patterns"[21] of the animal kingdom, which represent a compromise solution [*résultant d'un compromis*],

---

[19] Girard, *La violence et le sacré*.
[20] Schwager, *Glaube, der die Welt verwandelt*.
[21] English in the original French text.

are no longer possible. Hence, the crisis and transition to symbolic forms of culture begins with the surrogate victim, which I conceive of as the origin of symbolicity and the source of hominization. So it is possible that murder and human intelligence can be linked, but not as described by Hegel. The scapegoat mechanism could be the means by which a violent humanity raises itself up to the point where it would see this violence and renounce it … or perish. It is conceivable to think that, at every stage, there is a possibility for humanity to advance beyond [*d'accéder aux stades supérieurs sans*] sacrificial violence, but that man always chooses the sacrificial route, up to the point when this [advance] will no longer be possible.

One could see, therefore, the whole schema of the scapegoat at the heart of the cosmic march toward a greater awareness, as Teilhard [de Chardin] does, but without getting rid of the problem of evil, as he tends to do, since violence is never rehabilitated [*récupérée*] in the Hegelian sense. The moment must come when humanity has to confront it directly. I think this could be linked to a comprehensive vision of the Johannine Logos, as positioned behind [*derrière*] the violent Heraclitean Logos, at once hidden and banished by it. This doesn't suggest in the slightest the complicity of a nonviolent god, but rather a permission for human beings that—in spite of human violence—opens up redemptive possibilities leading toward Christ, as understood through the plenary revelation of the Logos as the one cast out, the Logos who truly gathers all together [*menant au Christ bien entendu c'a.d à la révélation plénière du Logos en tant qu'expulsé, le Logos qui rassemble vraiment*]. I think that the question of the law poses a problem for me. I believe that certain aspects of the Jewish law come from the expulsion of the victim—and Paul in a sense bears witness to this; but the text of the law is extremely complex and includes quasi-Christian elements (that you will love your neighbor as yourself), which shows that the evolution of the Law toward its *raison d'être* was already taking place in the OT.

I consider that primitive laws consist of refraining from all that could bring about a crisis, but in a way that is narrow, superstitious, engendered by terror. The law of love, as I see it, is the *truth* of all primitive laws—that is to say, how to get on with one's brother without all these nit-picking requirements, face to face, with love. Christ is the truth of the laws of all societies (contrary to Freud, Nietzsche, and all the moderns who see only oppression in prohibitions). To my mind, the superiority of the Jewish law lies not in its difference, but simply that it has always been more advanced than everybody else on the route that leads to the gospel.

Friendly greetings,
René

I'll be in California in July, perhaps in Paris in the second half of August; if you come, perhaps we can meet. I'll be staying with Dr. Oughourlian (J.-M.) [...].[22]

After September 1, I won't be there any more but teaching again at Hopkins. Here's my address in the Department of Romance Languages, The Johns Hopkins University [...]

Institut für weltanschauliche Fragen—ORIENTIERUNG—Redaktion und Verlag—Zürich

June 30, 1976

Dear Sir,

Thank you for your most interesting letter. I learnt with particular interest that you may come to Paris in August. In this event, I will try to get to Paris, as there are several questions that I would like to discuss with you. I am still looking for a publisher for the translation of your book.[23] But up until now all my attempts have failed. Given that I am more and more convinced that your analysis of society and aggression are of capital importance, particularly for theology, I have begun to write a new book, which will be completely centered on *La violence et le sacré*.[24] I hope to generate an interest in it in German

---

[22] Jean-Michel Oughourlian, one of the interlocutors in: Girard, *Des choses cachées*.
[23] Girard, *La violence et le sacré*.
[24] Schwager, *Brauchen wir einen Sündenbock?*.

theological circles. This is why I ask if you have published articles apart from you books. I know only the paper that you read in Geneva.

Could you let me know the exact date when you will be in Paris?

Friendly greetings,
Raymond Schwager

[Girard] East Aurora [New York], August 19, 1976

Dear Sir,

I received your letter, which arrived with some delay as I spent the summer in California and at the moment we are in the midst of our move back to Baltimore. I have not forgotten your request for articles. I will send what I have as soon as I am installed at Hopkins, as, for the moment, all my affairs are scattered and not yet sorted. I fear that my first articles, those before *Mensonge romantique*,[25] would not interest you. Some more recent articles have just appeared, along with an introductory essay—in a collection entitled *Critique dans un souterrain*, from the publisher L'âge d'homme in Lausanne.[26] I have only one copy and I don't dare part with it, as this publisher seems to be in quite an extraordinary state of disorder and incapacity. I have not received anything from them; they don't send books to newspapers or critics, but with a little luck you may be able to order it through your bookseller.

I am very happy with the idea that you are going to write a book for which *La violence et le sacré* will be useful to you. I think that the trail we are blazing [*la voie dans laquelle nous travaillons*] is too new on the religious plane, too radical, and at the same time too "classical," to assert itself at the present moment, given that the slopes of linguistic nihilism are not as yet conquered [*à la fois trop radicale et trop "classique" pour s'imposer à l'heure actuelle tant que les pentes du nihilisme linguistique ne sont pas complètement gravies*].

---

[25] Girard, *Mensonge romantique et vérité romanesque* [literally, Romantic lie and novelistic truth], was Girard's first book, appearing later in English as *Deceit, Desire, and the Novel*.
[26] Girard, *Critique dans un souterrain*.

But I am personally completely convinced of the fruitfulness of this path—I can't help taking great comfort from the idea that minds such as your own are also committed to this approach. The isolation [*dispersion*] and often extreme vanity of university life make this indispensable. I hope that one of these days we will be able to have you here.

I'm afraid that it won't be possible to come to Paris in the near future, as I indicated in my last letter. This house moving business, and the fact that my wife is now working, will keep me here for now—but this is only a postponement.

Best wishes,
René Girard

From August 30 my address is as follows: [...]

Zürich, August/September, 1976[27]

Dear Sir,

Thank you for your letter of August 19. Your book, *Critique dans un souterrain*, to which you drew my attention, arrived very quickly. Reading this book was exciting for me; it was above all the article on Dostoevsky that gave me the most help in understanding your thinking. Reading this book, I also discerned that your first work, *Mensonge romantique et vérité romanesque*, was a direct preparation for *La violence et le sacré*. I have not yet read it and, for the moment, am having difficulties in getting it.

My efforts to find a German publisher who could translate *La violence et le sacré* continue to be in vain. A few days ago I received another negative

---

[27] In the French original, Schwager dates this letter August 10, 1967, which is obviously wrong. He changed the last digits of the year by accident. However, considering the time required for mail to cross the Atlantic, the month seems to be incorrect, too, because Schwager reacts to Girard's letter of August 19. It is likely that he wrote in September and, mentioning Girard's August letter, wrote the wrong month. Theoretically, the letter could also have been written in October or November, but not later.

response—after waiting several months. Despite these difficulties I will keep looking.

My new book is making progress.[28] I have almost finished the chapter that presents your thoughts on the Old Testament. I am truly totally convinced that the intelligence of the collective transfer of violence onto an arbitrary victim brings comprehension and organization to all the great themes of the Old and New Testaments. For example, I have collected all the verses that deal somehow with divine wrath (there are about 1,000). They fall into four categories.

1. Some rare texts that speak of a completely irrational divine anger (mythical texts).
2. Many texts that figure divine anger as a reaction to human action. Violence comes from God, but it is *man* who provokes divine anger.
3. Many texts that attribute to men the arousal and execution of violence—but it is God who makes the link between the two. Man triggers divine anger by a bad action, and this anger is used by *other men* to punish the wrongdoer (or wrongdoers).
4. Around thirty texts where the violence is a purely human affair: *the bad action falls upon the head of the wrongdoer.*

I consider the four categories as four stages in the draining away [*l'exode*] of violence and the progress of revelation (which becomes crystal clear from the New Testament on [*tout à fait clair à partir du Nouveau Testament*]). There are many other themes here that your thinking helps me to see in a new light.

Progressive universalization presents me with a particular problem. The Prophets, and above all the New Testament, speak in a manner that goes beyond empirical data. The Acts of the Apostles tells us for example: "This is what has come true: in this very city, Herod and Pontius Pilate plotted together *with the Gentile nations* and *the peoples* of Israel, against your holy servant Jesus, whom you anointed" (Acts 4:27). But it is not scientifically verifiable data that the Gentile nations (all nations) were in league against Jesus. From an historical perspective, one can speak only of a plot between

---

[28] Schwager, *Brauchen wir einen Sündenbock?*.

one representative of a Gentile nation and the Jews. The perspective of faith distinguishes itself from the scientific perspective by the degree of universalization (or generalization) in operation. According to my judgment, there is, therefore, both continuity and rupture between the scientific perspective and the perspective of faith.

These reflections I hope permit you to gain some impression of my new book.

I would also like to tell you that I have been in contact with a Jesuit who works in Abidjan (Ivory Coast), on certain African rites.[29] He has read your book[30] and is very impressed with it. I have given him your address so that he can send you a paper on healers.

Permit me to finish with a very personal remark: I thank God in my prayers that he has given you this wisdom. At the same time this prayer is "the means" for me to avoid falling into an absurd rivalry by taking you as model (master of thought).

Friendly greetings,
　Raymond Schwager

I hope to see you in Paris in the near future with Dr. Oughourlian, with whom I have made contact.

THE JOHNS HOPKINS UNIVERSITY—Baltimore, Maryland

December 6, 1976

Dear Friend,

Thank you very much for sending me this text by E. de Rosny. He has already sent me one of his publications. I sent him a word of thanks to the Ivory Coast address he gave me, but the letter has come back to me marked "not known at this address." If you have his address, could you please forward it to me?

---

[29] Éric de Rosny, SJ.
[30] Girard, *La violence et le sacré*.

I would like to thank you also for your last letter, which both interested and touched me greatly. It is very comforting for me to know that there is someone like you who is interested in the kind of theorizing that also interests me. One day, I would very much like to have a meeting of the several minds who are working in this direction. At certain moments one really needs to know that kindred spirits exist. It would be hard for you to imagine, I think, to what extent university life, of which I am a part, and of which, by the way, I cannot complain about on a personal level, is profoundly closed to research such as ours.

I have been working very hard recently, despite our move to Hopkins. Several of my texts, unfinished by the way, are in English, and these are part of the book that I am thinking through—this time truly centered on the Judeo-Christian.[31] To simplify things, I may publish the English version of the book first.[32]

I hope that your work[33] is progressing and that you are satisfied with it. If it is not too much to ask, would you send me those parts of it that are most likely to interest me? I would be most grateful.

With all my friendship, from,
    René Girard

Zürich, January 31, 1977

Dear Sir,

Several days ago I was in Louvain-la-Neuve (Belgium) for a conference on "The Divine in Society."[34] We talked a lot about your book *La violence et le sacré*. I was very surprised to discover that there are many misunderstandings

---

[31] Girard, *Des choses cachées*.
[32] This he did not do. A very slightly changed English version (*Things Hidden since the Foundation of the World*) was published in 1987.
[33] This refers to Schwager's work, *Brauchen wir einen Sündenbock?*.
[34] *Les nouvelles problematiques du divin en anthropologie / Neue Problematik des Göttlichen in der Anthropologie* [New issues for the Divine in anthropology], January 19–20, 1977.

about your analyses (e.g., founding violence ≈ Bergson's *elan vital*).³⁵ There is still a great deal of work to be done to disperse these clouds.

My book is finished.³⁶ The main conclusion is simple. An analysis of *La violence et le sacré* truly allows for an interpretive synthesis of all the major themes (and many of the details) of the Old and New Testaments.

Only two questions arise:

a. Universalization: in the Acts of the Apostles 4:27 Luke says that *all* the Jews and *all* the Gentiles plotted against the anointed one. This is not an empirical fact. It is necessary to make a distinction between the scientific sphere [*niveau*] and the sphere of faith.
b. Prior to this, in the New Testament, it is not really Jesus' reproach to his detractors that they are violent that triggers their violence, but his declaration that he is one with the Father (Jn 8:58-59; 10:38-39; Mt. 21:38; 26:63-66). From this I deduced that, according to the New Testament—behind human violence and "in" human violence—there is malice against God. Violence would then be a primary and foundational given on the empirical level, but in the perspective of the Old and New Testament, it is the fruit of the first sin against the true God (cf. the story of Paradise³⁷ and Cain and Abel;³⁸ Rom. 1:18-32).

One particularly interesting point: your analysis of sacrifice accords very well with the Epistle to the Hebrews, which at first appears to be saying the opposite.

As for the whole work: if you are interested in the German text, I can send you a photocopy of my manuscript.

I have already shown my text to an Old Testament specialist.³⁹ He was very impressed, but had a few problems related to the historical-critical method. In setting it out, I was careful not to confront the specialists of this approach (nearly all the scientifically minded exegetes in the main churches), but I think now that your synthetic approach should be presented in an even more

---

³⁵ The mathematical symbol ≈ stands for "is approximately equal to."
³⁶ Schwager, *Brauchen wir einen Sündenbock?*.
³⁷ Gen. 2:4b–3:24.
³⁸ Gen. 4:1-16.
³⁹ Norbert Lohfink, SJ.

cautious manner to those minds accustomed to the Bultmannian attitude. But I think that will be possible—at least in a few years' time. I notice that more and more people are preoccupied with the problem of violence, and I think that at least Christians can no longer hide from the evidence of the texts. I realize that research in the universities is very closed to this kind of research; nevertheless I am quite optimistic about the future.

I must say that the encounter with your thought has influenced in a decisive way my thinking, my work, and even my way of experiencing the world. I am more and more grateful to you.

With all my friendship,
   Raymond Schwager

The address of: Éric Rosny [...]

THE JOHNS HOPKINS UNIVERSITY—Baltimore, Maryland

February 12, 1977

Dear Friend,

I am happy to know that you have finished your book,[40] and of course I would very much like to read it, even before publication, which I hope will be very soon.

What you tell me about your discussions in Louvain doesn't surprise me at all. This makes me believe that the critical aspect of *La v. et le s.*[41] completely eludes quite a few people. How can anyone believe that it's a return to [Bergson's] *élan vital*?!

What you have to say about universalization, apropos Acts 4:27 "that all the Jews and all the Gentiles plotted against the anointed one": could it not be read as another formulation of the same principle of the scapegoat, and the refusal of its revelation through Christ?—a refusal, for a while at least, that serves to enclose a circle of unanimity against him [*refus qui referme, au moins pour un*

---

[40] Schwager, *Brauchen wir einen Sündenbock?*.
[41] Girard, *La violence et le sacré*.

temps, le cercle de l'unanimité contre lui], a unanimity whose "virtue" can be read in the elements of complicity between a certain sacrificial reading of the NT, and the other forms of refusal of the gospel?

Where faith is secure, surely, is in the humanly confounding fact of human violence against Christ, which is revealed in the gospel text—proof through Christ that man is unjust [*c'est dans le fait que la révélation de la violence humaine contre le Christ c'est la confusion de l'homme par le texte évangélique, la preuve que lui est injuste*]. But this revelation, which hands man over to his own violence [*qui laisse l'homme livré à sa violence*], has not of itself any redemptive value. Therefore, one could believe that the gospels are there only as an indictment of humanity [*on pourrait donc croire que les évangiles ne sont là que pour mettre en accusation l'humanité*], offering consistent proof that man offers nothing other than the divinizing of his own violence, which he has always put back onto God [*et prouver par leur cohérence que l'homme n'a rien qu'il puisse dire sien sinon cette violence qu'il a toujours rejetée sur Dieu, divinisée*].

But faith would consist then of seeing that this text can't be directed against man, but is concerned, once again, with saving him, by demonstrating what Christ has done for all men, what no other has been capable of doing: leaving violence behind, no longer contaminated by it at all, to reconnect with [the] God who asks only that [of us] [*sortir de la violence, ne se laisser contaminer par elle en rien, pour rejoindre Dieu qui ne demande que cela*], and who puts no barriers between man and God. Thus, Christ has completed for humanity the journey that God requires humanity to undertake freely [*a accompli pour les hommes le trajet que Dieu demande à l'humanité d'accomplir librement*]. Faith consists in thinking that the success of Christ as the God-man, given that we would be incapable of repeating this ourselves, is assured for all humanity.

I am looking forward to seeing what you have to say about the Epistle to the Hebrews. I am not sure what I think about this.

I will be in France, in Paris, from March 25 to April 5, in contact with Jean-Michel Oughourlian, who tells me that you have his address, in the event that we should be able to see each other. I look forward to reading your book.

Friendly greetings,
René G.

Zürich, March 3, 1977

Dear Friend,

I sent you a photocopy of my manuscript[42] about two weeks ago. I hope that in the meantime you have received it.

I am very glad that you are coming to Paris from March 25 to April 5. I can arrange to be in Paris for at least two or three days. I'll get in contact with Mr. Oughourlian.

I am very interested to hear your thoughts on my manuscript. I don't know if my way of applying *La violence et le sacré* to biblical texts is slightly different from yours. In any event I am looking forward to the moment when I can discuss this with you.

Meanwhile, my very best to you,
    Raymond Schwager

THE JOHNS HOPKINS UNIVERSITY—Baltimore, Maryland

May 18, 1977

Dear Friend,

I have been terribly busy recently with end of the [academic] year activities, manuscripts that I am obliged professionally to read in a very short period of time, all sorts of inescapable obligations.

But I am spending as much time as I can reading your manuscript,[43] which I am, of course, finding enormously interesting. What has struck me most of all to date is the novelty and force of your reading of the penitential psalms as an expression of the victim [itself]. All this is very striking.

I'll finish your book in about a month from now. For the moment I'm in

---

[42] Manuscript of: Schwager, *Brauchen wir einen Sündenbock?*.
[43] Manuscript of: Schwager, *Brauchen wir einen Sündenbock?*.

agreement with your analyses. Your contrasting of [*Votre opposition entre*] Job and the Servant of Y [Yahweh] is perhaps stronger than I would see it myself; either way, though, it's a minor matter. But I have not read everything in the part on the OT, and I have not begun looking at Christianity. This word is just to let you know that I am working my way through your book—the word "working" is not too strong, and you will soon have from me a more detailed letter. Let me know where you are with the publication.

All the best to you,
René

Zürich, May 26, 1977

Dear Friend,

I found your letter on my return from Frankfurt (Germany) and it gave me great pleasure. I was happy to learn that my manuscript[44] interests you and I now await your more detailed response.

I was in Frankfurt for a session on "Violence and the Sacred and the OT." A professor,[45] who was to have given a course of lectures on the theology of the OT, changed the course into one seminar and invited me to prepare and give the talk with him (two other professors[46] also participated). Everybody (including the students) was very pleased at the end, and much was said at the faculty about this session. There will be an article in a journal that will speak of your book[47] and this particular discussion.[48] This event convinced me that we can interest "the theological world" in your thought.

I will be working this summer on the second chapter of my manuscript. As far as the content is concerned, I don't have much to change, but the manner

---

[44] Manuscript of: Schwager, *Brauchen wir einen Sündenbock?*.
[45] Norbert Lohfink, SJ.
[46] Rudolf Pesch and, very likely, Peter Knauer, SJ. Schwager credits them along with Norbert Lohfink, SJ, in the foreword to *Brauchen wir einen Sündenbock?*.
[47] Girard, *La violence et le sacré*.
[48] It is not quite clear what Schwager means here. He is probably referring to Knauer's review of *Brauchen wir einen Sündenbock?*, by Schwager.

of presenting the analysis should proceed differently, to better adapt it to minds closed by the historical-critical method.

The professor with whom I did the session regrets that you have not yet elaborated your thinking so as to encompass societies such as the Assyrians, Babylonians, and the ancient Egyptians, because there are enormous influences of these societies on the OT. But, in the final analysis, he found that your thinking helps him to see many texts in a new light.

Two days ago I learnt that the Bishop of Innsbruck[49] has finally given his "placet" for my appointment as professor.[50] So in the future I will also have the possibilities a university offers to pursue this line of research that you have opened up.

The text of J.-M. Oughourlian and G. Lefort that you sent me is not easy to translate.[51] But I find it important as it shows your thinking to be different from that of my text. So I consider it a real enrichment for my book.

As to things practical, I continue to analyze conflict according to the model of "triangular desire." For me, the results are astonishing.

I am leaving now for a month in Innsbruck to give a course on eschatology. I will be back in Zürich in July (for several months).

I am having difficulties with the publisher I had intended. They think that the book will not sell, and they want me to reduce it to 100 pages. But I think they are wrong, so I'll look for another publisher.

All the best to you,
Raymond Schwager

---

[49] Paulus Rusch, Bishop of Innsbruck from 1964 to 1980.
[50] In Austria, for a university to appoint a new professor of Catholic Theology, the approval (*placet*) of the local bishop is required.
[51] In the Raymund Schwager Archive, Innsbruck, a short manuscript by Oughourlian and Lefort ("La révélation girardienne") is preserved, but no translation by Schwager.

THE JOHNS HOPKINS UNIVERSITY—Baltimore, Maryland

June 2, 1977

Dear Friend,

Congratulations on your appointment in Innsbruck. It is important for you and for our work. Congratulations also for the seminar in Frankfurt. Please don't forget to send me the article planned to follow on from the debate when it appears.

I have a project here myself—an issue of a journal from Hopkins, entitled *MLN* (formerly *Modern Language Notes*), will be dedicated to all those ideas that interest us, from mimetic desire to the scapegoat. Each year this review (originally concerned with literary history) has an issue in French, others in Spanish and Italian, and one on comparative literature. It's the French issue that will be dedicated to our project.

I would be happy if you would agree to participate in this issue. The piece has to be fairly brief, roughly between twelve and fifteen pages, double-spaced. This is an audience very different from your theologians, of course, more *au fait* with contemporary criticism, but strangers to the Bible.

You may do as you please, but if you would like to take from your book certain of your analyses of the OT, those on the psalms for example, with a small theoretical introduction and conclusion, that would be fine, I think.[52]

At a pinch we could publish in German, because there will be German in the issue dedicated to German literature, but hardly anyone will understand it. If you would like to write in French, I will take care, if need be, of revising your text. The deadline for the submission of the manuscript is September '78. There is still time as you can see; the issue will come out in spring '79.

I am pleased that, despite the difficulties, my text with J.-M. Oughourlian and G. Lefort will be translated and published by yourself.[53] I hope that you yourself will soon find a publisher more understanding than the one you spoke of.[54]

---

[52] The following article was published: Schwager, "La bande des violents."
[53] This did not come to pass; see the relevant earlier footnote in the previous letter.
[54] For: Schwager, *Brauchen wir einen Sündenbock?*.

J.-M. Oughourlian will be here in July and the beginning of August to finish with me the book we have been working on for two years.[55] Lefort will also be here, but only briefly.

Best wishes,
René Girard

Zürich, July 4, 1977

Dear Friend,

I'm back from Innsbruck and am starting to correct my manuscript.[56] A specialist in the New Testament (a professor from Frankfurt) has just read my text.[57] He is very happy with it and is interested in working along similar lines. He made a few comments about the text. Corrections for the chapter on the NT are modest.—I now have a publisher. The theological faculty at Innsbruck is launching a new series (with the collaboration of a publishing house from Innsbruck). My text will be the first installment in the series.[58]

The corrections for the chapter on the OT are presenting me with a few problems. But I think I'll be able to sort these out.

Your proposal to write a short text for the journal *MLN*[59] really interests me. I will try to continue my analyses of the psalms.[60] Could you tell me the exact date for the submission of the manuscript? I would like to concentrate first on rewriting my text on the OT and then turn my attention to this. Next year I have to give a course on redemption. I will focus my lectures on the scapegoat. Also I have set a two-day meeting on *La violence et le sacré* with some specialists in atheism. So I think your thought is slowly entering the German world.

Best wishes,
Raymond Schwager

---

[55] Girard, *Des choses cachées*.
[56] Schwager's *Brauchen wir einen Sündenbock?*.
[57] Rudolf Pesch.
[58] In the end, it was published elsewhere.
[59] *Modern Language Notes*.
[60] The result was Schwager's "La bande des violents."

THE JOHNS HOPKINS UNIVERSITY—Baltimore, Maryland

September 1, 1977

Dear Friend,

Thank you for your text.[61] The content is perfect; as for your French, my secretary, who is French, and I, will, if you permit us, make the little changes that are necessary. We will of course, send the result of this to you before it is published; we'll be guided by your suggestions. I can't do anything for the moment, as I am overwhelmed with work, but this is not a pressing matter. The issue will not appear until the spring of '79. I am very happy to have a contribution so innovative and important. And its presence in a French literary publication is justified, given the importance of the biblical psalms and their influence upon all of Western literature!

During the summer, J.-M. Oughourlian, Guy Lefort and I transformed the "dialogues" project into a more elaborate manuscript, which will result in a book of about 600 pages, of which more than a third is dedicated to the OT and, above all, the NT.[62] I'm longing to send it to you (January '78, I hope) and get your impressions, especially the reading of the gospel text as non-sacrificial but more transcendental than ever [*surtout sur la lecture non-sacrificielle mais + transcendantale que jamais du texte évangélique*]. There is much in it that is in agreement with your thesis, and some that is not. I have not been able to read and contemplate your text with as much leisure as I would have liked, but I think I have grasped the essence of it. I am counting on being able to get back to it with more time this winter, but I am more and more persuaded that the whole thesis on mimeticism, the scapegoat, and anthropology is going in the direction of the complete dissolution of the sacrificial reading, which *respects* and moreover justifies, comparatively and historically, the continued reading of medieval theology as sacrificial [*dissolution qui respecte d'ailleurs et justifie de façon relative et historique la lecture encore sacrificielle de la théologie médiévale*].

It seems to me that all the great dogmas of the early councils emerge reinforced and better integrated in this mimetic reading. It is presumptuous

---

[61] Schwager, "La bande des violents."
[62] Girard, *Des choses cachées.*

of course to speak like this, given my limited exegetical knowledge, but even so I hope to be able put forward decisive arguments in terms of the "deconstruction" of the sacrificial. Recently I received from two Frenchmen texts that are very much in line with your own analysis of this precise point, rather than with mine. Sacrifice remains. I alerted them to your work and gave them your address in Zürich. In any event I'll give you their names and addresses.

Mr. Pierre Gardeil [...] (text to come out in *Nouvelle Revue Théologique*[63])
Mr. René Huvet[64] [...]
Don't forget to send me your address in Innsbruck.

Warmest regards and every best wish for your new university post. Congratulations on the book.[65]
René Girard

JESUITENKOLLEG INNSBRUCK

Innsbruck, October 12, 1977

Dear Friend,

I have been back in Innsbruck for several days now and have finally begun my work at the university. A week ago I sent my manuscript[66] to the publisher, who is very interested. The other professors who have read the text are very pleased with the work that I did in the summer. We are all awaiting the reactions of the public.

In your last letter, you wrote that your interpretation of the NT goes toward a complete dissolution of the sacrificial reading. I had already felt previously that there is a difference of opinion between your interpretation and mine (based on your book). For the moment I am completely convinced by what I wrote. But I now look forward to reading the text that you wrote with Mr.

---

[63] Gardeil, "Le christianisme est-il une religion du sacrifice?."
[64] Huvet, "Autour de René Girard."
[65] Schwager, *Brauchen wir einen Sündenbock?.*
[66] Manuscript for: Schwager, *Brauchen wir einen Sündenbock?.*

Oughourlian and Mr. Lefort.[67] I wonder if you will manage to shake off my convictions and have me change my point of view. This question really fascinates me and I am constantly reworking my texts.

The manuscript that I have just finished will be the basis of a course that I will give next year.

I am now in contact with Mr. Huvet, whose address you gave me. I think that his work in theater[68] will give weight to your thesis on the mimetic character of the scapegoat; his reflections on the theme of the King are quite interesting.

I have no grand projects for the moment; university work takes up all my time. I am thinking of a study on "the Word" for the future.[69] It's through the Word that the prophets and Christ revealed the play of violence, and it's the Word that can create community and communion that transcends violence. I think that the Word gains strength by virtue of exposing violence. But these are rather vague ideas.

I wish you great success with your work and look forward to your next text.

Best wishes,
Raymond Schwager

JESUITENKOLLEG INNSBRUCK

Innsbruck, January 1, 1978

Dear Friend,

A new year has begun. I wish you all good things and pray to God for you and your work, which is so important.

My new work at the university is well under way. My book, *Brauchen wir einen Sündenbock? Gewalt und Erlösung in den biblischen Schriften*, is coming out in two months. As soon as I have it, I will send you a copy.

---

[67] Girard, *Des choses cachées*.
[68] René Huvet was director at the Comédie Française in Paris.
[69] In the end, he did not do a specific study on this subject.

I will speak in detail about *La violence et le sacré* in my summer semester course. Unfortunately, few of the students read French; there are more that know some English. I would like to ask if you could send me the book in English so that I can make it available to the students.

What is happening with your other projects? Is the book with Oughourlian and Lefort coming out soon?[70] I am most interested to read other texts of yours. I await this moment keenly.

Best wishes to you,
Raymond Schwager

THE JOHNS HOPKINS UNIVERSITY—Baltimore, Maryland

January 14, 1978

Dear Friend,

Your letter of the first arrived on the eleventh! I will send you immediately a copy of *Violence and the Sacred* [i.e., the English translation of *La violence et le sacré*] (several pages of the [French] original have been removed).

If I have understood well, the title of your book[71] has been changed.[72] I am very much looking forward to receiving it, because I am also going to do a course on "Mythology and the Biblical Text," where I will use it. You can't count on all the students here understanding German. I'll be your interpreter for them. *Des choses cachées depuis la fondation du monde* will come out on March 1 and I am waiting for this publication with more impatience than I've had with my previous books. I have the impression, perhaps mistaken, that I have clarified what I have to say and dispelled early misunderstandings. There will be others, of course, that I have not envisaged and will certainly

---

[70] Girard, *Des choses cachées*.
[71] Schwager, *Brauchen wir einen Sündenbock?*.
[72] Schwager had suggested the title *Jesus, der Sündenbock der Welt: Die biblischen Schriften im Lichte der Theorie René Girards* [Jesus, the scapegoat of the world: The biblical writings in the light of René Girard's theory], but changed it following suggestions from Norbert Lohfink and others.

show up, but that's inevitable. I am very eager to have your reaction, above all on the non-sacrificial reading of the gospels, and on the great religious question that flows from it—you will see that my reading is neither humanist nor progressive in the sense of the current blandness one finds with so many French Catholics. It is today's most essential question, necessarily the one that dominates all the others.

You will see, I think, that the elimination of the sacrificial schema does not at all entail a renunciation of the great dogmas of patristic orthodoxy and the early councils. Quite the opposite. It's therefore here, too, that the question of the disunity of the churches takes its bearings [*qui se repère ici*], and primarily, of course, the original fracture: the one between Jews and Christians. In this light you will view my interpretation [*Vous verrez donc ma lecture*] of the Epistle to the Hebrews and the notion of the Logos. This was all done a little too quickly perhaps, but even so I think the essential elements are there and I keenly await your thoughts about this. I would very much like to be able to speak with you more frequently, because around me the incomprehension concerning all religious matters is total. Best wishes for your work in Innsbruck and for the success of your book. It should also come out in French and English. Unfortunately I have no contacts in theological circles.

With all my affection,
René Girard

I am pleased to know that you are in contact with Mr. Huvet and I would like to indicate another contact whom I perhaps disappointed in revealing the anti-sacrificial direction of my work. He has sent me an extremely interesting text that I suggested he send also to you. He is a friend of Michel Serres—name and address: P. Gardeil [...].[73]

---

[73] Concerning Huvet and Gardeil, see the relevant footnotes to Girard's letter of September 1, 1977.

Innsbruck, January 28, 1978

Dear Friend,

Thank you very much for your letter and your book,[74] which I've now received. I am waiting impatiently for the publication of your book, *Des choses cachées depuis la fondation du monde*. I haven't, as yet, been able to form a precise idea of your anti-sacrificial interpretation of the death of Jesus. I understand my own interpretation to be also anti-sacrificial (in a certain sense). So I have a great interest in grasping the difference.

The two professors from Frankfurt who read my manuscript[75] gave some lectures a week ago in Munich on "Violence and Nonviolence in the Bible."[76] One gave a brief introduction to *La violence et le sacré*, after which they followed my book exclusively. They quoted my text at length, and this was publicity for the book that's about to appear. I greatly hope that your theory is going to solicit discussion at least in theological circles—we'll see. I feel resistance already in the university where I work. But that's normal. You are having the same experience, only in a more pronounced way. I understand that it's not easy for you if there is no response from those in your intellectual milieu, because the topic of religion is itself problematic. If you are coming to France this summer I would be very happy to see you again and to discuss your forthcoming book. An academy in Munich[77] has shown an interest in inviting you to give papers. The problem is the language. You have to speak German, and I don't know if that would be convenient for you.

The publisher of my book has not yet summoned up the courage to translate *La violence et le sacré*, but he is extremely interested in your next book, *Des choses cachées*. Could you let me know which publisher is publishing your book? Mine wants to order a copy immediately, to see if he can get it translated (depending on the financial situation).

My book is coming out at almost the same time as yours; I'll send you a copy

---

[74] The English translation of *La violence et le sacré* (Girard, *Violence and the Sacred*); cf. Girard's letter of January 14, 1978.
[75] Schwager, *Brauchen wir einen Sündenbock?*.
[76] They published a book of proceedings from this conference: Lohfink and Pesch, *Weltgestaltung und Gewaltlosigkeit*.
[77] Very likely the Katholische Akademie in Bayern (Catholic Academy in Bavaria).

as soon as I can get my hands on it. I'll also give you the reactions to it later on. Further, I'm hoping to elicit interest in your theory in non-theological circles. But this is certainly more difficult. In Germany there isn't much interest in French thought.

For me personally and for my work, it has been so important that I have had the chance to discover your thought. I thank you for it most warmly.

With all my affection,
Raymond Schwager

THE JOHNS HOPKINS UNIVERSITY—Baltimore, Maryland

February 22, 1978

Dear Friend,

Reading your letters is always a great pleasure for me, and the last is no exception. I intend to send you my book as soon as it appears[78]—the date is now fixed for March 15. The publisher is Grasset, as always. They have put a cover on the book—fortunately not attached—that I find a bit ridiculous (a painting of Magritte that portrays a man looking at an enormous apple) and I don't think it works at all, but it is too late to change it, and besides it is very difficult to intervene effectively in these things when one is on a different continent!

I am also impatient to have your reactions on the question of sacrifice. Given the tripartite nature of the book, concerning anthropology, psychology, and religion, the suspicion of theologians, who like all "specialists" do not like that which extends beyond their "speciality," will be even greater. However, I am beginning to observe, here and there, in Paris and in the United States, a certain interest in the anthropological theses of *La violence et le sacré*.

The intellectual climate in France is changing considerably. The extreme leftist Marxist dogmatism is starting to cave in more or less everywhere. A

---

[78] Girard, *Des choses cachées*.

certain kind of religiosity is now almost fashionable, but I think that this is going to produce quite a lot of banalities, as well as other quite aberrant things.

In my new book, you will see, I introduce the notion of intermediary texts, which I call "texts of persecution," into the problematic of archaic religion, mythology, and the Bible, and upon which rests, I think more and more, the articulation of two kinds of text, as well as the historic passage from one to the other: we have no more myths because we read potential myths as collective persecution (racial, religious, political, etc.) and this demythologizing reading seems to me to be governed always by the Bible. So there is an effort to explain the still ambiguous, historic uniqueness of our time, the world in which we live, and the idea that all history is moving toward the complete revelation of the nonviolent God of the gospels.

With all affection,
   René Girard

Innsbruck, March 29, 1978

Dear Friend,

Your book[79] has arrived. I started to read it immediately (almost devouring it). I'm at page 304. My congratulations. I find the entire text excellent. You have clarified very well the anthropological thesis. Your chapters on hominization convince me, and they contribute a great deal to the broadening of your fundamental thesis. While I was reading, I often thought of Maurice Leenhardt's book, *Do kamo* (Gallimard, 1947),[80] which could give added proof of the link between the corpse and God, [and] on the place of the skull as center of the world, etc.

I very much liked your analysis of texts of persecution. This finding is very important. I have only one question: are you completely sure that there are no

---

[79] Girard, *Des choses cachées*.
[80] Leenhardt, *Do kamo*.

texts of persecution outside of the Western world? In the Indies? In China? I recall vaguely having heard of such texts, but I don't have any specific details.

And the biblical texts? I am absolutely in agreement with your anti-sacrificial interpretation of the death of Jesus. I can only underline what you say of the nonviolence of the Father, and of human responsibility. I sensed all this before discovering your theory, and your thinking helped me to *understand*. What remains, though, is the possibility of a misunderstanding. I think that there will be people who will object to your reduction of the cross of Christ to an *epistemological* revelation, whereas the New Testament and the tradition speak of the cross as a source *of life*. I think that a large number of theologians are ready today to accept a *non-sacrificial* interpretation of the death of Jesus, but would refuse a reduction of the cross to a *source of knowledge*. What you say about *love* is central, but I have the impression that that would not be enough to take away the possibility of a misunderstanding.

From the line that you have drawn, I think that one could demonstrate very well that the cross is also a source of life. There are some texts and details that you don't mention much, but which could be easily integrated.

(1) When Jesus unveils violence in the heart of his opponents, they become agitated, but they don't react violently. The violence breaks out when Christ says that he is *one* with the Father (cf. Jn 8: 58-59; 10:30-31). So the violence is aimed at the nonviolent God. It is he that the violence wants finally to strike. From this datum of the Gospels, a new light falls on your anthropological thesis. You say that the victim is *innocent*. It is true, in this sense: that the victim is no more *guilty* than *the others*. Nevertheless, it is also true that the victim, in a certain sense, is completely innocent. The gospels demonstrate that violence, in the final analysis, is always aimed at this *victim*, who is Christ, the beloved Son, the one who is completely outside of the world of violence.

Throughout all history, men have expelled one victim after another. In all these victims, they expelled—without knowing it—*the* victim, who, in the final analysis, is truly innocent. That is exactly what a text from the Acts of the Apostles is saying:

> This is what has come true: in this very city, Herod and Pontius Pilate plotted together with *the* Gentile *nations* and *the peoples* of Israel, against your holy servant Jesus. (4:27)

Since discovering your thesis, this text seems to me to be of great importance. It demonstrates that the alliance against Jesus has a truly universal character. Not only the Jews who lived in the time of Jesus and several Gentiles, but *all the tribes* of Israel and *all the nations* of the Gentiles formed an alliance against him. It is the whole of humanity that transferred its own violence onto him, or else it's violence itself that threw itself upon him.

From here, other texts of the New Testament become intelligible:

> For our sake he made the sinless one a victim for sin, so that in him we might become the righteousness of God. (2 Cor. 5:21)

Hebrew does not make a distinction between a *direct action* and *what is allowed,* which has certainly also influenced the text of Paul. But in its context, the text seems perfectly clear to me. God has permitted that the Son was made a victim for sin, by the fact that the whole of humanity had transferred its own violence onto him.

(2) I think that this view confirms utterly the anti-sacrificial interpretation of the death of Jesus. Jesus announced—as you have so well shown—a nonviolent God. But the question of how God would react if men dared to kill the Son remains open. He sent the Spirit to them. You never mention the Spirit in your analysis. But I think this theme is very important from the perspective that you have opened up.

You say that men are utterly incapable of renouncing violence, and, in this fact, that Christ is not involved in this violence, you see the *proof* of his divinity. I find that to be very true. But the question remains: how are men able to renounce violence? The answer is: the Spirit slowly transforms the hearts of men and renders them capable of this renunciation. By the Spirit we are able to understand that we have transferred our violence onto Christ when we were still blind (and we continue to do this to the extent that we remain blind).

Therefore the cross is the *source of life* in a double sense. (1) Christ remained faithful to the message of the Father, even when the whole of humanity projected its violence onto him. He bore this violence and did not react against it with counterviolence. (2) The Father reacted against the violence by sending the Spirit.

Here I add another theme that I don't find in your text: *prayer*. This is a very important theme in all the NT writings. In the final analysis, prayer is always a prayer about the coming of the *Spirit*. And the Spirit is the Spirit of liberty, love and *peace*, as Paul very often tells us. Peace between men finally becomes possible through the gift of the Spirit.

Here I add a very personal experience. I experience all truly personal and profound encounters as *gift*, as something that I cannot achieve, but as something that has been given to me.

I think that all I have just sketched out and developed in my book[81] is very much in line with your interpretation—and I think that we can remove the ambiguity of the subject of the cross in this way: source of knowledge // source of life [*source de savoir // source de vie*].

One last point then I'll finish: your interpretation of the Epistle to the Hebrews. There is certainly a sacrificial *vocabulary* in this epistle; but I think that we can demonstrate that it is only the *vocabulary* that remains sacrificial, and that the *content* is quite other than this.

I am supported by the following facts: (1) the epistle underlines at great length the difference between *the* sacrifices and the death of Jesus. (2) the same epistle shows a *continuity* between the Old and the New Testament, but this continuity does not appear under the *name* of sacrifice, but under the name of *faith* (11:1–12:4). And the epistle says clearly that the *believer* is one who withstands persecution. Jesus is the one who "persevered against such opposition from sinners" (12:3).

His "*sacrifice*" was that he had learnt obedience, and this obedience was his *faithfulness* to the message of nonviolence at the time of his greatest persecution.

Your interpretation certainly remains possible when we look at the Epistle to the Hebrews in isolation. But I assume that each text of the NT should be interpreted in the *context* of all the other New Testament writings. And I think that the Epistle to the Hebrews is—despite the sacrificial vocabulary— sufficiently clear to allow an anti-sacrificial interpretation (in the OT there is

---

[81] Schwager, *Brauchen wir einen Sündenbock?*.

already the phrase "sacrifice of praise," where the word sacrifice was utterly *emptied* of sacrificial meaning).

Your interpretation of the Epistle to the Hebrews will create some problems [in that] it will serve as an argument for those who defend a sacrificial interpretation. *They will use your own argument against you.* I think, however, that this difficulty can be avoided. In any event, I will defend your anti-sacrificial interpretation against any arguments to the contrary that can be drawn out of the epistle. The sacrificial vocabulary certainly affords one an opportunity to pursue a sacrificial interpretation—but the problem is the same with the apocalyptic texts. The apocalyptic vocabulary can be interpreted in the sense of divine anger. But, as you have well shown, the [nonviolent] *content* is nevertheless clear.

I haven't had much reaction to my book as yet. It seems that the chapter on the NT will be well received, whereas the chapter on the OT will create some difficulty (but it's an intrinsic difficulty, as this [*le texte*] is not yet as clear as [when] you present it, and as I understand it).

Thank you once again, for all that you have given me. I reiterate that I am completely in agreement with your anti-sacrificial interpretation. Consequently I'm very interested in what you have to say about my comments (above all on the issue of the "source of knowledge / source of life").

I will have several opportunities to speak about your book in the coming months: on the radio, in a group of professors, in journals, and to my students.

I hope to see you soon to discuss in depth these issues I have been talking about.

Sincerely,
   Raymond Schwager

THE JOHNS HOPKINS UNIVERSITY—Baltimore, Maryland

April 17, 1978

Dear Friend,

I have received your long letter of the twenty-ninth and, of course, it interests me enormously. I am completely in agreement with you, and I think that the slight divergence between the claims in your book,[82] which I have also received—and accept my congratulations for the superb sobriety of your presentation, for which I envy you—and in mine, does not amount to any essential difference. I also understand that you are disappointed not to find in my work the development of certain appropriately religious themes, but I think that this is properly your domain, not mine. Given my background (and) my intellectual roots in modern critical thought, my research necessarily has to remain in the continuing context of that critical tradition [*ma recherche doit rester dans un contexte qui reste celui de cette critique*]. This should no doubt make it accessible not only to many people, but to the sorts of minds [*certains esprits de la même famille*] for centuries totally shut off, you could say, from anything that touches directly or indirectly the Judeo-Christian tradition.

As for the Spirit, I understand very well what you want to say, but, if you have finished reading my book,[83] since you have sent your letter, you will see that in the last text, cited right at the end, is a text on the Spirit, and in truth I decided years ago to finish the book I was planning with this text.

What's essential in this book, I think, is how it shows that the rise of what I call *transcendence-over* [*sur-transcendance*] is evident from the outset in the reading of these texts, and solely in the reading; that it is never an a priori or perhaps arbitrary position on my part, a false superiority, from which one would leapfrog over the real [*à partir de laquelle on survolerait le réel*].

Yesterday I received a letter from Mr. Huvet, where he tells me that his son, a German scholar, is very interested in your book and may perhaps do a complete translation. I think that he has written to inform you of this project; I would be very happy if this comes to fruition.

---

[82] Schwager, *Brauchen wir einen Sündenbock?*.
[83] Girard, *Des choses cachées*.

For the moment, I think what's essential is to explain and unpack all that which is concealed in the notion of sacrifice, while allowing for the evolution of this term in the direction that you indicate. It may be that at this stage of my work I'm being too adamant about the term itself, but I also maintain that the term isn't important, provided one can see the gulf between the perspective of the gospels and the perspective of the persecutors; a rift that, paradoxically, doesn't preclude a continuity—not just between the Old and the New Testament, but across all the religions on the planet—a strictly mediated continuity, in respect of humanity [*une continuité, sous le rapport de l'homme, qui est proprement médiatrice*], yet without any implication of complicity with the religions of violence. There are also things, undoubtedly still insufficient, in the last pages of the book that you were not aware of when you wrote your letter.

If I were to do the book again, in addition to the Judgment of Solomon,[84] I would also include the scene in the story of Joseph[85] where the hero puts his brothers to the test by pretending to have decided to make of Benjamin, "the other youngest brother," a scapegoat—and where Judah puts himself forward as the victim in a gesture that could indeed qualify as sacrificial, outside of its context. But one cannot refer to this in the same terms, however, as the violence done to Joseph himself in the first part by his eleven brothers, violence that cannot be denied—since it has, historically and anthropologically, the same sacrificial character as the proposition of King Solomon to cut the infant in two. It seems to me that the essentials are present, and one has to assume, I think, that what is great and good in the anti-sacrificial tenor of modern thought, [is] that which goes in the direction of the most profound kind of biblical inspiration.

I certainly don't wish simply to restrict the cross to a source of knowledge, but if it is also a source of knowledge, and not simply evincing the same misunderstanding characteristic of all the primitive religions with which we confuse it, it is perhaps not a bad idea [*il n'est peut-être pas inutile*] to demonstrate this independently, without invoking anything that does not flow from this demonstration; otherwise, we might give the reader the impression of offering for consideration some archaic religious a priori that he or she [the

---

[84] 1 Kgs 3:16-28.
[85] Gen. 37:1–45:28.

reader] needn't worry about, given that this is simply a matter of personal experience, perhaps legitimate in its own domain, but impenetrable to those observing from the outside.

I appreciate that one should not exaggerate the impact that such a demonstration could have, even if history makes it all the more obvious every day. But equally, one should not jeopardize its possible effect by including here whatever would weaken it, for the possible few concerned, even if this has to do with sentiments and attitudes that are not only legitimate, but also entailed by this demonstration.

If perhaps, while I was drafting the book, I had some illusions about the possibilities of an audience who would be open to it—these days it's doubtless necessary to accept [*assumer*] that there is something overwhelming in works of this sort, as you know—all that has descended upon me again, visiting misunderstandings and rejections on me that are even more numerous than in the case of *La violence et le sacré*.

I have already had exactly the same negative reactions [*des reactions negatives jumelles*] from Christians and atheists, both outraged—and about exactly the same things. This is why I appreciate so much your own observations and the deep understanding you have about the entire project. I am really looking forward to getting back in touch with you when I come to Europe next year. And I hope to have some more time in the coming weeks to get back to reading your book, German dictionary in hand, while waiting for the French translation, the thought of which gives me great pleasure.

I think you are quite right about the misunderstanding concerning the apocalyptic language and the sacrificial language of Hebrews. It is up to you to make this clear and I await your works with impatience. I also hope that your book will have the wide audience that it merits. Keep me informed about the reactions in German circles; I will do the same thing on my side. And do let me have your thoughts about the last chapters of *Choses cachées*, especially the one on the *skandalon*.

Very best wishes,
René Girard

Innsbruck, April 22, 1978

Dear Friend,

I've just received your letter that I was waiting for impatiently. It gave me great pleasure as I see that we understand each other well.

Since I sent my last letter I've read part three of your book.[86] What you say about interdividual psychology has greatly impressed me. Of course, I am not really capable of expressing an opinion on a matter of psychology, but what you have to say is so coherent that I can't see how one could reasonably reject it. And after that, the "skandalon." Here, I follow you with all my heart. Since *La violence et le sacré*, I have begun to think and see the texts in more or less the same manner, although I have not managed to express this so clearly. After this reading my only observation is that there are still other texts that tell the same truth with equal clarity (e.g., Mt. 12: 22-30). People are stupefied because Jesus casts out demons. The Pharisees are secretly fascinated because their followers are trying to do the same thing (12:27), but they don't acknowledge this fascination; to the contrary, they condemn Jesus as acting in the name of the chief of the demons. But Jesus shows the contradiction inherent in the accusation of the Pharisees. And this contradiction is nothing other than the contradiction of all the sacred: to do good by evil! Jesus reveals this contradiction, and in this way the house of the sacred collapses.

I have just spoken about your analysis of the "skandalon" with a professor of New Testament at the University of Frankfurt,[87] who, at the moment, is giving a course on the Gospel of John, very much in line with your thinking (mediated by my book). He drew my attention to other texts in the same vein. In the Gospel of John, the Jews speak of Jesus before Pontius Pilate, "We have a law and according to this law, he must die."[88] The Jews take the letter of the law very seriously, because they do not enter into Pilate's house to avoid becoming impure (18:28). But when Pilate wants to release Jesus, they completely change their judgment. They advance an argument that is centered

---

[86] Girard, *Des choses cachées*.
[87] Rudolf Pesch.
[88] Jn 19:7.

on "being a friend of Caesar." The essence of the faith insists that everything is judged according to the will of Yahweh. But the rivalry of the Jews faced with Jesus is so powerful that they betray the essence of the faith and begin to argue, using the position of the enemy of Yahweh (Caesar). This corresponds exactly with your analysis of madness. The subject prefers to renounce his own reason rather than abandon the rivalry.

I was sensitive to the fact that you finished your book with the text of Ezekiel on the issue of the spirit and the resurrection of the dead.[89] My comment in my last letter was too hasty. What you said in your letter in response to my question "cross—source of knowledge / source of life" convinces me totally.

I completely understand that you had great hopes regarding the possibilities of an audience when you were drafting your book (I've had the same experience). But I believe that your hope was completely justified. Of course, your books demand a revolution in the way of looking at these problems, and this isn't something that happens quickly. I reckon in terms of years.

I am not surprised that you have had some negative reactions from Christians. But these reactions don't impress me. Your judgment on sacrificial Christianity is certainly a bit hard sometimes, and on the great authors of the tradition I feel that one should be a little more nuanced; what you say is surely worthy of the ideas of "traditional theology" and of popular piety. But I understand that you have not had the time to study these authors; so the task of bringing these refinements is mine as well as that of the theologians who will follow you.

The only point that continues to worry me is your judgment on the Epistle to the Hebrews. Frankly, here I see a trace of sacrificial thinking. To *unify* the NT, *you throw out a text*. The Epistle to the Hebrews ... your scapegoat?!? One could say that it is a minor point, but I attach a great importance to it, with respect to the reception of your thought in the theological world and in the church.

I can already see theologians totally accepting your interpretation of the Epistle to the Hebrews, saying [*mais eux, ils diront*] that this is the true interpretation of the cross. From this position, they will go and collect all the other

---

[89] Ezek. 37:1-10.

words that have sacrificial connotations in the other writings of the NT. They will construct an antagonistic position, which will pull you against your will into a position of rivalry, and behold, once again, the famous doubles.

I think that we can and should avoid this difficulty. My interpretation of the epistle remains entirely in line with your thinking (pp. 205–9 of my book[90]) and I could add further arguments. The professor from Frankfurt who I've mentioned [*viens de parler*] shares this interpretation and I think that it will be accepted without any great difficulty.

(The main difficulties will come from those who—in the world of politics—will defend counterviolence as a requirement of good sense.)

My book has not as yet attracted much attention: one reaction has been positive; another positive for the NT part and negative for the OT,[91] but this reader did not really understand the new approach represented by your thought. I have spoken a little about you to professors here in Innsbruck, but they are not yet capable of making a judgment.

At the moment, I am giving a course in which I introduce your theory and its application to biblical texts; the reactions from my students are very positive. My assistant[92] has just changed the theme of his doctoral thesis. He has also begun to orientate himself to your line of thinking. Several days ago I received an invitation to give a paper at the University of Saarbrücken; I'll use the occasion to speak of the scapegoat.[93]

In the long run, I am very optimistic. Your thought opens up so many possibilities for a better understanding of religion and human behavior that I don't see how, following basic principles, it could be rejected.

I would like to finish this letter by thanking you for all that you have given me and all that I continue to receive. I will think of you in my prayers and I would be very happy to see you again one day.

Best wishes,
Raymond Schwager

---

[90] Schwager, *Brauchen wir einen Sündenbock?*.
[91] Keel, "Wie böse ist Gewalt?"
[92] Józef Niewiadomski.
[93] This lecture, given on May 24, 1978, was later published: Schwager, "Der geliebte Sohn und die Rotte der Gewalttäter."

THE JOHNS HOPKINS UNIVERSITY—Baltimore, Maryland

May 19, 1978

Dear Friend,

Thank you for your long and interesting letter. You are probably—perhaps certainly—right about the presence of sacrificial elements in my book.[94] Its polemical character, and the fact that it is a book organized in a form necessarily related to the origin of ritual, assures us of that.

Nevertheless, I think that the entire dynamic of this thought demands that one consider as newer those texts that are *more* sacrificial (than the gospels) in the NT; in my opinion, the Epistle to the Hebrews is essential, because it formulates explicitly the sacrificial thesis. I think that you are right, and that, somehow, the epistle *wants to say something quite different about sacrifice* before even the gospels say it, but, in the end, it's sacrifice that it expresses, and in a very explicit way. I think that a more detailed analysis would reveal a close rapport here, and it seems to me that that is what you are demonstrating yourself: the relationship between the *last* of the sacrifices and *no more sacrifice at all* [*entre le* dernier *des sacr. et* plus de sacr. du tout].

And it seems to me that there is, even so, something nuanced in my reading, since I compare this text to the great Old Testament texts. I don't want to suppress or eliminate anything from the NT. (!?).

On the other hand, I see in the still slightly sacrificial form of expression a justification of revelation from a historical point of view, which demands, quite rightly, an equivalent of the OT for the Gentiles.

I realize that, from an orthodox point of view, this attitude poses a problem from the orthodox point of view vis-à-vis the word *sacrifice*. But the *word* is common to all the churches. The texts seem to indicate that at the beginning of the Protestant Reformation, there was in certain traditions an interpretation both anti-sacrificial and religious at the same time. But immediately, Luther in particular fell into ultra-sacrificial [*supersacrificielles*] definitions.

The basic point, I believe, is that the non-sacrificial reading not only illuminates, but reinforces, all the great orthodox and patristic dogmas, and

[94] Girard, *Des choses cachées*.

far from eliminating the idea that Jesus "sacrifices" himself for the salvation of man [*Jésus se "sacrifie" pour le salut des hommes*], it strengthens that also. The only thing to look at is the misunderstanding, from here on, in the *vocabulary*, and so I repeat my question. Can one use the same word for what the bad prostitute did in the Judgment of Solomon and for what the good one did?[95] Is it not essential today to achieve reconciliation, not only between Christians, but more essentially between Jews and Christians, to demonstrate to Jews as to Christians how the thing that is most essential [*que ce qu'il y a de + essential*] in Judaic inspiration demands the recognition of Christ as *fulfillment*, just as it was presented throughout the Middle Ages? [*la reconnaissance du Christ comme* accomplissement *ainsi que l'a pressenti tout le Moyen Age?*]. Is it not essential to dispel what seems to me to be the inevitable sacrificial *misunderstanding*?

I think that all this, in spite of the still [*encore*] abrupt and hazardous character of certain formulations, is moving in the direction of the current evolution of the church and its own self-examination [*sa propre mise en question*], of which the blandness of the progressives is only a caricature.

I am aware that my book provokes parallel, negative reactions, often expressed almost identically by people from completely opposing sides, believers and atheists, Jews and Christians. Those of my friends who are involved in current thinking are very often dismayed by the religious content of my book.

There is no doubt that we need to rethink and ameliorate all that, to get beyond it in every way [*le dépasser dans tous les sens*], and that's your task, but broadly I hope it's already moving past the completely sterile oppositions of the moment, to actually attain something that, in one sense, no one wants to concede, while in another, obscure sense, *everyone* wants to concede it [*pour atteindre vraiment quelque chose à quoi personne en un sens ne veut accéder, et en un autre sens tout le monde obscurément veut aussi accéder*]. I don't know if I am making myself understood.

I'll be in Paris from June 5 or 6 until the seventeenth. I think mainly for a TV program (!). I can tell you that the book is doing better from a sales point

---

[95] 1 Kgs 3:16-28.

of view than anything that I have done up until now, thanks in part to several sensational reviews, in part to the efforts of my publisher, who hasn't done a thing before now, and in part, I hope, because of the book itself.

I think I'll descend on my usual hotel, Hotel d'Isly [...]. If by any chance I go elsewhere, I'll let you know.

Where are you with the contacts with Mr. Huvet and the project that he spoke to me about, to translate your book?[96]

Even if we don't see one another next month, there will certainly be opportunities next year as I'll be in Europe from October, in principle for the whole academic year.

Believe me that your work, your participation in the research that I'm working on, is as precious to me as it is to you. Above all in a period like this, where unexpected reactions from some people, and the extreme incomprehension of most people—even if these are to be expected—amount to no less than something of an emotional trial [*n'en constituent pas moins une certaine épreuve pour la sensibilité*]. I hope soon to have the great pleasure of seeing you again.

[not signed]

Innsbruck, May 28, 1978

Dear Friend,

Thank you for your letter, which gave me great joy. Unfortunately I cannot come to Paris between June 5 and 17, because I am taken up with work at the university. But your talk of a long stay in Paris next year has already given me the idea to have you come here for a lecture in Innsbruck. I'll try to arrange something with the Faculty of Arts and with the French consulate.

I wish you a very fruitful stay in Paris and I hope the TV show proves to be

---

[96] Girard writes in an earlier letter (April 17, 1978) that Huvet had written to him (exactly one week earlier) that his son wanted to translate Schwager's *Brauchen wir einen Sündenbock?*. In Huvet's letters to Schwager, there is actually no such proposal.

a success. *Could you send me from Paris the most interesting reactions to your book?* These will certainly help me find a publisher (translator) for your book.

The reaction to my book[97] remains modest—to date. I see more and more evidence that people are not accustomed to this kind of thinking. So it takes time. A few days ago I was at the University of Saarbrücken, where I took the opportunity to talk at length about your book.[98] The reactions of students and some faculty who were there were generally very favourable.

I can understand (because of my own experience) that negative reactions are testing for you. I guess it is primarily the reactions of people who are appalled by the religious aspect of your book that must affect you particularly. The religious part is the most intimate part of us, and negative reactions in this area wound us most easily—as for me, this is my "job," to talk about the religious, and yet I am also very sensitive on this point.

Your explications of your thinking about the Epistle to the Hebrews were for me very important. I think I can follow the substance of your thought. What remains is the question of vocabulary. You ask the question: "Can one use the same word for what the bad prostitute did in the Judgment of Solomon and for what the good one did?"[99] I think the answer is apparent. In fact, people *have always used* the same word. The problem is the same for other words. People use the word "love" both for the most egotistical pleasures and for total giving (and the same is also true for "freedom," "God," etc.). I think a single word, examined in isolation, remains ambiguous. It is only the context that can clarify things. I see in this the wisdom of biblical texts. They rarely offer us theory. They tell "stories" and the narrative [in question] gives the precise meaning of the words used.

People have sacrificed Christ; he accepted being sacrificed to reveal that God does not want sacrifice (Heb. 10:5-6). "Accepting to be sacrificed" (when one could resist violently or flee) is usually phrased "sacrifices himself." I see the significant problem attendant upon this vocabulary. But I do not see the opportunity to settle this problem. The event by which Christ reveals a

---

[97] Schwager, *Brauchen wir einen Sündenbock?*.
[98] For this, see the relevant editorial footnote to Schwager's letter of May 24, 1978.
[99] Taken from Girard's letter of May 19, 1978; cf. 1 Kgs 3:16-28.

nonviolent and non-sacrificial God is a sacrificial event *from the perspective of the people*. Christ does not share this *view*; his intention is entirely otherwise, but he *accepts* utterly what the people are doing. He consents to being sacrificed.

At the substantive level, there is a complete break between the intention of the people and the intention of Christ, but at the level of the concrete event there is continuity. Because these two levels must remain, an isolated word must remain ambiguous.

In my course on salvation I have almost finished the presentation of your theory and my book. I am now beginning to engage with [*la confrontation avec*] the tradition. The central idea of the Church Fathers was: redemption = *paideia* (education) through the Logos. There is the whole problem of the Logos, as you show in your book. But there is also the whole problem of *paideia*. The excellent book by Werner Jaeger, *Paideia*,[100] shows that all Greek thinking was dominated by the issue of *paideia*. Plato especially sought nothing other than the man *of virtue*, the mastery of desire and of violence through the education of man; and education is made possible, according to him, by the knowledge of the good. Jaeger shows that "the State" of Plato was nothing but a corporation engaged in the business of education (albeit a company that closely resembles a concentration camp). Jaeger also shows that the Greek idea of the "paideia" was totally centered on the "paradeigma" (model) and "mimesis."

But that idea of mimesis was very different from your idea of mimesis. The Greek idea: the one who imitates a virtuous man becomes virtuous and the man who imitates bad people becomes bad. The problem of rivalry is not in evidence.—But it is easily shown anyway. There are texts in Seneca where the idea of imitating the gods leads to the idea of surpassing the gods.

I see now in the idea of *education* the great tendency of humanity to try to overcome rivalry and violence without getting to the truth of the scapegoat. The great ideal of the Age of Enlightenment: the education of humanity (Rousseau, Lessing, Herder, Goethe). The great ideal of Mao: the education of the new man (in a state that looks a bit like the state of Plato).

---

[100] Jaeger, *Paideia*.

Another track:

The Fathers of the Church said: Christ defeated the devil on the cross. The gospels—where do they talk about this victory? The Jews condemned Christ by relying on the argument: we have a law, and according to that law he ought to die, because *he made himself Son of God*. To make oneself God is exactly the definition of Satan. So you have Christ being accused of being Satan. Satan is, therefore, the projection of one's own violent desire, the desire of the Jews and indeed of all humanity, projected onto Christ, who is made a scapegoat. In this way Christ has defeated Satan *by revealing his true nature!*

Sincerely, and with greetings from Mr. Oughourlian and Mr. Lefort,
    Raymond Schwager

I have no further responses from Mr. Huvet!!

THE JOHNS HOPKINS UNIVERSITY—Baltimore, Maryland

July 6, 1978

Dear Friend,

I am back in Baltimore after three weeks in France. The success of the book[101] has exceeded all expectations, especially considering that it had begun so slowly. I did several TV programs, quite a bit of radio, and interviews with numerous newspapers. In another TV program, on which I did not appear, the book was chosen from seven others to be "book of the month." It was presented by an economist called Jean Boissonat, the Editor of a journal entitled *Expansion*! I have been surprised by the interest taken in my book by economists. And also Parisian intellectuals, until quite recently very antireligious, who are in the process of changing, although it is perhaps, I fear, just another passing fad. One should hope that there is also a deeper movement and I hope that the relative success of the sales (they have already printed

---

[101] Girard, *Des choses cachées*.

more than 15,000 but have sold fewer than that) testifies to something other than the efforts of Grasset's publicity department.

Here in America, where the evolution of thinking is slower, the religious dimension of the work frightens the intelligentsia much more than it does in Paris. And the commercial success in Paris risks provoking people's resentment. But I am nevertheless very happy with the much wider distribution than I have had for my two other books.

For the moment we have no secretaries; they have all gone on holidays, but, as soon as I can, I'll photocopy some of the better articles to send you and perhaps they could aid in your efforts to elicit a translation. Italian, Japanese, and Spanish translations are already under way.[102] I will soon bring out a volume of essays here in English and won't forget to send it to you.[103]

I have been very happy with the theological exchanges in our last letters. In this regard, there is at the moment total silence in France, but just before my departure I learnt that the main Catholic bookshops in Paris, which up until now have shown very little commercial interest, have sold quite a lot of *Choses cachées*. In addition, I hear from Grasset that they are getting orders from individual priests, sometimes from isolated rural areas.

I am sorry that we were not in direct contact during this brief stay, but this is just a postponement. I hope that you have been able to arrange for next year the meeting that we have talked about. I will be in France from about October 1 to December 15, then again from the end of January to at least the end of March.

I hope that you are having a good summer and that your spiritual research is on track. Dr. Oughourlian, whom I saw in Paris, has serious concerns for his father, who is very ill, and who is in Paris for major cardiac surgery. I've had a letter from Mr. Huvet, but he wasn't clear; I have the impression that he must be in disagreement on several points.

Very best wishes,
René

---

[102] These translations were published several years later: the Spanish translation, *El misterio de nuestro mundo*, in 1982; the Italian, *Delle cose nascoste sin dalla fondazione del mondo*, in 1983; and the Japanese, *Yo no hajime kara kakusarete iru koto*, in 1984.
[103] Girard, *To Double Business Bound*.

On the television program with me was an elderly French writer, Roger Caillois, very cynical and nihilistic, who is interested now only in stones, precious or otherwise. Because they have no sense at all, he maintains. At the time, I did not know how to respond to him, but the following day, on entering the Church of Saint Germain des Près (next to the café where we met), where I always go when I am in Paris, always in this part of the city, I was struck immediately by a painting—not, by the way very beautiful, representing Christ entering Jerusalem, and below, there was a citation from the Vulgate, of course, the response that I had not thought of the day before on television, the perfect response on the topic of stones: *Lapides clamabunt*. If men do not speak, the stones will cry out ... [104]

THE JOHNS HOPKINS UNIVERSITY—Baltimore, Maryland

July 18, 1978

Dear Friend,

I have the impression that I replied to your last letter. So much of your argument on Satan, as projection of human desires onto Christ, struck me— the [scapegoat] victim expelled. And also what you had to say about mimesis and your reading of *Paideia* from W. Jaeger. It is a book that I also appreciate very much.

I think I did reply and told you all about my stay in Paris. According to the latest news, *Des choses cachées* is on the list of French "bestsellers" published by *L'Express*, in eighth position on July 10 and seventh on July 17. This is to say, things are going well, and even if I have not written to you the letter that I thought I had, indications are good [*l'indication vous suffira pour comprendre*] that the distribution of this book far exceeds that of the other two.[105]

I am writing or else writing again to you to let you know I'll be sending some articles on *Des choses cachées* to you separately. Please excuse my having made you wait. I am sending the most important things from a publicity point

---

[104] Cf. Lk. 19:40.
[105] Girard is referring to *Mensonge romantique et vérité romanesque* and to *La violence et le sacré*.

of view and the most interesting—which are not always the same. The article in *France Catholique* is very good.

Please excuse me also for not having called you from Paris. I really did not have a moment to myself. But now all is calm and I've got back to work. For the moment it is not intolerably hot, as is often the case in Baltimore in summer, so it's best to make the most of it.

Thank you for your invitation and the possibility of a visit [*invitation possible*] to Innsbruck. It would be a great pleasure for me if this could happen. I think warmly of you and of your work, which I feel will continue to develop.

Very best wishes,
René Girard

I don't know what I should put on the envelope to address you correctly when I write. I'd be very grateful if you could inform me about this. Thank you.

Zürich, August 9, 1978

Dear Friend,

I have been in Zürich for two months, where I have received your letter after some delay. It was a very great joy for me to hear about your success in Paris. It's a small reward for the very great work you have accomplished, writing such a very rich book.[106] Certainly, success is something that is very fragile, but the many responses in the "media" allow at least a large number of people to come into contact with your book, and I have no doubt that many people will feel inspired and will carry on thinking along the lines that you have traced.

With regard to my book[107] there is also an occasional positive response. It is not a great success. For "German minds," it is not easy to familiarize oneself with your way of thinking. Here there is still a strict, dogmatic separation of different branches of the humanities (purity of method). But I have no doubt that this dogma will meet its demise sooner or later.

---

[106] Girard, *Des choses cachées*.
[107] Schwager, *Brauchen wir einen Sündenbock?*

I have just written an article in which I mention some French reactions to your book and introduce several of your fundamental ideas. I am now looking to place this article in an important periodical. If successful, I will send this piece along with the French reactions to a publisher to finally elicit a translation. But I understand that it takes patience. For next semester I am preparing a course on the Holy Spirit and baptism. I'm trying to continue thinking along the path you have opened. I will highlight Paul's statements on the Holy Spirit, the Spirit *of peace*, the Spirit as the force that makes peace possible among people who are prone to violence.

I am finding it difficult to develop this course. I have the impression that it is easier to describe negative behavior (rivalry, jealousy, violence, etc.) than to describe positive behavior (love, freedom, peace). Negative behavior can be described using sharp juxtapositions (e.g., all against one), whereas describing positive behavior [*pour décrire le comportement positif*] requires one to "see together" different aspects.

Like you, I will have a few calmer weeks in these summer months. I'd like to rest a little and at the same time read works that I need for my next lecture series.

On August 20, I will have a half hour on South-west German Radio, to talk about my book. I'll be talking above all about you.

Friendly regards,
Raymond Schwager

Innsbruck, December 20 [1978][108]

Dear Friend,

The months pass by so quickly; the end of the year is getting closer and Christmas awaits us. I hope that you will be given a little of that peace that was announced at the birth of the child in Bethlehem, that peace that is so precious to us, and so difficult to achieve.

---

[108] The year is reconstructed from the content of the letter. In the winter semester of 1978–9 Schwager gave a course on the Holy Spirit and baptism.

In recent months, I was very preoccupied with my classes (about the Holy Spirit, baptism, etc.). I am continuing in the direction that you have opened up. What strikes me is that Paul designates *the law* as πνευματικός (i.e., as a reality belonging to the Spirit), and that at the same time he says that sin has deceived and killed people by this law. The ruse of sin is so deep that it can make use of a spiritual reality to deceive and kill. (A pattern [*schéma*] to explain the "dark" history of the church?)

It is a great joy for me to hear that your last book[109] is a success. It will allow many people to get in touch with your thought, and I hope that our collective intellectual and spiritual life will be changed somewhat as a result. Here, in the German-speaking world, the soil is not well prepared. I have written an article of ten pages and have tried to publish it in a major journal. But so far without success. Sometimes I have to wait a long time for a response—all negative at present. I have also sent a small dossier to a large publishing house.—So far no reply. I'll wait a little longer. If no response is forthcoming, I will send the same file to another publisher.

My book[110] is not selling well! But that no longer surprises me. I observe with my students that it always takes a few months of work before they enter into the perspective of your thought. Currently I am doing a seminar on *Violence et le sacré* (a very international group: two from Korea, two from Nigeria, one Australian, one Pole, one Italian, one from Bolivia, and some Austrians). I thought that your book would appeal most immediately to Africans, but it is they who have the most difficulties.

So I understand that it takes patience, but there are also positive signs. H. U. von Balthasar, the theologian who probably has the greatest influence in the Catholic world for the moment, has handed down a very positive verdict on my book. Likewise, K. Lehmann, who is the theologian of the German Bishops' Conference. So I think that your thinking will gradually prevail, even if there is resistance and difficulties for the moment.

I am delighted that you are coming to Innsbruck next year—the ideal time for us would be the month of November. What do you think?—For my part, I think of three lectures, one in French and two in English (one in English

---

[109] Girard, *Des choses cachées*.
[110] Schwager, *Brauchen wir einen Sündenbock?*.

at our Faculty of Theology, on Judeo-Christian thought; one in French on French literature in the context of the French Institute in Innsbruck; and one in English in the context of psychiatry).

Few people understand French and also the number of those who feel comfortable with English is limited. We therefore cannot count on a large audience, but your presentations will be an opportunity to talk about you on the radio and in newspapers.

Is an English translation of *Des choses cachées* in preparation?[111] My students are asking me about it.

With best wishes for the coming year. Sincerely,
Raymond Schwager

[Girard] February 10, 1979

My dear Friend,

I received your letter in Baltimore. I am in Paris at the moment at […]. I'll be here until April 13, apart from some short trips in the country. As I have a lot of engagements and am a little tired, I don't know if I will be able to come and see you in Austria as I had hoped to do, but I would very much like for us to get together and chat about the all those things that interest us.

The sales of my book[112] and the dissemination in the press, radio, and television have been even more considerable than I had hoped, and I've had lots of meetings, notably in Catholic circles. Next to my place, at the rue de Sèvres, there are Jesuits who deal with exegesis, notably Father Xavier Léon-Dufour. They have already invited me once, and I am going back next month to speak to the students. I think that in ecclesiastical circles they are asking questions about my thesis, but are wary of taking a position. But they are interested and that is no mean feat. I have also spoken at the *Centre des*

---

[111] An English translation appeared only several years later: Girard, *Things Hidden*.
[112] Girard, *Des choses cachées*.

intellectuels catholiques [*françaises*], but I am a bit tired of this too hectic life that you have to lead here, and yearn to leave and return to work in Baltimore.[113]

The course that you are giving appears very interesting to me. I'll give you my phone number in any case. It is in Paris,

[...]

I hope that we will soon have the opportunity to see one another.

Friendly greetings, and all my best wishes for your work.
René Girard

Innsbruck, June 27, 1979

Dear Friend,

I hope that you had a safe return to the United States and that you have managed to find a calm atmosphere in which to work. I remember with great fondness our meeting in Paris.

A few days ago I had the joy to learn that the publisher Herder in Freiburg has decided to translate *Des choses cachées*.[114] This is an important step forward. "Mimesis will now come into play." Very soon there will probably be another publisher who will translate *La violence et le sacré*. I am, in any case, in contact with another publisher in Switzerland.

My book[115] has just been included in the program of the "Wissenschaftliche Buchgemeinschaft" [Scholarly Book Club] in Darmstadt, the main organization in Germany for scholarly books. So there is also "some progress" in the German world.

---

[113] Girard had lectured at the *Centre des intellectuels catholiques* in 1976. This institution, however, was dissolved in 1976/77. He may have confused the memory of this lecture in 1976 with a lecture he had just recently given in 1979.

[114] This translation—using only parts of Girard's book—was published several years later, in 1983: Girard, *Das Ende der Gewalt*. A complete and better translation was published in 2009.

[115] Schwager, *Brauchen wir einen Sündenbock?*.

One of my students, who spent several months in Paris, has just brought me your interview in *Le Monde* (May 27–28, 1979),[116] which I am using here for publicity; as well as *Esprit* (April '79)[117] and *Tel Quel* ('78/'79).[118]

What do you think of the criticism of your work that *Esprit* published? Manuel de Diéguez:[119] it's hardly worth talking about. What a vision of Christianity?! But I think that you have made "his task" easier by your rejection of the Epistle to the Hebrews.

Richard Kearney and Northern Ireland:[120] I find this article interesting. What he does not seem to understand is precisely the imitation of Christ; in making themselves the victim the terrorists are imitating the rejected Christ. But this imitation of Christ entails a regression into violence. Kearney gives an impressive example to illustrate the difference between [mere] "*Nachahmung*" [imitation of Jesus] and "*Nachfolge Jesu*" [following Jesus].[121] The latter is done in the freedom of the Spirit and it is that which alone avoids the regression [into violence].

Stiker and the mode of thought:[122] this article signals several points that demand—in my opinion—further explanation (e.g., the problem of language and the problem of otherness). I see a double otherness, one that is governed by mimesis and that hides its identity, and the other, nonviolent love that accepts the other as other: trinitarian love. I see in *trinitarian* love the final answer to the mimetic *triangle*. But the central problem for Stiker: "global theorization is a dream." This is the objection that I find everywhere. And I answer: if one wants to actually *think*, one must dare to argue for universalization. If one limits oneself to some "important aspects" of a phenomenon, one can't judge if these aspects are independent of each other; if they intersect or if they *contra*dict one another. If the question of the contradiction can no longer be asked, it's all over for science [*c'est fini avec la science*]. Who decides what constitutes "the *important*"? Current impressions?!—Pure subjectivity?!!

---

[116] Buillebaud, "Le 'scandale' René Girard."
[117] *Esprit* 28 (April 1979) partially focused on Girard's thinking (several articles were published under the heading, "Sur René Girard: les sciences humaines, le sacré, le terrorisme et les sociétés modernes").
[118] Cf. Muray, "Quand les choses commenceront …"
[119] Diéguez, "Une ethnologie charismatique?."
[120] Kearney, "Terrorisme et sacrifice."
[121] The words in quotation marks are German in the French original.
[122] Stiker, "Sur le mode de penser de René Girard."

Science then transforms itself into bad poetry! But people don't want to accept this truth.

In my course, I have been dealing with the sacraments. The sacramental ritual?—Does it work in terms of transference [*fonctionne dans le sens du transfert*]? I've tried to demonstrate that the sacraments are the expression of the prayer/faith of the universal church, which is joined in the [Holy] Spirit to the prayer of Jesus during his passion (cf. Heb. 5:7). I see in the rite the expression (the sign) of the church's conviction that her prayer will be "infallibly" fulfilled. The church's true prayer (expressive of a non-mimetic relationship, which opens itself to the other as other) therefore allows the overcoming of mimesis. But even prayer can easily fall back into mimetism.

I have given one of my courses in collaboration with another professor. So the problem of rivalry presented itself existentially! Did I manage to overcome it ...? Who knows?

Another comment: H. U. v. Balthasar, of whom I have already spoken to you once, let me know that he will give you a "*place of honor*" in his forthcoming book.[123] This theologian from Basel is one of the most important in the Catholic world, and it is said that his work is read by the current Pope.[124] On the whole he is very impressed with your book [*Des choses cachées*]. His criticisms: natural knowledge of God and eschatology. I have tried to explain more of your thinking to him, but I don't know if I have succeeded.

When one attaches oneself to an "important aspect" (any aspect at all) one can attack your thinking from every direction (and the attacks are contradictory). I am preparing myself for a little "battle" after the publication of your book in German!!

I wish you deep serenity and much strength for your work.

Together in prayer,
Warmly,
    Raymond Schwager

---

[123] Schwager corresponded with him from 1977 to right before his death in 1988 (Raymund Schwager Archive, Innsbruck, II.6). Cf. Balthasar, *Theodramatik III*.
[124] John Paul II.

The School of Criticism and Theory—University of California, Irvine

August 1, 1979

Dear Friend,

I received your letter of June 27 very late here in California, where I am taking part in a summer school. Congratulations for the inclusion of your book[125] in the Wissenschaftliche Buchgemeinschaft [Scholarly Book Club]. Your commentaries on the articles that appeared in *Esprit* about *Choses cachées*[126] bring me back to a universe that is fortunately far from me at this moment. I have found here a solitude and tranquility that I appreciate very much. I expected a certain hostility from *Esprit*, but even so, not to this extent.[127]

I am thinking a great deal about what you said to me in Paris about the role of the scapegoat that Christ agrees to play, if mankind still has need of a scapegoat. I am completely in agreement with you. At the same time, when I go back to the great texts of the OT, like the Judgment of Solomon,[128] or when I see the kind of criticism that is leveled at me by all these people who want Christianity to be the same as all the other religions when it comes to sacrifice, it seems to me always necessary to insist on the non-sacrificial definition that cuts short this kind of criticism, and that could finally put an end to these secular misunderstandings, without damage to the church, which, after all, has self-criticism as its primary vocation. I am seeking formulations that would reconcile all of the various claims, but what you said to me in Paris will count a great deal in what I can do in the future.

For the moment, instead of "Ce que je crois" [What I believe],[129] I have gone back to a new formulation of the entire thesis, which will be more simple than the previous ones, and which will take into account Eastern religions, in particular the great Hindu reflection on sacrifice—especially

---

[125] Schwager, *Brauchen wir einen Sündenbock?*.
[126] Girard, *Des choses cachées*.
[127] For this, see Schwager's letter of June 27, 1979.
[128] 1 Kgs 3:16-28.
[129] Girard mentions his plan to write such a book several times later on (October 19, 1986; October 30, 1991). He never actually wrote it.

the Brahmanas—which is exceptional, but which never takes the prophetic direction toward the revelation of the scapegoat.[130] It has everything except the truth.

You are right about the problem of globalization. Our era is characterized by a refusal of risk in interpretation, which passes for prudence, but which is prudent only with respect to the mimetic game, in which it has no interest per se. It is, in short, an attempt to establish a kind of democracy of exegesis, where everything is "interesting" and nothing is ever decisive. It claims to respect the rights of all individuals, but in putting all on the same level, it reduces ideas and theses to the same nothingness. There is no real attention. It is the perfect doctrine for a bureaucratic age like ours.

What you tell me about Hans Urs von Balthasar also interests me greatly. His attitude comes from the fact that he sees in me, above all, a theologian, when in reality my roots are in literary and ethnological texts. It is an intellectual journey that must be recognized. The problem with Christians is that they either live in an intellectual ghetto and don't see what is happening around them, or, it seems to me, they do see this and then run the risk of adopting theses incompatible with their faith. They let themselves be swallowed by the monster of modernity.

Of course, this is not the case of [Hans] Urs von Balthasar, but the contact with existentialism has played an important role in his work, which, if I am not mistaken, he interpreted in a Christian light. At the time when he began to write, theology must have been rather alarmed.

There will be more simplicity in my next work. I hope that despite quite an effort to demonstrate that many of the questions posed by current criticism are legitimate in their context, it is clear that they can be answered. This is rather similar to what I do here with the students, and I have the impression that it will soon be possible to speak of Scripture without being taken for [being] incurably outmoded or insane.

It is true that this re-emergence of Scripture in the context of the current criticism does run the risk of having undesirable consequences.

---

[130] A result of Girard's efforts in this area was published decades later: Girard, *Le sacrifice*. The Brahmanas are a collection of ancient Indian texts with commentaries on the hymns of the four Vedas, incorporating myths, legends, the explanation of Vedic rituals, and in some cases philosophy.

If I have understood what the people from Grasset tell me, the German translation will contain only the first two parts. I thought that it was better to accept this than to have nothing at all.[131]

I feel in intellectual and spiritual communion with you. I wish you every good thing for your work and much success with your efforts.

Warmly,
René Girard

By the time you receive this letter I will be back in Baltimore.

JESUITENKOLLEG INNSBRUCK

Innsbruck, August 19, 1979

Dear Friend,

Thank you for your letter from California.

The news that you have put to one side "Ce que je crois" [What I believe] and begun a new formulation of your entire thesis makes me doubly joyful.

(1) My publisher has asked me if I would be able to do a Girard Reader, that is, a collection of texts from your books to introduce your ideas to those who don't as yet know your work. He told me that he would have the will [*courage*] to translate *La violence et le sacré* if the public had been prepared by such a means [i.e. via a "reader"] to receive your book [i.e. a German translation of *La violence*] [*si le public était préparé de cette manière à recevoir votre livre*].

I don't find this idea very persuasive. I think it would be very difficult to make a selection that would really give an accurate idea of your thesis. And there would probably also be difficulties with the copyright.

But if you are now yourself in the process of doing "a simpler formulation than offered previously" [*une formulation plus simple que les précédents*], then

---

[131] The first German translation was published without the third part of the book (Girard, *Das Ende der Gewalt*, 1983), but in 2009 a complete and new translation was published (with the same title).

that is exactly what my publisher is looking for. Perhaps he would be ready to do an immediate translation of your text (if it is *easier* than the two previous books[132]). Would you send me a copy of your text when you have worked up one part [*élaboré une partie*]? In this way my publisher would be able to form some idea, and perhaps the translation could be able to appear immediately after its appearance in French.

(2) I am also happy that you are taking Eastern religions into account in the reformulation of your thesis. This was a "lack" that I felt myself, and I have also been asked questions about this in discussions. Among my students is an Indian who wants to begin a thesis and would very much like to work on a subject that involves, at the same time, both Hinduism and Christianity. I have been very hesitant up until now with regard to his project. I was afraid that he would lose himself in a topic that is limitless. I think now that he could begin with the theme that you are dealing with yourself (sacrifice in Hinduism and your thesis), and your next book would help him to produce a result.

The non-sacrificial definition of Christianity? More and more I think that there are two very different *forms* of sacrifice. The first is the case of a violent mob; for them, sacrifice is a transfer of their collective violence onto a victim. The other concerns the reaction of the victim. Normally, the victim is resigned to his fate and so shares the view of the malicious mob. But the "righteous" of the OT "rebelled" against their enemies. And Christ? This is a completely new attitude. On the one hand he is ready to accept the *transfer* [of violence]; he is ready to bear the sins, the violence, and human lies. But at the same time he does not at all share his enemies' viewpoint.

The reaction of Christ concerning the behavior of these enemies—it's *prayer*. I find this text very important: Hebrews 5: 7-10. The *priest* (and so the sacrifice) is *here defined by prayer*. And I think that the Epistle to the Hebrews refers to this prayer as that which rises to the Father, when it speaks of the sacrifice of Christ. Psalms 50 and 119 already speak of the *sacrifice* of praise, praise from the *lips*, and the Epistle to the Hebrews picks up this text (13:15). Thus, this concerns a completely different form of sacrifice. And I understand the "*sacrifice*" of Christ as the *prayer* of one who is ready to bear the violence

---

[132] Schwager is referring to: Girard, *La violence et le sacré*; Girard, *Des choses cachées*.

of others. So I personally have no difficulty in accepting your "non-sacrificial" definition of Christianity, because I think that your thought is directed against the *first form of sacrifice*. And on this point I am completely in agreement with you, that one must reject this.

The problem is thus a problem of vocabulary. Why is the name of sacrifice given to this prayer? My reply: because the Scriptures have spoken like this. Even if her primary vocation is self-criticism, the church never ceases to speak of the *sacrifice* of the Christ because she addresses herself to [*se tiendre aux*] the Scriptures.

One could again ask the question: why does the Epistle to the Hebrews (and also other writings) speak in this manner? I am thinking of underlining the extraordinary aspect of this prayer: it is the prayer of the one who takes away the sins of the others, who has been overwhelmed by an onslaught of violence and lies and who accepts this death (although not by resignation) and prays for these enemies; who *makes of his death a prayer, a gift*. All truly Christian prayer is said "in the name of Christ" (Jn 14:13; 16:24-26); that is to say, all prayer rests on the prayer of Christ (on his "sacrifice"). That the death of Christ is to be seen in the context of prayer is demonstrated by Jesus in chapter 17, the chapter that is commonly known as *"priestly* prayer" (The priesthood defined by prayer).

Perhaps you will say: but these two conceptions of sacrifice create confusion! However, I think that it is impossible to "finally put an end to these secular misunderstandings."[133] I think that there are always misunderstandings. It's inherent in the story.

The lie is so cunning it will always find a way to obscure the truth. And the reaction to your book demonstrates that the definition of Christianity as non-sacrificial also creates misunderstandings. Beneath this formula one will always suspect a reduction of Christianity to a philosophy! So I continue to think that one can (and *"must"*) maintain the word sacrifice, *while declaring* [*en disant*] very *clearly* that which one *must exclude* and that which one *must affirm*.

Another question: In *To Double Business Bound* you write "imitation

---

[133] This is a quotation from Girard's letter of August 1, 1979.

operates with a *quasi-osmotic* immediacy."[134] This expression is a little vague for me. Could you clarify it?

I ask myself if we should not completely rethink the concept of freedom. One thinks normally of an autonomous being, but in the Christian tradition there is the concept of *original* sin. If one has the usual conception of freedom, the concept of original sin is "nonsense." In this case, one should say that man is the *victim* of the sin of another, rather than that there is original *sin*. But this concept is justified if one accepts that the freedom of an individual is always linked to the freedom of others. Even more, that the freedom of an individual is determined by the free acts of others [*les actes des autres libertés*]. Only in this case could one say that a freedom is sinful because of the sins of others. If a freedom is constituted by the freedom of others, one can also understand that an individual perceives in a quasi-osmotic manner "the activity" [*le mouvement*] of another.—But this is perhaps already "philosophy."

Sincerely, with my best wishes for your work,
    Raymond Schwager

JESUITENKOLLEG INNSBRUCK

Innsbruck, November 27, 1979

Dear Friend,

Khomeini is arousing much emotion, even in Europe.[135] This case shows once again the close relationship between religion and violence. It also shows that aggression arouses counteraggression. However the majority of people—even in our community—do not want to see this link (or that identity).

For my part, I continue to explain to my students how the Church has been both linked to the world of violence and how at the same time there were

---

[134] Girard, *To Double Business Bound*, 89.
[135] After the successful Islamic Revolution against the Shah, Ayatollah Khomeini returned to Iran from his French exile.

always attempts on its part to break free of this [*il y avait toujours des essais à s'en libérer*].

And you? How is your work progressing? And your plans for next summer? I would like to ask you whether there is still a possibility of your coming to Austria, as we discussed in Paris? I would be glad if you could give me any details. There is a French Institute in Innsbruck, and it would take time to prepare a joint lecture; the same with the Faculty of Arts. I would be very grateful if you could give me an answer about this in coming days.

One of my students asked me if there is already a translation of *Des choses cachées depuis* in English.[136] Most students here read English better than French.

A colleague from Paris wrote to me that he gave a course about your book to the Jesuits at the rue de Sèvres.[137] He would have liked to have been able to discuss it with me at more length.[138] Maybe I'll take a little trip to Paris next February.

I wish you Merry Christmas and feel in communion with you.

Sincerely,
Raymond Schwager

THE JOHNS HOPKINS UNIVERSITY—Baltimore, Maryland

December 10, 1979

Dear Friend,

Thank you for your last letter. It is always a pleasure for me to receive an echo of your reflections and thoughts.

I have just received the last book of Father Xavier Léon-Dufour,[139] which relates to our common project, and refers to it in a complimentary manner.

---

[136] For this, cf. Schwager's letter of December 6, 1976.
[137] The Centre Sèvres is a private Jesuit university, founded in 1974, and approved by the Pope in 1986.
[138] This is either Michel Corbin or Xavier Léon-Dufour, though it is more likely to be Corbin.
[139] This should be: Léon-Dufour, *Face à la mort*.

I am going to read this book very carefully because there is a great deal in it on sacrifice.

I am working quite well but I don't have the sense that I'm making much progress. I am reworking in French my basic argument about mythology, starting with the falsified reports of violence coming from the perspective of the persecutors (the texts called "persecution texts" in *Des choses cachées*).[140] I want to analyze closely the mental processes that one carries out automatically, almost without thinking, when one analyzes such a text—about Jews or lepers being responsible for plague in the Middle Ages—and show that it's these same processes [*les mêmes opérations*] that we can't help but recognize in the scapegoat role [*que réclame la déduction du rôle du bouc émissaire*] played by the victim-hero in myths. What is surprising is not really my hypothesis, but the fact that it should appear surprising at all.

I'm also working again on Shakespeare. I have some papers to give and this seems to me much easier to do … because it is Shakespeare who does all the work.[141]

I'm finally working on some OT and NT texts—including Job, about which you seem to me to be a little too harsh [*sévère*] in your book.[142] It seems to me that one can't approach this as a unified text. [I'm working] also on the synoptic texts of "the kingdom divided against itself" and the expulsion of the demons[143] either by God or by Satan. I think this is absolutely essential.

I envy you your trip to Paris in February. I'd forgotten your suggestion of Austria, and I think that it is better to abandon the project for this summer as I have to be in Jerusalem for two months, if I go to Europe—(and Asia). I have overcommitted myself recently and I'm afraid that my university obligations will call me back here faster than I would have wanted. To be honest, my travel plans aren't yet finalized, and it could be that I spend the entire summer here, continuing to write, and also staying for family reasons. Given

---

[140] From this emerged: Girard, *Le bouc émissaire*.
[141] Girard wrote several articles and essays on Shakespeare. This work eventually resulted in a book: Girard, *A Theater of Envy*.
[142] Girard is referring to the manuscript of Schwager's *Brauchen wir einen Sündenbock?*. From Schwager's letter of March 4, 1980, it becomes clear that the passage to which Girard referred was not part of the published version of Schwager's book.
[143] Mt. 12:25-30.

these uncertainties, it is better not to commit myself, for which I apologize. But I hope nevertheless that we meet up somewhere soon. Johns Hopkins is planning a translation of *Des choses cachées* but, as yet, they haven't even found a translator.

I also wish you the best Christmas, and I feel very close to you.

Best wishes,
René Girard

JESUITENKOLLEG INNSBRUCK

Innsbruck, March 4, 1980

Dear Friend,

I've just spent four days in Paris. It was a very fruitful stay for me. I spoke a great deal with Michel Corbin, who is a professor at the Institut Catholique. He considers your work to be an intellectual event of the first order. I got on very well with him. He is a specialist on the work of Anselm of Canterbury and St. Thomas Aquinas. I explained to him a little of my idea of working gradually towards organizing [*d'organiser lentement*] an international effort to pursue detailed research on the basis of your central hypothesis.[144] He said that he was very ready to take part in this. I would like to discuss this project in detail with you one day.

Another result of my stay in Paris. X. Léon-Dufour proposed that I get my book translated for the collection "Parole de Dieu," published by Editions du Seuil. Of course he can't decide this on his own. The publisher also has a say, and no decision has been taken as yet. But it is likely. Father Léon-Dufour now wishes to add to my book a short dialogue between you and me on the question of sacrifice, to make a link between my book and yours (*Des choses cachées depuis la fondation du monde*). Hence my question: are you coming to

---

[144] These thoughts eventually led to the foundation of the Colloquium on Violence and Religion (COV&R) in 1990.

Paris this summer? The text must be ready by July this year to enable the book to come out in January 1981.

Another idea: the "Bundesministerium für Wissenschaft und Forschung" in Vienna[145] has informed us that the "National Endowment for the Humanities" (Washington, DC, 20508) has a translation program and funding set aside for foreign books. All that is necessary for translation is that a university propose a work. So the idea came to me that you might write something to the organization in question about this.

Just by chance, I stumbled upon the novel *The Slave* by Isaac B. Singer (Farrar, Straus, and Cudahy, New York). In the book there is a short description of a village fête (Poland, Middle Ages) that corresponds to your thesis almost word for word. The author explicitly describes the "Queen" of the fête as a scapegoat (in the German translation at page 47–8).[146]

Another very interesting book: Rosemary [Radford] Ruether, *Faith and Fratricide: The Theological Roots of Anti-Semitism*, The Seabury Press, New York, 1974. The author (a Catholic nun who converted to Judaism[147]) maintains that the roots of anti-Semitism are to be found in the NT. Any exegesis of the NT that accepts the Christ as a "cornerstone" would be responsible for all the evils to the Jews through history.

It's a vigorous attack. I think that it is only by an interpretation along the lines of the surrogate victim that one could demonstrate the weak point of this attack. Your comments (in your last letter) apropos of Job are fair. I myself saw the weakness in my text on Job and dropped this paragraph from the book. (The text that I sent you is not identical in my book. I reworked it before publication.)

I've just had published a short article "Geschichtsphilosophie und Erlösungslehre."[148] I've returned to the ideas of a German philosopher who demonstrates that the "philosophy of history," which considers man as both the subject of history and an actor in it, leads necessarily to the hunt for a

---

[145] The Federal Ministry of Science and Research of the Republic of Austria.
[146] Singer, *The Slave*.
[147] This is not the case; Ruether was never a nun, never converted to Judaism, and is still a member of the Roman Catholic Church. We cannot say how Schwager obtained such incorrect information.
[148] Schwager, "Geschichtsphilosophie und Erlösungslehre".

scapegoat (because mankind, in the end [*à la longue*], will not put up with being responsible for the crimes of history).

This philosopher (Odo Marquard) did not like his own conclusions, so he abandoned the "philosophy of history" that he himself had previously defended, and sank into skepticism. I try to show that only a theology of redemption can get us out of this dead-end. (I will send you a reprint.)

Other matters must wait for another time (I have to leave for a talk on my book). I await a word on your travels in summer. I'll be very happy to see you soon.

Together in prayer,
Raymond Schwager

JESUITENKOLLEG INNSBRUCK

Innsbruck, April 20, 1980

Dear Friend,

Time flies. I have just received a letter from Father Léon-Dufour, in which he informs me finally that a translation of my book will not be possible. The publisher (Seuil) is being difficult. They think that the translation won't be a commercial success. So Fr. Léon-Dufour has to bow down before this "higher reason." The plan for a short dialogue on the notion of sacrifice, which I spoke to you about, thereby loses its justification.

I'm now following up on another project. An Austrian scientific association publishes a book every year, in which about thirty projects of scientific research are presented to the public. This year I have been invited to present my work, and that of our institute.[149] I'd previously informed them that I was working, with the assistance of your theory, on the theme "violence–religion–society." I would like now to mention in my text other work that is being carried out

---

[149] Cf. the published paper: Schwager, "Religion, Gesellschaft und Gewalt."

with the aid of your theory. (I am acquainted with Paul Dumouchel and J. P. Dupuy, L'enfer des choses;[150] and V. Descombes, "Une solution de la stratégie atomique: la télépathie", Critique, 1979.[151]) *Could you let me know if there are other important books or articles treating a problem with the aid of your theory?* I have one month to write my manuscript.

In my last letter I wrote to you that I would be happy if we could establish some kind of communication between people who are working with the aid of your theory. This could perhaps strengthen the research program that you have opened up.

In this context, I have another question: One of my students—an Indonesian—will finish his thesis this summer.[152] From the month of January 1981 until June 1981 he will be in Chicago. Before returning to his country he could spend several more months in Baltimore. He wants to do research on an important Javanese text with the help of your theory, and he would be happy to be able to prepare himself for this work through personal contact with you. *Would you let me know what sorts of activities you will have at the University of Baltimore from September 1981 to January 1982* (courses, seminars, discussion groups)?

Among the reactions to your work, there is quite a discussion concerning your concept of "union in love" ["*amour fusion*"]. In this context, I often think of a text of Richard of St. Victor concerning trinitarian love.[153] (Trinitarian love—is it not the final response to triangular desire?)

I thank you once again for all that you have given me through your work. I realize more and more that this has had a decisive influence on my life.

Sincerely,
R. Schwager

---

[150] Dumouchel and Dupuy, *L'enfer des choses*.
[151] Descombes, "Une solution de la stratégie atomique."
[152] This thesis was published a year later: Banawiratma, *Der Heilige Geist*.
[153] Richard of St. Victor, *De trinitate*, esp. bks 3 and 4.

THE JOHNS HOPKINS UNIVERSITY—Baltimore, Maryland

May 7, 1980

Dear Friend,

You asked me to let you know of books and important articles about my work, or from the same or a similar perspective. Eric Gans, author of *Essais d'esthétique paradoxale* (Paris: Gallimard, 1978[154]), is bringing out a book in English on the elementary structures of language, from a modified mimetic perspective (University of California Press). Another American, Bruce Basoff, publishes on contemporary English and French literature from a mimetic perspective. Cesáreo Bandera has published *Mimesis conflictiva* (Madrid, Gredos, 1975). A former student of mine is also working from this perspective: Sandor Goodhart has published an article on Sophocles, "Leskas Ephaske: Oedipus' and Laius' Many Murderers," *Diacritics* 8(1) (Spring 1978): 55–71. He also works on Shakespeare. Josué Harari has provided some commentary on me in his *Textual Strategies* (Ithaca, New York: Cornell University Press, 1979) and he is preparing a review of *Choses cachées*.[155]

Michel Deguy is preparing an anthology with articles by himself, Eric Gans, Pierre Pachet, Jean-Pierre Dupuy, Paul Dumouchel, etc.[156] Dumouchel, for his part, is working on projects in the areas of sociology and economics. Dupuy is looking to formalize the logic of mimetic desire, which he thinks, as you know, approaches some of the most recent [philosophical] logics.

I'll also mention two very good students here who are finishing theses that will be published: Paisley Livingston on mimetic desire in the films of Ingmar Bergman,[157] and Tobin Siebers on the evil eye.[158]

All things considered, I think it would be better if I send you my *curriculum vitae*, which will give you all details known to me. There are lots of things that will not be of interest to you, but others, perhaps, you may find useful.

I think we will be able, in a year or so, to have the symposium on the entire

---

[154] First edition: 1977.
[155] Girard, *Des choses cachées*.
[156] Deguy and Dupuy, eds, *René Girard et le problème du mal*.
[157] Livingston, *Ingmar Bergman and the Rituals of Art*.
[158] Siebers, *The Mirror of Medusa*.

mimetic problematic, probably here at Hopkins.[159] I hope that there will be sufficient funds to get you here.

Thank you for the text of Richard of Saint Victor, which is very beautiful. I have not received the article that you promised me, on the Geschichtsphilosophie [philosophy of history].[160]

I have thought about what you said to me in one of your last letters on the non-sacrificial interpretation,[161] and I think that you are right; it must also engender misunderstandings—the opposite misunderstandings to those that give rise to the sacrificial interpretation, but similar in the long run precisely because of this opposition [*des malentendus inverses à ceux que suscite la lecture sacrificielle mais analogues en fin de compte justement parce qu'inverses*]. But it is only a matter of vocabulary, and finally, one is obliged to say that no vocabulary is adequate, nor could it be, from the fact that human thinking and language are rooted entirely in sacrifice, in the founding violence. I think that, at this level, we are perfectly in agreement.

I am still not certain that I will go to Paris, but if I go it will be June 15 because of travel costs. I confess to you that I am feeling very lazy now about traveling.

I am sorry that the translation of your book[162] did not work out with Seuil. With the threats that are weighing on the economy, publishers are more cautious than ever.

It will be with the greatest pleasure that we welcome your student here, but in 1981–2 it is more or less certain that I will be in France for most of the year. Your student should write to us so that we can see where he is exactly. If I am in Paris, it will be at this address […]

With all my friendship,
René Girard

---

[159] This conference did not take place at Johns Hopkins University, but at Stanford University. The title was *Disorder and Order*. The results were published under the same title.
[160] In German in the French original. Girard is referring to: Schwager, "Geschichtsphilosophie und Erlösungslehre."
[161] Girard is referring to Schwager's letter of August 19, 1979.
[162] Schwager, *Brauchen wir einen Sündenbock?*.

[Girard] Paris [June 1980][163]

Dear Friend,

Here I am, already in Paris for two—almost three—weeks, and I have not had the time to get in touch with you! I'll be in France until July 3. I'll have a little more time in the week beginning the thirtieth, which will finish with my departure on Thursday, July 3. I would very much like to see you, but I don't have the time to visit Innsbruck. Would it be possible for you to come to Paris? A little trip?

I came here because I've been invited, to my great surprise, to a breakfast with John Paul II, during his visit to Paris.[164] There were about twenty intellectuals of every stripe, but the majority were Catholic. But also Protestants, Jews, several atheists.

In Grasset, I saw various articles of yours in German periodicals on my writings, some of which I didn't know, and I thank you for this effort that you are making to disseminate my work. I hope the German translation will be good, despite the mutilation.[165]

The review by Hans Urs von Balthasar[166] has aroused great interest and I think he sees the explanatory importance of the thesis, despite his reservations on the question of sacrifice. I would have liked, of course, to see him discuss this at greater length.

I hope to see you soon. I send my most sincere affection.
René Girard

---

[163] Undated letter; month and year can be deduced from its content.
[164] The Pope was in Paris from May 30 to June 2, 1980; afterward he traveled to Lisieux.
[165] Girard is referring to the first German translation (1983) of *Des choses cachées*, which included only a part of the original French text: Girard, *Das Ende der Gewalt*.
[166] Balthasar, "Die neue Theorie von Jesus als Sündenbock."

JESUITENKOLLEG INNSBRUCK

Innsbruck, August 3, 1980

Dear Friend,

Thank you for the news you sent me from Paris. The meeting with the Pope was certainly a sign for you that your work finds a resonance in the Church. I'm very happy about that; I hope, too, that you had a good trip back to the US and that your move to San Francisco will go well.

We are on holidays here: I'll make use of August to write one or two articles on the history of the theology of redemption. It was a great theme with the Fathers of the Church: the cross as victory over Satan. But none of the Fathers manage to formulate a coherent theory; in one of my articles I show how this theme was so widespread that we are obliged to take it seriously; and after that I am trying to prove that it is only through your theory that one will arrive at a coherent articulation. Jesus told the Jews (and all men) that they had Satan as father (Jn 8[167]). But they return this accusation; they demand the death of Jesus with the words, "we have a Law and according to this Law, he must die; he *has made himself Son* of God" (Jn 19:7) or "because of blasphemy: *though you are only a man, you make yourself God*" (Jn 10:33). Being a man and making oneself God is the essence of Satan. So the Jews accuse Jesus of being filled with satanic essence. Satan is, at the same time, the murderer from the beginning and the father of lies. In accusing Jesus of being Satan the Jews themselves react according to the satanic spirit, because they kill him falsely [*En accusant Jésus d'être le Satan, les juifs agissent eux-mêmes selon l'esprit satanique, car ils le tuent mensongèrement*]. Satan, therefore, would be this hidden will of the Jews and of all humanity that transfers its own perversion onto Jesus. He is the scapegoat of his enemies; but because Jesus is without fault, his enemies do not succeed in sacralizing him; they have to "*satanize*" him. The essence of Satan becomes manifest in the death of Jesus.

---

[167] Jn 8:44.

And another idea: St. Athanasius was the first to work out a very precise notion of the "sacrifice of Christ." He says that God has given a *Law* to mankind, and that he was bound to a sentence of death by this Law that he transgressed [*et qu'il a lié une sentence de mort à cette Loi en cas de transgression*]. In fact, mankind (Adam and Eve) violated this Law. What are the consequences? If God carries out his own sentence, he destroys his work (which is unacceptable); if he does not carry it out, he is not truthful (which is even more unacceptable). What solution remains? The Son of God will come and he will accept that the sentence of death will fall on him, in our place. The death of Jesus therefore—for Athanasius—is, in this sense, a sacrifice: that he offers his body, in our place, so that the demands of the law are met. St. Athanasius says: *The judge comes first of all to be judged himself.*

And a very interesting book: H. Koller, *Die Mimesis in der Antike*, Francke Verlag, Bern, 1954. The author shows that there are two conceptions of mimesis in Plato: mimesis as imitation and mimesis as representation (actors in the theater). According to Keller the idea of imitation is secondary. He points out that the verb μίμεσθαι [mímesthai] comes from sacred dance. Originally it referred to the action of actors in sacred games. Koller formulates the hypothesis that the word "mimos" designated the actors in the Dionysian festivals.

Koller says—albeit only in passing—that in these sacred dances there were always two choirs. But it seems to me that it is exactly this element that permitted "represent" to morph into "imitate." The choirs, which represented the sacred action, imitated each other. The word "mimesis," therefore, comes from ritual.

Koller also mentions a book that I don't have access to, but that would be perhaps interesting for you. L. von Schroeder, *Mysterium und Mimus im Rig Veda*, H. Hassel, Leipzig, 1908.

Likewise a book of *Cardinal Ratzinger* (Munich) could be interesting for you. *Einführung in das Christentum*, the chapter "Gelitten unter Pontius Pilatus." There is certainly an English translation of this book.[168]

---

[168] Ratzinger, *Introduction to Christianity* (part 2, Ch. II.2, "Suffered under Pontius Pilate, was crucified, died and was buried").

When are you leaving Baltimore? What will your new address be?
I wish you well for your work in San Francisco.

Sincerely,
   Raymond Schwager

THE JOHNS HOPKINS UNIVERSITY—Baltimore, Maryland

August 18, 1980

Dear Friend,

We are in the process of working on the same subjects. Satan is above all the enemy, the accuser (of Job, for example), and this is the real meaning of the word "diabolos." *Diabolè* means, first of all, dissension, discord, and from there, accusation in the legal sense, often slanderous accusation. And then I think of the *Paraclete*, which means defender, advocate, and for me, the spirit of *truth*; it's the spirit who defends all victims, the one who inspires first of all Christ himself—for example, in the episode of the adulterous woman[169]— and afterward the disciples, allowing them to take back [*de rapporter*], in a spirit of truth, what in the gospels was always related to a spirit of diabolical accusation: [i.e.] the passion itself; the collective murder, which appears in cultures only under the form of mythology, in which the representations engendered by standard religions show themselves to be, at the same time, accusatory and idolatrous.

I am working on a book[170] that will lay quite a deal of stress on our power to read *truthfully* [*de lire* en vérité], as a performance [*comme representation*] inspired by the scapegoat—giving an account [*les comptes rendus*] of persecution in our world—in order to demonstrate that my reading does not, in principle, bring forward a new interpretation, but only extends to the mythological text, and all the archaic religions, a method that we have practiced for

---

[169] Jn 8:1-8.
[170] Girard, *Le bouc émissaire*.

centuries in the Western world, since we gave up hunting witches and don't believe any more in sorcery. [All this] to demonstrate that this interpretation, in appearance anti-Christian, is in fact quite unique in our world and necessarily [*forcément*] inspired by the Paraclete, the defender of victims who has never done the same in any other cultural universe.

It is the development of the chapters of *Choses cachées*[171] that immediately precede the Christian part, but have a closer logical connection between the Christian texts and the new biblical texts. And this time I think I can start with the Christian texts and follow an entirely logical order.

And I am going to try to express more clearly the difference between the text structured by the effect of the scapegoat—an account of a witch trial, for example, written by judges who believe in the guilt of the victim and therefore don't say that she is a scapegoat—and the text of the historian who demystifies the first text, and who says "the victim is a scapegoat." A text structured by the scapegoat effect cannot make a theme of this; [and in turn] a text that makes a theme of the scapegoat cannot be structured by this effect. In the gospels, Christ is so obviously the scapegoat of everyone [in the text] that he can no longer be the scapegoat *of the text*, just as the sixteenth-century witch isn't the scapegoat of the twentieth-century historian.

This is really why I always have difficulties with all sacrificial formulations that suppose a scapegoat effect that is still active and yet not revealed. I am prepared to accept Christ's willingness to be the scapegoat even of Christians in the course of history. But by the very fact that we say this, we escape, if only ideally, from the scapegoat structure—and theology necessarily represents this ideal [*mais, du fait même que nous le disons, nous échappons, ne serait-ce qu'idéalement à la structure du bouc émissaire et la théologie c'est forcément cette idéalité*]. Even if Christ is our scapegoat, he is not that of the Father, and [so] the sacrificial understanding is always relative, while the absolute is that which is beyond all sacrifice. Tell me what you think. Is it that the definition of perfect love between the Father and the Son, or the identity of loving one's neighbor and the love of God, realized only by Christ himself, mightn't be what's beyond sacrifice [*ne serait pas cet au-delà du sacrifice*]? This does not

---

[171] Girard, *Des choses cachées*.

exclude, of course, the imperative to "give his life for his friends."[172] I ask myself if, in orthodox Christian circles, one does not run the risk of losing something essential to save the sacrificial formulation, which scandalizes non-Christians—and not without reason [*qui ne scandalise pas les non-chrétiens sans raison*]. And after all, this formulation has no dogmatic sanction; we can't rule out that the church won't decide to renounce sacrifice—one day, after long examination [*on ne peut pas exclure qu'un jour, après de longs examens, l'église ne décide pas*]—faced with the evidence that the elimination of sacrifice bears fruit on so many levels (if this is understood, not in the insipid and saccharine sense that "progressives" envisage it, but from the conception of sacrifice that we present, for the renunciation of sacrifice).

I ask myself, if, by an excessive desire for continuity, theological thinking does not take sufficiently into consideration the formidable weapon that "sacrificialism" constitutes in the hands of enemies of Christianity, because it [theological thinking] risks thinking inside a Christian "ghetto," and forfeits an excellent chance to show the universality and limitless power of the NT text.

This does not entail, by the way, a condemnation of sacrifice, either in historic Christianity, or even in primitive religions—which can only be what they are. I think that the sacrificial formulation perennially defers every decisive opportunity [*diffère toujours tous les moments décisifs*], with the most sacrificial churches in history counted as the most successful because they held literally to the [sacrificial] texts, even in the darkest times [*et la supériorité des églises les plus sacrificielles dans l'histoire, même dans les moments les plus noirs c'est qu'elles ont préservé les textes dans leur lettre exacte*]. Whereas philosophical and moralistic movements, in keeping with the fashions of various epochs—from ancient gnosticism through to Enlightenment thought—result in the suppression of the cross. The orthodoxy of the major churches—Orthodox, "high church" Protestant, and above all Roman Catholic—could reside in [*serait dans*] this preservation of what's essential, allowing the future spiritual campaigns of the Holy Paraclete to emerge more fully into revelation [*permettant aux opérations futures de l'esprit saint Paraclet, d'avancer dans la*

---

[172] Jn 15:3.

revelation]. Whereas the gnosis of every age destroys everything because it does not respect the "mystery" of the cross.

I am not saying all of this in the spirit of "provocation," I hope, but merely to try out these reflections on you, because I am not yet sure of what I am saying, and I want to look again at the problem of sacrifice, in the light of criticism, of course. I remember very well what you wrote to me about the fact that Christ always serves [*se faisait*] as a scapegoat in Christian history, and I agree with you. But having said that, is it not correct to say, in the final analysis—in a way that anybody today can understand [*que personne ne l'est plus dans le niveau de compréhension aujourd'hui possible*]—that he *is* not that?

In fact, I think that the word we use has not much importance, or rather it is inevitably poor [*mauvais*], because the whole language is permeated with "sacrificialism" in the worst sense of the term—language emerges entirely from this.

Thank you for your comments. I think you are right about the accusation made against Christ of his being essentially satanic, when he is accused of desiring "to become God," and about this process of "satanizing" instead of "sacralizing." The essence of Satan thus manifests clearly in the death of Jesus, but it is also the sacred essence without the "good side," the beneficial and peaceful side, that is rightly no longer there from the moment that all is revealed.

A thousand greetings. I am not leaving for Stanford until before the end of December or January and hope that you will write to me here before that date.

In any event, my university address over there is: Department of French and Italian, Stanford University, Stanford, California, 94305.

René Girard

JESUITENKOLLEG INNSBRUCK

Innsbruck, September 3, 1980

Dear Friend,

Thank you very much for your last letter, which I read with great interest. I await—almost with impatience—your forthcoming book.[173] The link that you see between the Western scientific method and Christian inspiration is, in my opinion, of great importance. This will show that the Spirit does not work only in the church and among Christians, but blows where it wills [*partout où il veut*]!

What you have to say about the Spirit as defender, I see in the same manner; but I had not yet seen the direct link between the *words* "accuser" and "defender." Thank you!

And sacrifice?

The difference between a text that *speaks* of the scapegoat and another that is *structured* by the scapegoat is certainly of paramount importance. In this sense, I am completely in agreement with you that Christ is no longer—in the Gospels—an unrevealed scapegoat. It's the opposite: now he is spoken of openly as the scapegoat!

Therefore I am completely in agreement with your phrase: "Even if Christ is our scapegoat, he is not that of the Father, and the sacrificial understanding is always relative, while the absolute is that which is beyond all sacrifice."[174]

What is left to specify is "the absolute"! Is it not the Kingdom of God in its full (pan-terrestrial) [*trans-terrestre*] realization? And I would say that theology (and preaching) is *the announcement* of this completely non-sacrificial Kingdom [*Règne*]—an announcement that is already at work in history and that slowly transforms this history!

But theology is not only an *announcement* of the future; it must also look back and *speak* of what *we still are*. And with this, there is something that I have not formulated clearly enough up to now: Christ is our scapegoat, but—and

---

[173] Girard, *Le bouc émissaire*.
[174] This quotation is from Girard's letter of August 18, 1980.

here I am in complete agreement with you—*the positive effect* doesn't come any more from the fact that once more we have found a scapegoat; *the positive effect only comes from the fact* that Christ transforms violence and hatred and falsehood into love, and that he *sends* us the Spirit of Truth and Love.

The sacrificial mechanism, as such, no longer has any positive effect! But the overcoming of sacrifice does not begin *outside of the sacred*. For a start, Christ completely accepts [*Le Christ accepte d'abord totalement*] "the old game," in an acceptance that is not merely a game, but very real.

The death of Christ has a salvific effect only in the sense that it *transforms* and *reverses* the sacrificial mechanism, but by *entering totally into this mechanism*, or by allowing himself to be captured by the mechanism!

"Is it that the definition of perfect love between the Father and the Son, or the identity of loving one's neighbour and the love of God, realized only by Christ himself, mightn't be what's beyond sacrifice?"[175]

I am in agreement, adding that the actualization of love in Christ shows how far [*jusqu'où*] perfect love can and should go. It includes *solidarity with those* who still need a scapegoat—and in that sense it gets mingled up in [*se mêle*] the sacrificial world.

The Father does not desire sacrifice; but mankind needs it! The Father gives men a victim, who initially enters into their game, and that liberates them from the inside.

H. U. v. Balthasar strongly underlines that the true measure [*dimension*] of the love between the Son and the Father is revealed to us uniquely by the fact that Christ is in solidarity with sinners right to the end. This is an idea that I find very profound!

So Christ's acceptance of becoming a scapegoat for men has, at the same time, *two* dimensions:

1. liberating men, in accepting what they have done, right until the end;
2. revealing by this acceptance what the love of God truly is, of a God who does not distance himself from the world of sinners, and thus from the sacrificial mechanism.

Do you see these things in the same way?

---

[175] This quotation is from Girard's letter of August 18, 1980.

Another word on the subject of "the idealism of theology." In fact, traditional theology has not only *spoken* of the scapegoat, but the texts remain in a certain manner structured by the scapegoat, as you have shown! Will a future theology escape this fate entirely? The historian who demonstrates that a "witch" was not in truth a "witch," but a scapegoat, certainly does not—in this sense—enact a sacrificial reading. But these historians, don't they use their works to accuse other people (people of this period, the church, etc.) and to transform these into a scapegoat?

And what of ourselves? Are we really completely outside this mechanism? The people who come after us, won't they find aspects of sacrificial thinking even in the way we use anti-sacrificial theory?

I think that theology, even in its idealism, remains inside "this world"; it [theology] is the announcement of the Kingdom of God, but [it] will always be in need of conversion—it is not yet in the Kingdom of God!

And the question of the word "sacrifice"? I see the weight of your arguments, and it won't finally be us who decide this question. I think the dangers of misunderstanding still remain. If we abandon the word sacrifice, the danger would be to not sufficiently underline the *solidarity* of Christ with *us*, who are still terribly embedded in a sacrificial world. Besides, the Council of Trent defined the *Mass* as *sacrifice*, which obviously [*évidemment*] implies that the cross is also a sacrifice. The church would therefore have a lot of trouble in abandoning this word. But it's finally a question of tactics!!

And another question: is the project for a conference on the theme of "mimesis" going to come off [*se laisse réaliser*] in 1981?[176] If so, could you let me have the exact date soon? The chance of getting the cost of the trip from the Austrian Government would be greater if I could do a small presentation at the conference. I don't think that I have a great deal to say, but it would make my application easier.

I wish you strength in your work—in deep union.
Raymond Schwager

---

[176] For this, see the relevant editorial footnote to Girard's letter of May 7, 1980.

JESUITENKOLLEG INNSBRUCK

Innsbruck, December 8, 1980

Dear Friend,

The time for your departure from Baltimore is approaching. I hope that the move will be calm, and that things will begin well for you in San Francisco. And your work? Is it making good progress?

For my part, I began the cycle of my courses (a cycle of three years) at the beginning of October, and I began with a quick presentation of your theory. The majority of the students were very interested, but for a certain number it is too demanding. During the semester I have no free time to pursue my personal work. For that I have to wait until the end of teaching [*la fin des cours*]. Of course, the preparation of the courses helps me deepen that which I have already written in my book.[177] Lately, I have been occupied with the Jewish position, which reproaches the New Testament writers with vigor for having falsely interpreted the Old Testament. I find that your theory is essential in finding a valid response to this criticism. If one considers the Old Testament as a mixture of sacrality [*sacralité*] and revelation, an argument with the *letter* of the OT becomes impossible. I think that the Jewish point of view does not take seriously enough the "contradictions" within the OT.

And the conference in San Francisco? Given that I have not received a response to my last letter, I presume that the preparations have not proceeded such that a date has been fixed. So I suppose it is planned for later. Would that be correct?

For this Christmas season, I wish much peace and profound grace for you, your family, and your work.

Very sincerely,
 Raymond Schwager

---

[177] Schwager, *Brauchen wir einen Sündenbock?*.

THE JOHNS HOPKINS UNIVERSITY—Baltimore, Maryland

December 28, 1980

Dear Friend,

Thank you for your letter and your good wishes. I send you mine, especially for an intellectual and, above all, spiritual life always fertile and close to the true Spirit, nourished by him.[178]—Recently, my reflection has turned very much on the Spirit. I don't know if I spoke of this in my last letter, but from the moment I grasped the opposition—Satan = the accuser, and the Paraclete = the defender, the defense counsel in a trial—many things in passages from that great final prayer in John[179] have become clearer. Also on the role of Satan in Job.

In my new work[180] I will also have something on the demons of Gerasa[181]—about the *crowd* of demons expelled—the expulsion of expulsion, and the terrified reaction of the Gerasenes, who are pagan and do not want to see their sacrificial system destroyed.

We are just at the point of leaving for California, and even though it should be a good decision, I think, it is a trial. All our children were here with us for Christmas and it was a great joy for us to see how much they love these family gatherings and we hope to all get together again soon in California.

I'm thinking about calling my forthcoming book simply, *Le bouc émissaire*. As far as I know, the title has not been used in France except for the publication of a part of the big [*grand*] book of Frazer.[182]

I will hope to see you this summer. I have to go to Switzerland for a colloquium, and they are paying for my travel. I think it's about August 15.

Again, I send you all my best wishes and affection.
René Girard

---

[178] While the French "lui" allows a translation of "her" as readily as "him," and while some Feminist theologians, hymn writers, and others during the period of this correspondence began referring to the Holy Spirit with the words "she" and "her" (in part, because the Hebrew "ruach" is feminine), we can be confident that our reasonably conservative Catholic correspondents would not have done so. Hence, despite any editorial preference, we are using "him."
[179] Jn 17.
[180] Girard, *Le bouc émissaire*.
[181] Mk 5:1-20 and parallels.
[182] Frazer, *The Golden Bough*.

STANFORD UNIVERSITY—Stanford, California

Stanford, May 13, 1981

Dear Friend,

Thank you for the news you sent. Would you be able to let me know the reference for the Balthasar piece, or even, if it is possible, to send me a photocopy of the twenty pages on our ideas in his last book?[183] The professor[184] who translated *Des choses cachées* into English[185] is here in Stanford; he studied theology in Germany and I would be very happy to have him read these pages.

Congratulations on your activities and your television program.[186] What you tell me about my translator isn't very encouraging, but even so I hope he will finish the German translation one of these days and that the book will come out.

My next book[187] is taking shape, but not as rapidly as I would have hoped. I have thrown myself into mimetic readings of certain passages, such as the denial of Peter,[188] and especially the death of John the Baptist, in Mark.[189] This allows me to take up the problem of mimetic scandal and to clarify and restate the essentials of the thesis at the beginning of the book, without centering myself on the text of the passion, which I have spoken about directly. I'd prefer not to hurry and to produce a book a little tidier than the last one.[190] I will also have a reading of miracles, and in particular of the demons of Gerasa,[191] which I hope will allow me to show that the texts are a very long way from the magical thinking that the ethnologists claim to find in them.

I am sending you an invitation to the colloquium that we will be holding here at Stanford in September.[192] It will be centered on the natural sciences

---

[183] Balthasar, *Theodramatik III*, 276–91.
[184] There were two translators for this book (Stephen Bann and Michael Metteer); Girard seems to refer to Stephen Bann.
[185] Girard, *Things Hidden*.
[186] On February 27, 1981, *Austrian Broadcasting* (Österreichischer Rundfunk, ORF) aired a discussion with the psychologist Wilfried Daim about Schwager's *Brauchen wir einen Sündenbock?*.
[187] Girard, *Le bouc émissaire*.
[188] Mk 14:66-72 and parallels.
[189] Mk 6:17-29 and parallels.
[190] Girard, *Des choses cachées*.
[191] Mk 5:1-20 and parallels.
[192] Symposium *Disorder and Order*, Stanford University, September 14–16, 1981. Cf. Girard's letter of

and economics. There will be, no doubt, a little on mimetic desire, as the economist Jean-Pierre Dupuy, who has written a book on the subject,[193] will be there; but nothing in a theological vein, nor anything religious per se. I am not saying this to discourage you from coming, but to let you know what sort of meeting this will be. I hope, subsequently, to be able to organize another meeting that will directly concern the topics that interest us most.

The phrases that you cited in your letter interest me very much, in particular, "they have exchanged the glory of an incorruptible God for a *representation*" ["*ils ont changé la gloire de Dieu incorruptible contre une représentation*"]. Everything related to a fall into the sacrificial world, which would precede hominization, remains very obscure for me, and I don't know how to reply to you.

I have go to France from June 10 to 20 for a meeting in Normandy[194] that is a bit similar to the one we will have here in September. Perhaps you could come to Paris. Life here is very pleasant, and I am very happy to be here.

With my best wishes for your work and your thinking.
In friendship,
René Girard

JESUITENKOLLEG INNSBRUCK

Innsbruck, May 24, 1981

Dear Friend,

I was happy to hear your news and hope that you are happy with your work at Stanford and that you feel at home in that part of the world.

Attached are pages from Balthasar's book that discuss your book.[195] I've started a little dialogue with him on his criticisms of you (natural theology,

---

May 7, 1980.
[193] Probably: Dumouchel and Dupuy, *L'enfer des choses*.
[194] This meeting took place in Cerisy-la-Salle, June 10–17, 1981. A publication emerged from it: Dumouchel and Dupuy, eds, *L'auto-organisation*.
[195] Balthasar, *Theodramatik III*, 276–91.

God's wrath, etc.).[196] I know teachers who are starting to take you seriously because Balthasar finds your ideas at least very interesting. So this criticism is beneficial when people engage with your books.

The symposium at Stanford on natural sciences would interest me, even if it does not deal with questions in my discipline.[197] But I cannot make it there. I agreed to participate in a conference on "Violence and Nonviolence in the OT,"[198] a conference that will probably be big enough [*assez important*] to make your ideas known to a wider audience. In addition, it is too late to apply for funds for the trip. But I believe that the lectures from the conference will be published and that I'll have the opportunity to read the texts.

Similarly it is impossible for me to come to Paris between June 10 and 20. We'll still be having classes and examinations at that time. But in your letter before last you wrote that you'll be coming to Switzerland in August. Is this plan still in place? I would be very happy to see you then. Otherwise I expect to see you in Paris some time during the coming academic year.

One of my students is now in Denver; he is very interested in your work. Could you send him a detailed program for the Stanford conference? I don't know if he has time to participate, but maybe he can come to California.

J. B. Banawiratma

[...]

For the moment I do not have much time to continue my research. But during the summer I would like to work on the Pelagian crisis (Pelagius–St. Augustine) and interpret this as a mimetic crisis.[199]

Pelagius tried to understand redemption through the Greek idea of "paideia" (paradeigma–mimesis). St. Augustine strongly criticized this theology. I have found in Seneca texts that show that the imitation of God (or the gods) leads to a rivalry with God. (So there is rivalry not only when the object of desire is limited—imitation seems necessarily to arouse rivalry—can we say that the imitation of God is the fundamental sin?). The subtle forms

---

[196] Raymund Schwager Archive, Innsbruck, II.6.
[197] Symposium *Disorder and Order*, Stanford University, September 14–16, 1981; cf. the relevant editorial footnote to Schwager's letter to Girard of May 7, 1980.
[198] Meeting of the German-speaking Old Testament scholars in Brixen (South Tyrol), August 24–28, 1981. The papers were published in Lohfink, ed., *Gewalt und Gewaltlosigkeit im Alten Testament*.
[199] Based upon this, he published an article: Schwager, "Unfehlbare Gnade gegen göttliche Erziehung."

of rivalry interest me more and more. In my course on Christology I try to show that the great christological controversies were the result of a tradition of thought dominated by rivalry (siding either with God or man) and that the great progress of the Council of Chalcedon was to posit a "true God" and "true Man" in a state of perfect personal unity [*une parfaite Unité (Personne)*], a unity that includes otherness.[200]

And what do you think of the new US government?[201] Over here there is a growing number of people who see the mimetic behavior of the two superpowers. But we don't see an outcome. It seems that the US government is preparing the ground for a possible war limited to Europe and the USSR. But who will survive? A future that is not very comforting! It is essential for me to believe that even this future is in the hands of God!

Very sincerely,
Raymond Schwager

STANFORD UNIVERSITY—Stanford, California

August 9, 1981

Dear Friend,

We have had two visits here from Father Banawiratma, who is a charming young man, and who gave us much pleasure. Yesterday we all ate as a family; my children were there and it was truly an excellent day.

I am trying to finish the book that I spoke of to you,[202] but the preparations for the colloquium that I was telling you about[203] and the aftereffects of our getting settled [*installation*] here—without mentioning other interruptions

---

[200] He further developed this train of thought in a posthumously published book: Schwager, *Dogma und dramatische Geschichte*.
[201] From 1981 to 1989, Ronald Reagan was President of the United States of America.
[202] Girard, *Le bouc émissaire*.
[203] Symposium *Disorder and Order*, Stanford University, September 14–16, 1981; cf. the respective editorial footnote in Schwager's letter to Girard of May 7, 1980.

and the fact that my decreasing capacity to work, which is diminishing with age—are making these final stages difficult and delaying me considerably. The original book has divided itself into two, I think, the first focusing above all on myth, insofar as it is read by the passion, the second mainly containing interpretations of gospel texts, of which the majority have been ready for quite a while—the denial of Peter, the beheading of St. John the Baptist, the demons of Gerasa. These readings are more detailed than those undertaken in *Choses cachées*.

Father Bono,[204] as he told me to call him, tells me that, as far as he knows, the German translation of *Choses cachées* should be finished soon.[205] I would be very happy if the thing finally gets done [*si la chose finalement se fait*].

Summer here in California is really very agreeable, but for us the coming month is looking very busy because of the colloquium; I'll be spread very thin.

In the spring of 1983 there will be a conference in Cérisy-la-Salle conference center in Normandy—a week devoted to the problems raised by my work. Consider yourself invited [*D'ores et déjà je vous y invite*]. It will be in *June*.[206]

Please excuse me for not having responded to your last letter. I will send you soon, I hope, the texts comprising my forthcoming book, in which I would like to present the evidence for my theory as rigorously as possible, like a proof [*comme démonstration*], and without polemics not directly relevant to the central issues [*le problème*] of the book.

I hope your summer is good, and productive for your work.

I think often of you, and wish you much inspiration from the Holy Spirit.
René

---

[204] The earlier mentioned Johannes B. Banawiratma, SJ.
[205] Girard is referring to the German translation, finally published in 1983 (Girard, *Das Ende der Gewalt*).
[206] Interdisciplinary symposium *Colloque René Girard*, Centre Culturel International de Cerisy-la-Salle, June 11–18, 1983. The results were published: Dumouchel, ed., *Violence et vérité*.

JESUITENKOLLEG INNSBRUCK

Innsbruck, August 30, 1981

Dear Friend,

It was a joy to receive your letter, and I am very pleased that Father Bono[207] has met you, and that you had a good day with him. I hope that this meeting has given him an extra incentive to work in the direction of your thinking.

I wish you much success for the colloquium[208] and I would be very happy to hear the "results" one day.

Last week, I attended a conference on "Violence and Nonviolence in the OT," with professors of the German-speaking world who teach the OT.[209] They invited me to the closing session, which lasted half a day. At the beginning, there was a very short presentation of your thought by someone who is very favorably disposed toward you. Following that, there were three long papers, in which the results of very technical research were presented on "Holy War in Israel," "Enemies in the Psalms," and "The Servant Songs in Second Isaiah," followed by discussions. All the results of the research went in the direction of your thinking. Nevertheless, there was strong opposition to you, and to my book.[210] One professor from Münster, for example, who wrote a very negative review of my book,[211] told me afterward in private that he had not grasped before that I make a radical distinction between the sacred (violence) and the holiness [*sainteté*] of the Christian God. He was under the impression that I wanted to explain all of Christianity by violence. My jaw dropped!?!!

Many others were telling me that the theory of Girard is interesting in a certain way, but it wants to give a mono-causal explanation of all religious phenomena and, because of this, it must be rejected. The word "*mono-causal*"

---

[207] Johannes B. Banawiratma, SJ.
[208] Symposium *Disorder and Order*, Stanford University, September 14–16, 1981; cf. the respective editorial footnote in Schwager's letter to Girard of May 7, 1980.
[209] Meeting of the German-speaking Old Testament scholars in Brixen (South Tyrol), August 24–28, 1981. Cf. the respective footnote to Schwager's letter of May 24, 1981.
[210] Schwager, *Brauchen wir einen Sündenbock?*.
[211] Zenger, Review of *Brauchen wir einen Sündenbock?*, by Schwager.

was used repeatedly in the criticisms. The closing discussion was not about violence, but on questions of method.

I was able to clarify quite a few things and several have changed their minds and are now more favorably disposed to your thought. But I also observed that the question of violence touches personal emotions. That's why it is not just a matter of argument—an always-present emotional undercurrent has to be taken into account [*c'est toujours tout un arrière-fond d'émotion qui est mis en question*], and on this level one does not easily change minds. The three long papers will now be published in a book, and I have been invited to add a small text, which gives me the occasion to say a word to the readers. We also want to add this book to a list of your books, and others that take up your theory.[212] Therefore I prevail upon you to send me a list of the books that deal with your work (I have a list that goes until early 1980).

Thank you for your invitation to Cérisy-la-Salle. Is it correct that this session will be held in 1983 (not 1982)?

I am working at the moment on St. Augustine.[213] It is quite simple to demonstrate that his critique of Pelagius is fundamentally about mimesis.

What is more difficult to grasp is the true scope and import [*portée*] of Augustine's doctrine of grace.

In this doctrine there is a mix of a very strong sense of the generosity of God along with a vision of him that can horrify. What is interesting is also his definition of sacrifice: = each work, through which, one is united with God through [*par*] a holy community. Augustine underlines the communal character of Christian sacrifice. This is how he arrives at this surprising formula: *It is the sacrifice of Christians that forms one body* (*City of God*, X, 6).

Next week I will attend a meeting of Jesuits on the question of disarmament. The subject makes for a lively discussion and I am getting a little involved.[214] I would be able to spend my time giving lectures on this subject,

---

[212] The papers, Schwager's text "Eindrücke von einer Begegnung" (214–24), and a bibliography on Girard (245–7) were published in: Lohfink, ed., *Gewalt und Gewaltlosigkeit im Alten Testament*.

[213] Schwager later published a paper that resulted from this work: Schwager, "Unfehlbare Gnade gegen göttliche Erziehung."

[214] Schwager did quite some work on this topic, e.g., Schwager, "Der Heilige Stuhl und die Abrüstung"; Schwager, "Von der biblischen Lehre der Gewaltfreiheit."

and on the question of violence. But I refuse nearly all invitations, otherwise I wouldn't get any work done.

I wish you much courage for finishing your two books.[215] I await them with "impatience." You are in my prayers.

Very sincerely,
Raymond Schwager

STANFORD UNIVERSITY—Stanford, California

September 29, 1981

Dear Friend,

I always need a long time to reply to your letters, as my tasks are multiplying, and I also have the impression that it is taking more time to finish my ongoing work.

The colloquium[216] went very well from Stanford's point of view, a big success, but for me a lot of lost time, and ultimately little intellectual gain.

At the moment we have my friend the writer Michel Serres with us; he is a visiting professor at Stanford. It's upsetting for me to always be installed in university departments that basically are not mine, and not to be able to invite someone like you. But we will see one another in France next year.

Everything that you tell me about your activities interests me greatly. I am sorry about the resistance and incomprehension, above all on your account, because that could hinder you in your work, but I think that with time you will be able to clear up [*éclaircir*] the misunderstandings. People who think that you want to explain all Christianity by violence are truly very naïve. I come across quite a few things like that here. The mimetic is not mono-causal; it is rather a principle of complexity. To people who say "is there only mimetic

---

[215] Schwager is referring to Girard, *Le bouc émissaire*. Obviously, he misunderstood Girard's remark in his letter of August 9, 1981, according to which his book will consist of two parts.
[216] Symposium *Disorder and Order*, Stanford University, September 14–16, 1981; cf. the relevant editorial footnote to Schwager's letter to Girard of May 7, 1980.

desire?" I reply that the answer is probably [*sans doute*] "no," and that, in any event, that isn't what interests me. What interests me are the consequences of mimetic desire for the linking [*sur les rapports*] of individuals and societies.

The emotional undercurrent [*L'arrière-fond d'émotions*] that you spoke of is very important.

Please find attached the bibliography of reviews of my work.

One can see that the question of disarmament has become very important in German-speaking countries, and what you tell me about it interests me a great deal.

It is indeed in '83 and not '82 when the meeting will be held in Cerisy-la-Salle.[217]

I wrote recently to Professor Konrad Thomas of the Sociology Seminar at Georg August University, Göttingen; he is interested in my work, and in my very late reply, I spoke to him of you.

My work[218] is progressing, but less rapidly than I would like. I will send you soon a few fragments on the gospels.

With all my friendship,
René Girard

JESUITENKOLLEG INNSBRUCK

Innsbruck, October 26, 1981

Dear Friend,

Thank you for your letter. I am happy that the colloquium at your university went well and was a great success.[219] I am waiting now for the texts on the Gospels, and on the interpretation of myths, that you spoke of.[220]

---

[217] Symposium *Colloque René Girard*, Centre Culturel International de Cerisy-la-Salle, June 11–18, 1983. Cf. Girard's letter of August 9, 1981.
[218] He is referring to his work on: Girard, *Le bouc émissaire*.
[219] Symposium *Disorder and Order*, Stanford University, September 14–16, 1981; cf. the relevant editorial footnote to Schwager's letter to Girard of May 7, 1980.
[220] Texts, which Girard wrote for: Girard, *Le bouc émissaire*.

The translator of your book (*Des choses cachées*)[221] spent a few days on holiday recently near Innsbruck. I valued the opportunity to go and see him, and he showed me a part of his "translation." But what translation? Sometimes it's a summary, sometimes there is not even one-fifth of your text remaining, sometimes there is a certain fidelity to your text, sometimes there are errors. I said to this "translator" that his work cannot be published as a translation, that he can publish his work as a "confrontation with Girard" or as an "introduction," but not as your text. He pretty much accepted this criticism.

In the light of this I have written to the publisher. I think that no translation is preferable to this translation; I hope that I have acted in your best interests.

Professor Konrad Thomas (Göttingen), of whom you spoke, sent me a text that he has done for a publisher (Suhrkamp). I hope he will have more success than I have had in convincing this publisher to translate *La violence et le sacré*. I also hope that Herder will employ another translator for *Des choses cachées*. I know the first translator, and right from the outset I had my suspicions about him. Now, it is at least clear that his work isn't going ahead [*ne va pas*]. He said to me, "I am a free man and I only write what corresponds with my convictions." What a principle for a translation. In case Herder asks for the rights to translate several "extracts" from your book, I would advise you to be very cautious about it. As soon as I have any news, I will write to you.

Work has begun again at the university. I wasn't able to conclude all my projects during the summer, but overall I am very pleased with my work at the university; more and more I realize that I owe so much to you for my intellectual work, and I thank you very cordially.

With all my friendship,
Raymond Schwager

---

[221] Ladislaus Boros. This translation into German was not completed because Boros died suddenly (cf. Schwager's letter of January 10, 1982).

JESUITENKOLLEG INNSBRUCK

Innsbruck, January 10, 1982

Dear Friend,

The new year has begun and I hope that you are bearing up [*vous vous portez bien*]; I think of you in my prayers and hope profoundly that God will bless you, your family, and your work.

A friend who teaches at the Institut Catholique in Paris[222] wrote on a New Year's card he sent to me: "The older I get, the more I realize that René Girard has put his finger on something essential. Many educated Christians know this, but the learned don't want to hear about it. It's true that it throws light on the flimsiness of their ideas."

I am witness to the same resistance of the "learned" here. Nevertheless, I have the impression that there are people who are beginning to listen a little.

The saga of the translation of your book[223]—and it's really a saga—has taken a most unexpected turn. Several weeks ago the translator[224] died. I don't know if the publisher Herder has already hired another translator. Even prior to this unexpected event, I have forwarded two other names (as eventual translators) to Herder.[225]

His death has been very difficult for his wife (he was a former priest and Jesuit). But who knows? This small detour may give a little providential help to your work.

About E. de Rosny, who has described his experience in Africa with the help of your theory, I've just heard that his new book[226] is a huge success (15,000 copies sold in two weeks—eight pages in *Paris Match*). I don't yet know if he speaks much about you in the book—I hope so; that would be quite a help!

---

[222] Michel Corbin, SJ.
[223] Girard, *Des choses cachées*.
[224] Ladislaus Boros.
[225] In the end, neither of them was assigned the work of translation.
[226] Rosny, *Les yeux de ma chèvre*.

My article on St. Augustine is finished (with publication probably in a year's time).[227] I'm now working on Maximus the Confessor.[228] I realize more and more that the question of freedom is central to patristic thinking about redemption. But nobody managed to adequately formulate this problem. Freedom is also the positive counterbalance to the *sacrificial mechanism*.

Have you elaborated upon this issue at all [*développé un peu ce problème*]: freedom–mechanism / freedom–mimesis? I am looking for extra enlightenment on this.

The question of peace remains wildly popular in German-speaking countries. If I had the time, I would have many opportunities to speak about it. But the political question must remain marginal for me. I think that theological work is my calling.

Two books have just come out that are more or less directly aimed at you and me, even if they say little of us.[229] I have begun an epistolary dialogue with the two authors, who, again, have the same misunderstandings. But they are beginning to make concessions![230]

I wish you all the best.
With all my friendship,
    Raymund Schwager

Father Bono[231] arrived safely in Indonesia. He has begun to teach. I hope he will have enough time to do some research

---

[227] Schwager, "Unfehlbare Gnade gegen göttliche Erziehung."
[228] From this emerged: Schwager, "Das Mysterium der übernatürlichen Natur-Lehre."
[229] Schwager is referring to: Hoffmann, *Sühne*; Schenker, *Versöhnung und Sühne*.
[230] An adaption of one of Schwager's letters to Schenker was published: Schwager, "Versöhnung und Sühne."
[231] Johannes B. Banawiratma, SJ.

STANFORD UNIVERSITY—Stanford, California

January 26, 1982

Dear Friend,

Thank you for your last letter. And thank you for all that you are doing for the translation of *Des choses cachées*[232] and the dissemination of my work. There are also problems with the English translation.[233] The first translator never did anything and we are looking for a second. The psychological part will probably [*sans doute*] appear separately.

As for the German translation, I would really prefer that the dialogue format not be omitted, and that the names of Oughourlian and Lefort appear on the cover, as in the French version. It would not be fair to them, especially Oughourlian, if they are left out—and I ask myself, after a rather ambiguous indication from Paris, if this was not the intention of the first translator and publisher.[234] If it is ever to go ahead, we could perhaps slightly shorten certain things where there is repetition, but go no further than that.

I feel that a great weight has been lifted. The day before yesterday, my manuscript[235] finally left for Paris (feast day of the conversion of St. Paul!).[236] Please excuse my not having sent you anything, but I have had secretary problems lately and I was absolutely overwhelmed by my mail, and all sorts of things that have remained in suspension while I finished this book. I am going to send something now.

This term—I am giving a course on the Bible, which is going very well. As always here, there is an extraordinary mixture of Protestants, Catholics, lots of Jews, Asians, and atheists, but the reactions, particularly with the Jews, are often passionate. Yesterday, I spent two hours on the Judgment

---

[232] Girard refers to the German translation, which was published (if only partially) in 1983 (Girard, *Das Ende der Gewalt*).
[233] This was only published in 1987: Girard, *Things Hidden*.
[234] In the end, in the 1983 German translation (Girard, *Das Ende der Gewalt*) the dialogue format was omitted, not crediting Oughourlian and Lefort. This was finally put right in the completely new translation of 2009 under the same title.
[235] For: Girard, *Le bouc émissaire*.
[236] The feast day of the Conversion of St. Paul is actually January 25.

of Solomon,²³⁷ and it is a marvelous text to attack all the pseudoscientific attitudes: anthropologism, Freudianism (and freedom, as you say, [as] the positive counterbalance to sacrifice), sociologism, etc. The students here, as everywhere, don't know much. But Stanford is a little like the Harvard of California and [so], the selection [process] being strong, they are ignorant and very intelligent at the same time. This makes for a much better combination than the majority of our colleagues (!).

If there is no problem with Grasset, my new book should be published at the end of April. It could be that it will be entitled *Qu'un seul homme meure* (It is better that one man should die, than that the whole people should perish²³⁸). I did not finally include the texts on Job that I had begun. But the last chapter is on the Paraclete (a bit too fast perhaps). The gospel section is on the passion, the beheading of John,²³⁹ the denial of Peter,²⁴⁰ the demons of Gerasa,²⁴¹ Satan expelling Satan,²⁴² and the Paraclete. There is virtually nothing on the OT. And the first part is entirely on persecution and myth, with quite a few readings of the great myths. I am looking forward to seeing you in Europe next year.

In greatest friendship,
René

I am curious about these books you mention that are directed against us. If you can, please give the references in your next letter.²⁴³

E. de Rosny doesn't really mention me in his book.²⁴⁴ I can't wait [*il me tarde*] to see your article on St. Augustine.

---

[237] 1 Kgs 3:16-28.
[238] With this, Girard quotes—partially—from the words of Caiaphas according to Jn 18:14. In the end, the book was entitled *Le bouc émissaire*.
[239] Mk 6:17-29 and parallels.
[240] Mk 14:66-72 and parallels.
[241] Mk 5:1-20 and parallels.
[242] Mt. 12:25-30.
[243] See the relevant editorial footnote to Schwager's letter of January 10, 1982.
[244] Rosny, *Les yeux de ma chèvre*.

[Girard] Paris, June 20, 1982[245]

Very dear Friend,

Here I am in Paris for a stay of more than a year, and very happy to be in France, despite my attachment to the United States, and California in particular, where we have been for a year and a half.

The news on the topic of the German translation[246] is certainly very good, and I won't insist on the original format, as you tell me that it creates a problem. In any event, it's Grasset's business, who own the rights, and who have agreed to enter into a specific contract with the German publisher. Thank you for "keeping an eye on" [*surveiller*] the translator.[247]

I don't remember if you have mentioned receiving the invitation to the "week" in Cérisy-la-Salle, which will be held from June 11 to 18, '83, on all the problems that touch on my work, from economics to theology. Cérisy is a castle in Normandy where, every summer, symposia are held on subjects mostly literary and philosophical, with sometimes one hundred people present, who are accommodated in the castle itself, or in houses in the grounds. If you haven't yet received the invitation, you will soon, and I hope that you will respond. I hope also that we will have the chance to see each other before this and be able to chat at our leisure, now that we are geographically closer to each other.

I was very touched by your reaction to *Bouc émissaire*.[248] The book is sometimes attacked in the press, perhaps more than the preceding one,[249] effectively because, as you say, it necessitates a decision. But it is doing very well with the public.

A book of Dr. Oughourlian's on desire will be coming out in September,[250] as will a book of articles on my work,[251] both with Grasset. A mimetic theory

---

[245] The content of this letter shows that one letter by Schwager was lost. Girard probably lost it when he traveled from France back to the United States of America.
[246] Girard refers to the German translation of *Des choses cachées*, which—using only parts of Girard's book—was published in 1983 (Girard, *Das Ende der Gewalt*).
[247] August Berz.
[248] Girard, *Le bouc émissaire*.
[249] Girard, *Des choses cachées*.
[250] Oughourlian, *Un mime nommé désir*.
[251] Probably Deguy and Dupuy, eds., *René Girard et le problème du mal*.

of money has just appeared, *La violence de la monnaie*, by Michel Aglietta and André Orléan (Presses universitaires de France).[252] Also, in the United States, there's a mimetic interpretation of Ingmar Bergman, by one of my former students (Cornell University).[253] There will also soon be a book on the evil eye, *The Evil Eye*, from another student at the University of California.[254] But, from French theologians, not much. Do you know *Mort pour nos péchés* (publication of the Facultés universitaires Saint-Louis, Bruxelles)?[255] The text predates both your book[256] and mine,[257] but there are several allusions to *La violence et le sacré* in it.

I hope soon to have the pleasure of seeing you, perhaps here. I have a "studio" (a one-room apartment) here, and adjacent there is a small hotel where lots of German-speaking people come to stay. I will be away at the beginning of August but I'll spend the best part of summer here, in Paris. It is at [...]. From September 20 I'll be living in a bigger apartment rented by Stanford [...].

Thinking of you,
René Girard

[Girard] Paris, November 2, 1982

Dear Friend,

Thank you for your letter[258] and the packet. I really hope to see you in January, but I will be in the United States from December 22 to January 2 (arriving on the evening of the third) and I'd be very sorry to miss you. Could you lengthen your stay or put your trip off for two or three days? Let me know soon. If this

---

[252] Paris, 1982.
[253] Livingston, *Ingmar Bergman and the Rituals of Art*.
[254] The actual title was: Siebers, *The Mirror of Medusa*.
[255] Léon-Dufour et al., *Mort pour nos péchés*.
[256] Schwager, *Brauchen wir einen Sündenbock?*.
[257] Girard, *Des choses cachées*.
[258] This letter by Schwager has not been preserved. Girard probably lost it when he moved back from France to the United States of America.

isn't possible, I will come back a day earlier. But, I'd prefer, if possible, to spend January 1 at home, as there will be a family reunion.

I know the book by Adolf Jensen well, as I used it at the time of *La violence et le sacré*.[259] There is some quite remarkable material there, but his thesis is a sort of justification of sacred murder, a bit analogous in certain respects to that of Otto,[260] or of Walter Burkert in *Homo necans*,[261] if I remember correctly.

Apropos of this, have I spoken to you about the meeting in Stanford next September/October on "Religion and Ritual"?[262] Walter Burkert, Jonathan Smith of Chicago, the English ethnologist Victor Turner, and Burton Mack of Religion Studies (at Claremont College) in Los Angeles will be there. If all goes well, it should be possible to pay your fare. Obviously there will be the obstacle of the English language, which will be the language used. But certainly some theological issues will arise.

Thank you for the idea for a response to [the editor of] *Études*.[263] I had dinner with him[264] last week, at the home of some mutual friends, who were all rather well disposed toward me. The discussion was very animated, but he was on the defensive.

You are also in my prayers. I hope to hear news from you soon.

René

Norbert Lohfink will be getting an invitation to Cerisy.[265]

I draw your attention to two books on my work that have just come out in France; one self-published, which I have not yet read: *Comprendre Girard* by J.-B. Fages[266] (a pseudonym, it appears); and the other with Grasset, *R. Girard et le problème du mal*,[267] which contains some very good and some not so good work.

---

[259] References in *La violence et le sacré* are to: Jensen, *Mythos und Kult bei Naturvölkern*.
[260] Otto, *Das Heilige* [literally, The Holy, though translated in English as *The Idea of the Holy*].
[261] Burkert, *Homo necans*.
[262] This meeting took place in Pajaro Dunes, near Santa Cruz, California. The papers and discussions were published: Hamerton-Kelly, ed., *Violent Origins*.
[263] Girard refers to a text by the chief editor of *Études*: Valadier, "Bouc émissaire." Schwager corresponded with Valadier about this very critical text (Raymund Schwager Archive, Innsbruck, II.4/I).
[264] Paul Valadier, SJ.
[265] Symposium *Colloque René Girard*, Centre Culturel International de Cerisy-la-Salle, June 11–18, 1983. Cf. the relevant editorial footnote to Girard's letter of August 9, 1981.
[266] Fages, *Comprendre Girard*.
[267] Deguy and Dupuy, eds., *René Girard et le problème du mal*.

[Girard] Paris, November 13, 1982

Dear Friend,

All things considered, I have to come back to Paris on December 29, so you have no need to move your trip for us to see one another. But I will, of course, also be here at the beginning of January. Phone me when you can. If I'm not at home in the afternoon, I certainly will be there in the morning: [...]

In my last letter I am not sure I told you how much I appreciated your comments on the scapegoat and Christian revelation.[268] Everything that you said there contains the most essential response to be given to those who say that our reading "reduces" Christianity to sociology [*à un contenu sociologique*].

The passage in *Choses cachées* on the incarnation is essential for responding to the accusation of both reductionism and Gnosticism (!).[269] During a recent dinner with Father Valadier, organized by a mutual friend, I wanted to cite it, but I couldn't remember it exactly.

Perfect also [is] all that you say about scientific hypotheses, and also about the relationship between faith and the proposed hypothesis. This is truly marvelous and could be the basis of a paper at Cérisy[270] (if they ask you to speak, as I recommended, but it is not I who am organizing the meeting, and of course I don't want to put pressure on the organizers, or to influence you).

You say all that I wanted to say, responding to objections that we currently face [*qu'on me fait en ce moment*], in a way that I don't hesitate to call *inspired*.

I needed time to absorb the content of your comments in German, but now that's done, it's a *joy* for me and I thank you.

With all my affection,
I have many things to tell you; see you soon.
René Girard

---

[268] Here, and in the following letter, Girard refers to Schwager's answer to a critique from Valadier in the French journal *Études* (cf. the relevant footnote to Girard's letter of November 2, 1982).
[269] Girard appreciates Schwager's answer to Valadier, where he refers to Girard, *Des choses cachées*, 239.
[270] Symposium *Colloque René Girard*, Centre Culturel International de Cerisy-la-Salle, June 11–18, 1983. Cf. the relevant editorial footnote to Girard's letter of August 9, 1981.

[Girard] Paris, December 11, 1982

Dear Friend,

Please excuse me once again for bringing a change of plans relevant to your Paris trip in January but, because of a coincidence of circumstances too involved to explain, I will return to Paris only on the evening of January 5 (Roissy, about 5 p.m.).

I hope that it will be possible for you to change your trip a little or lengthen your stay sufficiently that we will have the time to chat together at great length [*copieusement*].

I remind you of my phone number in Paris [...]

See you soon, I hope.

Affectionately,
René

STANFORD UNIVERSITY—Stanford, California

Paris, May 12, 1983

Dear Friend,

Thank you for all that you say in your letter.[271] Cardinal Ratzinger is much talked about in France at the moment because of his warning concerning French methods of catechesis. Insofar as I have been able to judge, I understand the reservations of the cardinal.

I can't wait to see you at Cerisy.[272] I hope it will be for you an occasion to make useful contacts. That's the main purpose of this kind of thing.

I've come back via Stockholm and Copenhagen, where I gave some lectures under the auspices of the French Cultural Services, with very good reactions

---

[271] Girard refers to a letter that has not been preserved. Girard probably lost it when he moved from France back to the United States of America.
[272] Symposium *Colloque René Girard*, Centre Culturel International de Cerisy-la-Salle, June 11–18, 1983. Cf. the relevant editorial footnote to Girard's letter of August 9, 1981.

from the public. I have to go to Italy again around May 23–25 for the launch of *Choses cachées* in Italian.[273]

I won't be sad to return to California and my work habits after Cerisy at the end of June. Life is too hectic for me here.

I'm going to talk about Job at Cerisy.[274] Recently I read some Lev Shestov, whom I did not know, and who repeats himself a great deal, but whose supposed post-Kierkegaardian "irrationalism" seems to me to be relevant to many of our ideas. Here we see an absolute rejection of the God of the philosophers, of Kantian-Hegelian idealism—complete opposition between Athens and Jerusalem; it is full of good intuitions that don't ultimately manage to open up anything truly new, but instead goes around in circles, lacking a true foundation in biblical analysis [*faute de s'appuyer vraiment sur des analyses bibliques*].

See you soon, then, and with my best wishes,
René

I am going to look at the train timetable for getting to Cerisy, and to see also if there are cars that can take you. I will be there with a Spanish-American friend[275] and I'll try to organize a trip together.

JESUITENKOLLEG INNSBRUCK

Innsbruck, June 27, 1983

Dear Friend,

I have very fond memories of the colloquium at Cerisy-la-Salle.[276] Certainly

---

[273] Girard, *Delle cose nascoste sin dalla fondazione del mondo*.
[274] He gave the final paper: "Sur Job et la philosophie."
[275] Probably Cesáreo Bandera.
[276] Symposium *Colloque René Girard*, Centre Culturel International de Cerisy-la-Salle, June 11–18, 1983. Cf. the relevant editorial footnote to Girard's letter of August 9, 1981. Girard gave the final paper ("Sur Job et la philosophie"); Schwager gave a talk as well ("Théologie de la colère divine"). However, in the volume with the conference proceedings (Dumouchel, ed., *Violence et vérité*) another text by Girard is published (Girard, "La meurtre fondateur dans la pensée de Nietzsche").

there were people there who used a part of your thinking to expose several victims and who were, at the same time, beginning to hide the true victims in a more subtle manner. But that did not surprise me at all. I was expecting it.

I liked your final paper very much. What you had to say about Job seemed well-justified to me, and your distinction between science and faith is very important; to me this has always underlaid your thinking, but, up until now, you had never expressed it so clearly. This will help to avoid a whole series [*toute une série*] of confused discussions in the German theological world. So I am very pleased that we are able to publish this text at more or less the same time as the translation of *Des choses cachées*.[277] I see now two possibilities for this publication:

- a text of about 70–80 pages, as a small book
- a text of about 30 pages for a periodical

If you have enough time, the first possibility would be best for us (above all, if you add several comments on the problematic of sacrifice in the NT). In this case, I will try to win over H. U. v. Balthasar to do the translation. He is a master at this, and would give the text extra weight in the eyes of some theologians.[278]

Last night I talked to my colleagues here in our house about the colloquium. Two reacted emotionally (but without any coherent argument). The discussion lasted until midnight. And it will continue.

I think of you in my prayers.
Sincerely,
Raymund

The reason for this may be the fact that, at a conference in Geneva in January 1983, Girard had already presented a shorter version of this Job paper. This version was published in November 1983, two years before the Cerisy proceedings volume: Girard, "Job et le bouc émissaire."

[277] Schwager is referring to the 1983 German translation: Girard, *Das Ende der Gewalt*.
[278] Neither of the two suggestions was realized. Girard's thoughts on Job were available in German only when his book on Job (Girard, *La route antique des hommes pervers*) was translated and published in 1990.

STANFORD UNIVERSITY—Stanford, California

July 16, 1983

Very dear Friend,

All in all, I have fond memories of Cerisy.[279] Thank you for your courage and your encouragement. I see now that you understand better the intellectual milieu in which I live, and to what extent it is different and far from your own. And some of those who are, on the one hand, very attached to our theses, are only interested in de-Christianizing them.

Lately, I have above all been resting in the wonderful Californian sun, after a literary conference in Washington. It is delightful for me to be back with my family, my books, my habits, my house. My preoccupation at the moment is getting used to working on an IBM microcomputer, which in French we call a *machine à traitement de texte* [word processing machine]. I hope that this is going to make my work easier by saving me from typing almost the same things ten times, as I've done for thirty years. But perhaps I'm mistaken. In any event, next week I'll have my machine and will get back to work.

I have to prepare for a meeting at the end of the summer with several American experts on sacrifice, and a Swiss, Walter Burkert (*Homo necans*).[280] It's focused on the primitive side [*côté primitif*] of sacrifice and my presentation must be ready by the end of August. After that I'll go back to Job, but I wonder if the text is suitable for a general discussion on sacrifice, and I don't know if it will be long enough, even for a little book.[281] I'll do my best but I don't want to make it longer in an artificial way. Would it be perhaps possible

---

[279] Symposium *Colloque René Girard*, Centre Culturel International de Cerisy-la-Salle, June 11–18, 1983. Cf. the relevant editorial footnote to Girard's letter of August 9, 1981.
[280] Girard is referring to the meeting *Religion and Ritual*, October 1982, in Pajaro Dunes, near Santa Cruz, California.
[281] Girard published several times on the book of Job. Cf. Girard, "'The Ancient Trail Trodden by the Wicked'"; Girard, *La route antique*. Girard is referring to Schwager's ideas concerning a publication of Girard's thoughts on Job for the German-speaking world, which, in this form, did not come about. Cf. the relevant editorial footnote to Schwager's letter of June 27, 1983.

to add another text … on the adulterous woman in John,[282] for example? What do you think?

I wish you a very good summer. With love.
René

JESUITENKOLLEG INNSBRUCK

Innsbruck, August 12, 1983

Dear Friend,

I've just finished my article (eighty pages) on Luther.[283] Luther—just in quantitative terms—is an immense world (100 volumes) and then [there's] the literature on him. Nevertheless I've found some extremely interesting things of his for the scapegoat theory, and this is important for discussions with Protestant theologians. There is already an author who attacked me, saying that Luther knew only that Jesus had taken our sins upon himself. This is true; Luther strongly underlines this aspect, but there are also some extremely dense texts where he speaks of men who are blind, and who transfer their sins onto the victim.

But for the moment I am leaving the books in my room as I want to take in some mountain air, and I will also go to the sea for several days. I hope that you are having a good rest in the "wonderful Californian sun,"[284] as you call it.

Did the colloquium on sacrifice go well? And Job? Don't worry too much about the length of the article. There is the possibility in the German world to publish very short books (in large print). We would have difficulties finding a publisher for a longer book (for the moment). And, if the idea for a short book does not eventuate, I'll find a periodical to publish it. As soon as I have the text, I'll speak to Father Lohfink to explore the best way to proceed.[285]

---

[282] Jn 8:1-8.
[283] Schwager, "Der fröhliche Wechsel und Streit."
[284] Schwager quotes from Girard's letter of July 16, 1983.
[285] Cf. the relevant editorial footnote to Schwager's letter of June 27, 1983.

I think of you in my prayers. With love,
Raymund

Maria Assad, who was your student in Buffalo, wrote to me. She is interested in translating my book[286] into English.[287]

STANFORD UNIVERSITY—Stanford, California

September 12, 1983

Dear Friend,

Thank you for everything. Please send me your work on Luther when it appears.[288] I have just finished a text in English today that is a sort of general summary of my theory of myth for the symposium on sacrifice, which has not happened yet, but will be held in the first week of October.[289]

I typed this text entirely on my IBM computer, [the kind] that Stanford is pushing us to adopt. I think that it is really going to make some things easier. Imagine a typewriter without a fixed spatial reference. You can work at any time on any part of the text, in all directions, add, delete, modify, correct as much as you want, add an entire book to the third line of the first, if that appeals to you, and everything is reformatted and organizes itself right before your eyes, just by using several extra keys, or a combination of keys.

Before getting back to Job for you,[290] I have to finish an article on literature that I have promised my colleagues here, for a Stanford journal.[291] But this won't take much time, as it is half done.

I hope your holidays were good. Since my return here, it has been

---

[286] Schwager, *Brauchen wir einen Sündenbock?*.
[287] After quite some time, this project was eventually successful: Schwager, *Must There Be Scapegoats?*
[288] Schwager, *Der fröhliche Wechsel und Streit*.
[289] Girard is referring to the meeting *Religion and Ritual*, October 1982, in Pajaro Dunes, near Santa Cruz, California. According to the publication that emerged from this (Hammerton-Kelly, ed., *Violent Origins*, 73–105), Girard's paper was "Generative Scapegoating."
[290] Cf. the respective editorial footnote to Girard's letter of July 16, 1983.
[291] Probably: Girard, "Hamlet's Dull Revenge."

wonderful weather and I've been going to the pool every day. I am sleeping much better. I've had a bit too much of the Parisian, and even the European, climate. Besides, the world here, above all in California, is less dominated by resentment than is the Parisian intelligentsia, and that's refreshing.

I've recently been doing a lot of reading of modern classics of Christian faith—France, Maritain, Gilson, de Lubac (*La foi chrétienne sur le symbole des Apôtres*[292]). I'm more and more surprised, reading all this, that we're not seeing the potential in the church for anthropological rejuvenation, such as is offered to orthodox faith by the theory of the scapegoat.

Mr. Wieser of Geneva, from the World Council of Churches, has more or less finished his translation of *Bouc émissaire*.[293] More and more I dream, after this summary on the notion of myth in my work, to do an improved version of *Choses cachées*[294] in English rather than just a translation. This is perhaps more important than anything else.

I am pleased to know that Maria Assad is translating your book into English.[295] Perhaps to make Job longer, I could touch on the problematic of the Spirit.

With love [*Je vous embrasse*].
René

[Schwager] December 4, 1983

Dear Friend,

The weeks are passing so quickly that I am not able to finish all my projects. The translation of your book[296] appeared a month ago and, to date, I have not seen much reaction. Of course, the translation is bad and that inhibits the uptake. The text is very difficult to understand without the dialogues—and

---

[292] De Lubac, *La foi chrétienne*.
[293] He translated Chs. 13 and 14 of Girard, *Le bouc émissaire*, into English: Wieser, "Generative Violence."
[294] Girard, *Des choses cachées*.
[295] Maria Assad translated Schwager's *Brauchen wir einen Sündenbock?* into English as *Must There Be Scapegoats?*.
[296] Schwager is referring to the German translation in excerpts: Girard, *Das Ende der Gewalt*, 1983.

without the necessary background understanding of the French intellectual milieu. I have written four small articles for newspapers and periodicals about your thinking (as advertising for your book). Two of these articles will appear at the beginning of next year;[297] I haven't yet found a publication venue for the other two.

I think it is a very good idea to rewrite *Des choses cachées* in English. This book is very difficult to translate.

And your text on Job?[298] I've been waiting for weeks; I think that it could facilitate the dissemination of your book. Are you busy with other works?

A priest in Rome has written to me. He is currently the President of the Catholic Biblical Association (USA).[299] His presidential address to the 1984 congress will have as its theme "Girard and the Old Testament."[300]

For the moment I am working on Karl Barth with my students. It is interesting work, but overwhelming. There will be 20,000 pages to read—an impossible thing, but I hope I will get the gist [*à saisir l'essentiel*]. There are some very interesting aspects to pick up on for a theology of the scapegoat.[301]

Two weeks ago I was in Zürich and on this occasion I met Mr. and Mrs. Salberg,[302] who were also at Cerisy-la-Salle.[303] They are doing some interesting work in Lausanne but are also encountering a great deal of resistance. For my part, I have experienced the same resistance and, more and more, I think that one cannot accept the thinking about the scapegoat if one is not ready to face one's own buried aggression [*affronter sa propre agressivité souterraine*].

The feast of Christmas is coming. I wish you profound peace and several days of rest. I will think of you in my prayers.

In all friendship,
Raymond Schwager

---

[297] Schwager, "Der Nachahmer als Sündenbock"; Schwager, "Christliche Herausforderung."
[298] Cf. the relevant editorial footnote to Girard's letter of July 16, 1983.
[299] Robert North, SJ.
[300] This paper was published: North, "Violence and the Bible."
[301] From this emerged the following publication: Schwager, "Der Richter wird gerichtet."
[302] The name is difficult to read; it seems to be "Salberg-Beal." From Schwager's other correspondence, however, we know that he refers to Jean-François Salberg and his wife Pascale.
[303] Symposium *Colloque René Girard*, Centre Culturel International de Cerisy-la-Salle, June 11–18, 1983. Cf. the relevant editorial footnote to Girard's letter of August 9, 1981.

STANFORD UNIVERSITY—Office Memorandum

Stanford, December 7, 1983

Dear Friend,

I will send you a copy of my work on Job, which has come out in Geneva in French.[304] Unfortunately, it still does not seem to be a very good text. I am in the process of doing an English version, which I hope, of course, will be better. But it is not ready yet.[305]

Could the German translation be derived from the English text?[306] Or would you like to look at this [French] text? In any event I will send you the English text when it is finished.

I hope that all goes well. I will write again soon.

Until next time,
René

JESUITENKOLLEG INNSBRUCK

Innsbruck, December 21, 1983

Dear Friend,

I wish you a happy holiday and a few peaceful days in which you—in a world of violence—can feel a little Christmas peace: "Glory to God in the highest, and *peace* on earth."[307] It is a precarious peace, as the murder of the Bethlehem children[308] shows; but this peace can still give us a foretaste of a future world and orientation in such a turbulent world.

---

[304] Girard, "Job et le bouc émissaire."
[305] Girard, "The Ancient Trail Trodden by the Wicked."
[306] Cf. the relevant editorial footnote to Girard's letter of July 16, 1983.
[307] Cf. Lk. 2:14.
[308] Mt. 2:17-18.

Thank you for your letter and for sending "Job et le bouc émissaire." This seems like the text of your presentation in Geneva.

You had developed this further in Cerisy-la-Salle.[309] And you write that the final version will be in English,[310] so I await *that* version for translation into German.

Within hours I'll be leaving for Switzerland. I will spend Christmas with my mother; I also have many brothers and sisters and fifteen nieces and nephews[311] to see. I do hope I'll have a few hours of calm.

I'm thinking of you and your family and I ask God in my prayers that he bless you for '84.

Sincerely,
Raymond Schwager

STANFORD UNIVERSITY—Stanford, California

December 28, 1983

Dear Friend,

I don't remember if I sent you the paper from Geneva. I will send the English text of Job,[312] which should be of a size sufficient for a small book. I hope not to spend too much time, but I am trying to make a book that is self-explanatory, capable of being understood by people who have not read anything of mine, and that should be good for German readers. I lean toward the "literary" side of things, not being a linguist.

Things are very calm here, and I am making the most of the holidays to try and move forward on this work on Job. But all the family has been here

---

[309] Symposium *Colloque René Girard*, Centre Culturel International de Cerisy-la-Salle, June 11–18, 1983. Cf. the relevant editorial footnote to Girard's letter of August 9, 1981.
[310] Girard, "The Ancient Trail Trodden by the Wicked."
[311] In his letter of January 28, 1984, Schwager writes about fourteen nephews and nieces.
[312] Girard, "The Ancient Trail Trodden by the Wicked."

for Christmas and obviously this takes up time, but it is a great joy for me. The children have changed a lot since you saw them at Sauvterre, both self-employed [*indépendants*], in business and law, not intellectuals, but solid optimists. Our daughter is here and Daniel will be a "lawyer" in San Francisco, which is quite close to here.

I also received a letter from this researcher who is to speak on mimesis and the scapegoat at the biblical scholars' meeting that you mentioned.[313] He thinks that we differ on certain essential points. I think that he is wrong, and that he should reread my thesis on sacrifice in a more disciplined manner than I think he has done. Recently, I have read or reread quite a good amount of modern theology. De Lubac in particular, also Jean Guitton, who is not a theologian, but who is not without interest in what he says about the gospels; I find the reaction in theological circles very surprising.

I remember your letter to the Editor-in-Chief [*Directeur*] of *Études*[314] and I am sorry that it was not published. Could it not be inserted as a discussion somewhere in the book that is coming out on Cerisy?[315] Would you agree to add that to your contribution, or do you think that it would be out of place? Tell me what you think.

I wish you a happy Christmas retroactively [*rétroactivement*] and a good year in '84, actively [*activement*].

I will not forget you either in my prayers.

Affectionately,
René

---

[313] Robert North, SJ.
[314] Girard refers to the chief editor of *Études*, Paul Valadier, SJ. Valadier had criticzed Girard's thinking (Valadier, "Bouc émissaire"); Schwager reacted to this critique in a letter to Valadier. Cf. the relevant editorial footnote to Girard's letter of November 2, 1982.
[315] Symposium *Colloque René Girard*, Centre Culturel International de Cerisy-la-Salle, June 11–18, 1983. Cf. the relevant editorial footnote to Girard's letter of August 9, 1981. In the end, Schwager's letter was not published in the conference volume (cf. Schwager's letter of January 28, 1984).

STANFORD UNIVERSITY—Stanford, California

January 8, 1984

Dear Raymund,

I believe that the English version of Job[316] will soon be finished, and I will send it to you immediately. I'm working on it a lot at the moment, which means that I am neglecting everything else. I think that it will be much more logically coherent than previous versions, and comprehensible for people unfamiliar with the themes. In short, I've made a small book of it, and it's you who gave me the idea.

But for the moment I've got the flu and that's limiting my activities quite a bit.

I am reading Anders Nygren on the Epistle to the Romans[317]—radical Lutheranism with all sorts of things that I'm turning over in my mind; in particular, the distinction between the two ages (and the notion of sin as a powerful corruptor that triumphs over everything that is not redeemed by Christ). It is very difficult to speak of Romans without falling into the heated quarrels between Protestants and Catholics. It is extraordinary, however, that all the divisions between the two Pauls, between the one before and the one after, come out of Jesus' question to Paul on the road to Damascus: "Why do you persecute me?"[318] Until then, Paul did not know, not only that he persecuted Christ, but that he persecuted anyone at all. True knowledge is always knowing that we persecute Christ.

Life at Stanford is pleasant, but I find the teaching—even limited to two classes of 1 hour 50 minutes a week—more and more arduous, because it necessarily distances me from my real interests in a good many cases. Next year I am going to resume teaching on the Bible.

Nygren demonstrates well that the anger of God in Romans is not a punishment inflicted after the fact: it's the fact that man surrenders himself to

---

[316] Girard, "The Ancient Trail Trodden by the Wicked."
[317] Nygren, *Commentary on Romans.*
[318] Acts 9:4.

([via] mimetic desire) the interplay of sinful relationships [*jeu des rapports de péché*] that disintegrates and corrupts everything and results in idolatry.

This is very powerful, and likely dangerous for the average human ... it is the problem that you pose in your letter.[319]

I hope your work is going well. I understand that the translation of *Choses cachées*[320] is often incoherent. I am receiving things from France that show that there is interest in the mimetic–victimary theses, but very often at a woefully simplistic level.

Very best wishes for the New Year.
I am praying for you. With love.
    René

JESUITENKOLLEG INNSBRUCK

Innsbruck, January 28, 1984

Dear Friend,

A very big thank you for your letter; I'm glad you were able to enjoy your Christmas holidays and that you had a nice time with your family. I spent Christmas Day with my mother (seventy-seven years old) in the home of one of my (four) sisters. Then I visited my other sisters, my two brothers, and fourteen nieces and nephews. Overall there are no big problems at the moment. That's a comfort to my mother.

Since New Year I've resumed my work. I have a course on Christology/salvation and I spend weeks looking at the gospels. Your thought is always present and my students are able to understand it, more or less. I've also written two articles introducing your book;[321] I will send you copies.

In an issue of the journal *Christus*, on hatred, I've offered a brief analysis of

---

[319] It's unclear what Girard is referring to here; maybe an earlier letter was lost.
[320] Girard refers to the fragmentary German translation (Girard, *Das Ende der Gewalt*, 1983).
[321] Cf. the relevant editorial footnote to Schwager's letter of December 4, 1983.

mimesis and the scapegoat.[322] The translation, which I hadn't previously seen, is unfortunately not good and contains some contradictions; I still hope that it will help to dispel some misconceptions circulating in religious circles. (I'll send you a copy.)

You asked a question about the piece I wrote against Valadier, SJ.[323] I fear that this text is not comprehensible without Valadier's [original] article.[324] I shall write to Michel Corbin to see if he knows a magazine that would accept an article that indirectly corrects Valadier's words![325]

For now I wait above all for "Job."[326] I'm very pleased that you have drafted the text so that that it is understandable even for those who do not know your thinking.

You speak in your letter of publications on mimeticism in France. Please send me the necessary information so that I can buy them. I would like to make a collection of all publications concerning mimeticism, even if they do not directly relate to theology.

You also talk about Nygren. I have not read his book on Romans,[327] but I'm very preoccupied with this epistle. I think more and more—with St. Augustine and Luther, contrary to the majority of theologians—that the famous Chapter 7 speaks of Christians (struggle between two laws) and not just pagans. If Christians do not recognize that the law of sin remains active in them, they must necessarily remain blind and project their sins onto others.

Isn't it true that Christians need scapegoats, because they have not seen in Romans 7 a mirror of their own existence?

My assistant Niewiadomski, who was with me in Paris a year ago, did research on the image that Christians have of themselves, and on how anti-Semitism has been connected to this image.[328]

---

[322] Schwager, "Haine sans raison."
[323] Schwager is referring to Girard's letter of December 28, 1983.
[324] Valadier, "Bouc émissaire."
[325] It seems that this idea did not come to fruition.
[326] Girard, "'The Ancient Trail Trodden by the Wicked.'"
[327] Nygren, *Commentary on Romans*.
[328] Niewiadomski has published several articles in this field: Niewiadomski, "Vom dogmatischen Gegner zum verhaßten Feind"; Niewiadomski, "Die Mörder Gottes und die Gegner des christlichen Volkes"; Niewiadomski, "Die Juden im Neuen Testament."

In Rome, N. Lohfink, who was also in Cerisy-la-Salle,[329] held a large public lecture at the Biblical Institute[330] on "The Violent God of the Old Testament and the Quest for a Nonviolent Society." He talked a lot about you. Did I send you this text?[331] I do not remember!

I hope you're in good health and I wish you strength for your so-important work.

In all friendship,
Raymund

JESUITENKOLLEG INNSBRUCK

Innsbruck, February 26, 1984

Dear Friend,

We have two weeks of holidays; I am working on Barth,[332] where I find many ideas that are very close to yours; and nevertheless there is a clear difference. Barth speaks a great deal about the identification of the Christ condemned with sinners. I accept this formulation while adding an important distinction: Christ as the victim identifies with his enemies (sinners) as victims, but not as a participant (any action that is directed against another is also directed against oneself, as the example of Judas clearly shows).

In my article for *Semeia* (Chicago), I will speak a little about the issue of sacrifice.[333] I have heard from the [Pontifical] Biblical Institute[334] in Rome that there are professors there who are profoundly shocked by what you have said

---

[329] Symposium *Colloque René Girard*, Centre Culturel International de Cerisy-la-Salle, June 11–18, 1983. Cf. the relevant editorial footnote to Girard's letter of August 9, 1981.
[330] Schwager refers to the Pontifical Biblical Institute, the most important scholarly institution for biblical exegesis and theology in Rome. Founded in 1909, it has always been run by Jesuits. Lohfink (b. 1928), too, is a Jesuit.
[331] The original English version of this lecture was not published, but it appeared in Italian and Spanish as: Lohfink, "Il Dio violento dell'Antico Testamento"; Lohfink, "El Dios violento del Antiguo Testamento."
[332] A result of this work was: Schwager, "Der Richter wird gerichtet."
[333] Schwager, "Christ's Death and the Prophetic Critique of Sacrifice."
[334] See the footnote about this institution accompanying the previous letter.

about the Epistle to the Hebrews in *Des choses cachées*. Are you addressing this issue at all in your article on Job?[335] I hope that you will be able to finish this work soon; I am waiting for it impatiently.

In general, there remain many obstacles before us. Three major periodicals, to which I sent articles about you weeks ago, have not replied. But there is also positive news. A Protestant institution is organizing a session on your thinking at the beginning of November 1984.[336] Perhaps this meeting will help to set up more coherent work on your thought in the German-speaking world from now on [*à organiser un travail plus cohérent à partir de votre pensée dans le monde allemand*].

Have you received the three texts that I sent you?

I continue to work with patience, and hope this will bear fruit one day.

I feel ever closer to you [*en plus uni avec vous*].

Best wishes,
Raymund Schwager

STANFORD UNIVERSITY—Stanford, California

April 13, 1984

Dear Raymond,

My apologies for the text on Job, but I've had thousands of interruptions and have not managed to improve the presentation I gave in Cerisy[337] as much as I would like. Now I need to finish the Cerisy text, which should be about fifty pages, that is to say, too short for a book. But patience.

At the moment I'm interested in Nietzsche—can you imagine! I think more and more that his vision of the difference between the biblical and

---

[335] Girard, "'The Ancient Trail Trodden by the Wicked.'" Cf. the relevant editorial footnote to Girard's letter of July 16, 1983.

[336] This session, *Die Gesellschaft der Rivalen*, took place in the palace of Schönburg, Hofgeismar, November 2–4, 1984.

[337] Symposium *Colloque René Girard*, Centre Culturel International de Cerisy-la-Salle, June 11–18, 1983. Cf. the relevant editorial footnote to Girard's letter of August 9, 1981.

mythological, Dionysus against the Crucified, is accurate, aimed at the syncretism of the period, but that his moral choice (in favor of Dionysus) is a *disaster* that drags him toward positions progressively more and more *inhumane* (see the fragments at the end of *Twilight of the Idols*[338]) and that his madness is linked to a monstrous kind of *wager* in favor of the mythological, the inverse of Pascal's *wager*. I've just written a short text[339] on Aphorism 125 of *The Gay Science*,[340] which is above all not a text on the death of God, as is always said, but about the collective *murder* of God. The text (of the aphorism) functions symbolically—in terms of the primitive religious, of the Christian text, and of modern atheism conceived as a new version of the murder—from which re-emerges another form of the religious [*un texte (l'aphorisme) qui fonctionne symboliquement, sur le plan du religieux primitive, du texte Chrétien, de l'athéisme moderne conçu comme une nouvelle version du meurtre d'où ressurgit une autre forme de religieux*]. It's a truly strange text and, thus far, very enigmatic. Heidegger *did* everything to *suppress* the religious problematic in Nietzsche, to the benefit of traditional philosophy, and the French Nietzscheans have gone down this route, but it is very wrong. In particular he [Heidegger] wrote a very mistaken article about Aphorism 125— very powerfully mistaken [*puissamment faux*], in *Die fröhliche Wissenschaft* (in *Holzwege*).[341]

Moreover, in the fragments of the last year of Nietzsche's sanity, there are texts that bring together the *martyrdom* of Dionysus and that of Christ that assert that The Difference *is not* in the martyrdom, but in the interpretation; the Christian interpretation is defined as *slander* against life [*calomnie contre la vie*], and life defined as involving the worst suffering [*la vie est définie comme impliquant les pires souffrances*], in other words, the acceptance of violence. Nietzsche, in other words, sees that the sacrificial is on the side of Dionysus!!!!

I have a project for a book on the *modern/modernity* [*sur le* moderne] that

---

[338] In the French original letter, Girard used the German title of Nietzsche's book, *Götzen-Dämmerung*.
[339] Probably: Girard, "La meurtre fondateur dans le pensée de Nietzsche"; this paper was published in the conference volume from the Symposium *Colloque René Girard* in Cerisy: Dumouchel, ed., *Violence et vérité*, 597–613.
[340] In the original French, Girard used the German title of Nietzsche's book, *Die fröhliche Wissenschaft*.
[341] Girard uses the German original titles of Heidegger's writings, which are now available in the complete edition: Heidegger, *Holzwege*.

will be based on the Wagner–Nietzsche polarity. It's a project that is in the process of taking shape.[342]

I hope that everything is going well for you. I've received a letter from Austria, and another very interesting one from a woman in Fulda, in Germany. This is the only feedback I have had on the German translation,[343] but the letter from Fulda reminds me of the ones I received from France after *Des choses cachées*.

I hope that you will have a good Easter after a good Lent. Would it disturb you if we addressed each other more informally [*se dit tu*] [i.e. rather than using *vous*]?[344] There is a very beautiful Gregorian mass here given by the musicians at the university, and I go regularly with Martha, my wife, who has a Protestant background, but has never been interested in religion, but who is now attached to this mass, and I am very happy about this. Pray for us.

In deep friendship,
René

JESUITENKOLLEG INNSBRUCK

Innsbruck, April 22, 1984

Dear Friend,

Easter Day, the day of new life; I hope you've had some days of peace during this holiday. I feel more and more that we have a fundamental need of that strength that resuscitates us from the dead to overcome some of [*vaincre un peu*] the violence in humanity [i.e., in general] and in ourselves [*dans l'humanité et en nous*]—I feel resistance from these forces that want

---

[342] Actually, no book by Girard was focused on this topic. Cf. Girard, "Dionysus versus the Crucified." Neither does this article address the Wagner–Nietzsche polarity.
[343] Girard, *Das Ende der Gewalt*, 1983.
[344] The "tu" here is a reference to the informal term used in French for "you," as opposed to the more formal "vous." Girard is here extending an invitation to Schwager to abandon the formality of French public, commercial, and workplace exchanges for the informal address more typical of friendship. Note that it has taken ten years! However, Schwager only began to use the informal address in his letters from September 30, though with only a few exceptions afterward.

everything to remain somewhat unresolved [*un peu dans l'ombre*], for everything to remain mixed—a bit of new life and much of the life of this world. I feel this resistance also in myself; the in between is more convenient [*l'entre-deux est plus commode*].

And you? Your work, how is it progressing? I hope that you have received the text ("Christ's Death and the Prophetic Critique of Sacrifice") that I sent you a few days ago. What do you think of it? I would be very happy to hear your reaction. I have done this text for *Semeia*. I'll send it to Chicago in a fortnight. I could still rework my article if you have any changes to propose.

I am just finishing my article on Karl Barth.[345] That was a pretty tough job. On the question of predestination—it's Barth who has brought about a tremendous openness to the whole tradition starting with Augustine. He remains nevertheless—in a very subtle way—tied to the sacred.

In Rome, Father Lohfink has had two very animated debates [*discussions*] about your thought. Father Lyonnet, who has two students who write speeches for the Pope,[346] has slowly changed his mind. He is now quite well disposed toward you.

Thinking of you.
Best wishes,
    Raymund

May 8, 1984

Very dear Raymund,

I find your essay on sacrifice[347] excellent. I am completely in agreement with your theological formulations.

What strikes me especially is the theme of rivalry with God, and the fact that Christ should be condemned for all that he revealed amongst his enemies;

---

[345] Schwager, "Der Richter wird gerichtet."
[346] John Paul II.
[347] Schwager, "Christ's Death and the Prophetic Critique of Sacrifice."

the perfect redoubling of reciprocal accusations, though corresponding here with the greatest disparity [*le rédoublement parfait des accusations réciproques mais qui correspond ici à la plus grande différence*]. And the attitude that contents itself with demystifying the doubles and saying "they're alike" is as radically mistaken as Solomon would have been mistaken if he'd dismissed the two prostitutes without pronouncing in favor of either [*renvoyait dos à dos*] under the pretext that, since they were saying the same thing as each other, there was no need to differentiate between them.[348]

All your arguments on the subject of the non-resistance of Jesus and the corroborating citations (1 Pet. 2:22-24), and against the idea that God the Father identifies the Son with sinners, are excellent.

I am certain that you are being faithful to orthodoxy here [*Vous tenez ici, j'en suis certain, la voie véritablement orthodoxe*], and [that] your definitions are admirable in their fairness and moderation. The use you make of Father Lohfink's research is also very interesting. It's fortunate that you're there [*Heureusement que vous êtes là*] to dispel misunderstandings and defend what's true in our thesis—there, where it's important.

Also, what you say concerning the much-lauded justice [*Ce que vous dites sur la fameuse justice aussi*]. What are these principles of justice? It is always forms of revenge.

There is someone here who has just read your work and has much admiration for it. His name is Robert Hamerton-Kelly, "Dean of the Chapel" at Stanford, a specialist in New Testament and also in the Alexandrian literature; he seems to me very cultured and intelligent and will I think get in touch with you. He will be in Basel next summer for a conference and wants to see you.[349] He's a liberal Protestant, but sees many things as we do. I think that is important for us.

In Montreal, Paisley Livingston, Paul Dumouchel, Lucien Morin, and others, tell me that they are going to create a "Centre of Girardian Studies," under the auspices of the English department of McGill University (the large Anglophone university in Montreal). They want to organize a colloquium in

---

[348] Cf. 1 Kgs 3:16-28.
[349] Schwager and Hamerton-Kelly eventually met for the first time at the symposium *Myth, Literature, and Bible*, Provo, Utah, November 12-16, 1984.

'85–'86 to which they will bring over ninety-nine Europeans, yourself, and certainly more Americans and Canadians than were at Cerisy.[350]

No doubt you have a German version of your article[351] that will come out in your field.[352] It would be good if there were a French version.[353] The review *Semeia* is doubtless not the best platform for this kind of essay in English, but it will be a counterbalance to the attacks that will certainly be there. I'm working on Job in French[354] and in English[355] simultaneously, but I have been interrupted by many things, among them the article on Nietzsche,[356] which I believe I have spoken to you about.

In friendship,
René

JESUITENKOLLEG INNSBRUCK

Innsbruck, September 30, 1984

Dear Friend,

I've phoned Paris many times in the last weeks, but have never been able to reach you.

Fortunately we will see one another at Provo in a few weeks' time.[357] Did you have a good experience in Paris? I hope so.

I've received *Job*.[358] I have read it with a great deal of interest, and, with the exception of a few small details, I can follow you without reservation. I am very happy that you have done this work, and I hope it will find readers. For

---

[350] Symposium *Colloque René Girard*, Centre Culturel International de Cerisy-la-Salle, June 11–18, 1983. Cf. the relevant editorial footnote to Girard's letter of August 9, 1981.
[351] Schwager, "Christ's Death and the Prophetic Critique of Sacrifice."
[352] Cf. Schwager, "Der Tod Christi und die Opferkritik."
[353] Cf. Schwager, "La mort de Jésus."
[354] Girard, *La route antique des hommes pervers*.
[355] Girard, "The Ancient Trail Trodden by the Wicked."
[356] Cf. the relevant editorial footnotes to Girard's letter of April 13, 1984.
[357] Schwager is referring to the symposium *Myth, Literature, and Bible*, Provo, Utah, November 12–16, 1984. In the course of this trip, Schwager visited Girard at his home.
[358] Schwager is referring to the typescript of Girard, *La route antique des hommes pervers*.

the German translation, I've made contact with the publisher Herder. They show "interest," but not much else. And I don't know if I can find another publisher.[359] For the moment I await the reaction of Norbert Lohfink, who has more publishing contacts than I have.

I finished my work on Balthasar[360] during the summer. Now I am thinking of something small on the conflicting views of theologians on the subject of sacrifice.[361]

With this study, I want to finish my series on the theology of redemption, and I am thinking of publishing the eleven articles as one volume.[362] Will that help to dispel the misunderstandings about your thought in the theological world? There are other problems that remain; for example, the topic of freedom, which I will speak about in Provo. I've finished the text of my paper and the translation.[363] I await your reaction, as I give an interpretation of a few sentences in *Des choses cachées* that don't altogether accord with what you said on auto-organization in the discussion at the colloquium.[364] I came across this text after drafting my paper. I really hope that we're able to clarify this point.

See you soon.
In all friendship,
    Raymond

---

[359] In the end, the Swiss publishing house Benziger published the German translation: Girard, *Hiob*.
[360] Schwager, "Der Sohn Gottes und die Weltsünde."
[361] In the end, such an article was never published.
[362] Schwager, *Der wunderbare Tausch*. This volume consists of only ten articles: the eleventh, on sacrifice, was neither written nor published.
[363] In Provo, Schwager gave a paper on mimesis and freedom. It was published in its German original in 1985: Schwager, "Mimesis und Freiheit"; recently, an English version was published: Schwager, "Mimesis and Freedom."
[364] Schwager refers to a meeting that took place in Cerisy-la-Salle, June 10–17, 1981. A publication emerged from it: Dumouchel and Dupuy, eds, *L'auto-organisation*. Schwager is thinking of one of the following two texts: Girard, "La contingence"; Girard, "La danse de Salomé."

STANFORD UNIVERSITY—Stanford, California

February 23, 1985

Dear Raymund,

Many thanks for your two letters.[365] I have been overwhelmed lately with university meetings that hold no interest, but that add further to my obligations.

Congratulations on your position as Dean, despite what that means at the administrative level.

I'll be in France from March 15 to April 15, but as there's a risk that I'll have a number of appointments, phone or write a few days before coming to make sure that we can have one or two days without interruption.

Here is my address again.

[…]

and the telephone:

[…]

With love [*Je t'embrasse*] and I hope to see you soon.
René

STANFORD UNIVERSITY—Stanford, California

July 2, 1985

Very dear Raymund,

Between September and November '86, you say, is the symposium in Stuttgart.[366] I'll certainly try to come. The first half of September would be easier than after, because of classes. If this goes ahead, I can decide to come to France at that time.

All is well here. I love the summertime. I am in the process of reworking

---

[365] At least one of these two letters has not been preserved.
[366] Girard Symposium of the Catholic Academy Stuttgart-Hohenheim, September 25–28, 1986.

some of my contribution to a symposium that occurred here two years ago with Walter Burkert,[367] a Swiss classicist/ethnologist who is better disposed [*plus favorable*] to our theses than most. But he maintains that the rite originates in the *hunt*. It's Robert Hamerton-Kelly who ran the thing [*que dirige la chose*].

We have a small group reading the Epistle to the Romans on Monday evening with him, a Lutheran professor, and several other Stanfordians. I'm learning a great deal about justification by faith and Protestant/Catholic differences. You have to experience these things through personal contact to really appreciate them. It seems to me that, with convinced Protestants, there is a tense negativity, which foreshadows Sartreanism, etc. This is not the great serenity of Catholicism at its best.

I see in a book on vengeance that St. Thomas Aquinas justified certain forms of vengeance, up to a certain point. How do you see this doctrine?

I've received a work on St. Augustine and the mimetic system.[368] There are some interesting things, but hardly anything on sacrifice that isn't banal.

I'm intending to spend the rest of summer finishing my book on Shakespeare.[369]

Our son Martin is getting married at the end of July.

With love.
René

JESUITENKOLLEG INNSBRUCK

Innsbruck, September 20, 1985

Dear Friend,

Thank you so much for your letter of July 2. I hope that you had a good summer; for my part I spent several days at Ravenna, Italy. The churches

---

[367] This meeting took place in Pajaro Dunes, near Santa Cruz, California; cf. Girard's letter of November 2, 1982.
[368] Probably: Wohlman, "René Girard et Saint Augustin."
[369] Girard, *A Theater of Envy*.

and the mosaics of this town (fifth–sixth century) greatly impressed me. It is surprising to feel such religious and artistic strength [*force religieuse et artistique*] from an era that is usually thought of as decadent.

In July, I wrote an article on sacrifice and the death of Jesus for *Recherches des Sciences Religieuses* (Paris)[370]—in line with my contribution to *Semeia*,[371] and I am now in the process of finishing the manuscript for a small book (faith, justice, peace).[372]

And the symposium in Stuttgart—yesterday I received a first definitive response. The academy that is organizing the symposium has set the date from September 25 to 28, 1986. That does not correspond exactly with the time that is most convenient for you. I hope, nevertheless, that you can come and I have begun to sketch out a plan. Twenty-fifth to twenty-seventh (noon): work in German with a select group of people who know your work and who are particularly interested in it. Twenty-seventh (afternoon and evening): discussion in French or English with you and this group (about thirty people)—at the same time: an introduction to your thought for a wider public (twenty-seventh, afternoon and evening, and twenty-eighth, morning) with a lecture from you in German (twenty-eighth) in this context (we will translate the text).

What do you think of this idea? I think the academy in Stuttgart will accept this with joy (provided you're able to come).

Two days later, on October 1, 1986, classes begin at our university. It would be a great joy for me if you would be able to come with me from Stuttgart to Innsbruck to give (at the beginning of the semester / October 1/2) two or three lectures (one in German, the same as in Stuttgart). I've been waiting a good while for an opportunity for you to come to Innsbruck [*J'attends depuis longtemps un bon moment pour ta venue à Innsbruck*]!

Of course, there remains a small problem. The academy in Stuttgart isn't able to pay your flight from San Francisco on its own.[373]

---

[370] Schwager, "La mort de Jésus."
[371] Schwager, "Christ's Death and the Prophetic Critique of Sacrifice."
[372] Schwager, *Für Gerechtigkeit und Frieden*.
[373] The rest of the letter is missing.

JESUITENKOLLEG INNSBRUCK

Innsbruck, December 23, 1985

Dear Friend,

It's three days before Christmas, so you'll receive this letter after Christmastide; I hope much peace has been given to you, and also to your family. I wish you the same peace for the coming year; I wonder more and more, as the years pass quickly, if I have made of my life everything I could have. My encounter with you has been very important to me and I think that it is one of my duties to collaborate with you on your work [*de coopérer à ton œuvre*].

I thank you sincerely for the news that you can come to Stuttgart and I realize that you also have two days in Innsbruck. I'm looking forward to seeing you here.

During the time I'm required to act as Dean I have virtually no time for personal work, but I hope I that I can benefit from this new experience later on. I also have some ideas about improving the work of our faculty; but carrying them out [*la réalisation*] is very difficult.

The translation of *Le bouc émissaire* will be released in two months by Herder in Freiburg.[374] I hope it will help establish your thought in the theological world here, which is very difficult to penetrate and resistant to "conversion." My book finally has a (small) second edition.[375]

December 24

I just received this morning a letter from Stuttgart. The symposium program includes:

September 25–27: papers and discussion among those invited (in German)

September 27, afternoon and evening: discussion with you in French or English

---

[374] This announcement was a bit premature; the translation was published two years afterward, not by Herder, but by the publishing house Benziger: Girard, *Der Sündenbock*.

[375] Schwager, *Brauchen wir einen Sündenbock?*, 1986.

September 27 (afternoon) and September 28: session open to the public with a lecture from you in German (September 28) (I will translate your text).
I hope that all this suits you.

Tonight—Christmas Eve—I will think of you.
Sincerely,
Raymund

STANFORD UNIVERSITY—Stanford, California

January 10, 1986

Dear Raymund,

Thank you for your good wishes and please accept ours in return. I wish you, above all, tranquility and the opportunity to work.

All is well here. It is possible that, from this spring, the freedom and sphere of action of "the mimetic school" will be enhanced in Stanford with the appointment of Dupuy (one term each year) and Paisley Livingston (full time)—but theology is not represented here except by Bob Hamerton-Kelly (who might be getting an offer from Yale).

No doubt the university is going to give us enough money to do a summer school around our interests (six weeks in '87). Can you come in summer? (Get back to me about this.) Where's that book of articles of yours that should be coming out?[376] Bravo for the second edition!![377]

At the moment I am looking at a lot of very classical theology. I am reading St. Augustine and also Jacques Maritain. The relationship between Aristotelian thought and what we are trying to do interests me more and more. I have the impression that it is not at all incompatible, but that neo-Thomism (and Thomism) not only take as natural many things that are cultural, but they understate the tremendous revolution that is revelation [*la révolution*

---

[376] Schwager, *Der wunderbare Tausch*.
[377] Schwager, *Brauchen wir einen Sündenbock?*, 1986.

formidable de la révélation]. And yet their idea of a fundamental insufficiency of philosophy—faced with revelation—allows that the framework of their thought [*cadre de pensée*] remains excellent for many things. I realize this reading Maritain, or at least I think I realize it.

I read *Entretien sur la foi*[378] by Ratzinger. It's called *The Ratzinger Report*[379] in English, and although I am not in agreement with everything he says, I *feel* as he does about all that's happened since the [Second Vatican] Council. In America, as in France, I have the impression of a veritable dissolution of the church. In France, the *ressentiment* (in the mimetic–Nietzschean sense) of a portion of the clergy played a big role [*a beaucoup joué*]. Here, a profoundly repressive and Jansenist Catholicism, treated with contempt by Protestantism, is motivated by its desire for integration into American society. And at the same time, it's managing perfectly to bring about its own dissolution [*Il réussit parfaitement à s'y dissoudre, en ce moment même*].

On the theological plane, this crisis of the church has at its center the question of sacrifice. The essence is precisely there. But I can well see that neither progressivism, nor the wish to keep the church within the constraints of the old formulations [*dans la crispation sur les formulations anciennes*], can really hear what we try to say. Quite a lot more time is needed, but I'm sure it will come about one day.

Just before the conference in Stuttgart,[380] there will be a biblical conference in Florence, organized by the city of Florence.[381] I will be there with John Freccero, whom you met in Provo.[382] In principle, H. Urs von Balthasar should be there.

Konrad Thomas from Göttingen has been here for a month, and California suits him well. We talk a lot, and he comes to my classes; my only regret is not to have enough time with him because of the university, which takes up almost as much time at the moment as it would were I the Dean!

---

[378] Ratzinger, *Entretien sur la foi*.
[379] Ratzinger and Messori, *The Ratzinger Report*.
[380] Girard Symposium of the Catholic Academy Stuttgart-Hohenheim, September 25-28, 1986.
[381] This conference in Florence on *Dante e la Bibbia* took place from September 26 to 28, 1986. In the end, Girard did not participate, probably because of the overlap with the Stuttgart conference. Balthasar also is not in the table of contents of the publication that emerged from the Florence conference: Barblan, ed., *Dante e la Bibbia*.
[382] Symposium *Myth, Literature, and Bible*, Provo, Utah, November 12-16, 1984.

I think of you a great deal, and of what your friendship means to me. Once I've finished my Shakespeare,[383] which is, in a certain sense, dedicated to my academic life in the Anglophone world, I will write much more about religious problems. But I feel myself aging!

With love.
René

Undated [between January and May 1986]

Dear Raymond,

Mr. Doucet's commentary on Maximus the Confessor[384] is excellent. The key is there: "And his obedience, in confronting (death) refers to a divine will that does not lead to [*ne porte pas*] this death." This comes at the right moment for me, as I am thinking about this conference in Stuttgart,[385] and would like to speak about essential things. I am in the process of revising my whole argument, based only on the gospels, which has always been my goal. To show that the gospels are sufficient for everything, and that anthropology can truly be interpreted [*se lire*] in their light.

What you have to say about the difficult route between the denial of Greek philosophical thinking, which would amount to a rivalry with it, and dependency on it, seems to me to be absolutely correct. True Catholic thought is always a narrow road between two abysses, which aspire to truth through twin radicalisms, equally *heretical* in the original sense [*aspirent à la vérité par des radicalismes jumeaux également hérétiques au sens original*].

I have noted your possible contribution to the "mimetic" activities here in summer '87.[386] The situation seems to have really thawed, just at the moment

---

[383] Girard, *A Theater of Envy*.
[384] Doucet, *Dispute de Maxime le Confesseur avec Pyrrhus*.
[385] Girard Symposium of the Catholic Academy Stuttgart-Hohenheim, September 25-8, 1986. Girard's paper in the conference was "'Tragischer Konflikt'—in Literatur und Bibel" [Tragic conflict—in literature and Bible]; his public lecture was entitled "Gewalt und Selbstzerstörung" [Violence and self-destruction] and was published: Girard, "Der tragische Konflikt."
[386] These activities seem not to have eventuated in the summer of 1987—at least, Schwager did not

when I had more or less given up all new efforts to start a little group here. But as long as nothing is really established, nothing is ever certain, as the university environment is full of pitfalls and mimetic obstacles that appear and then reappear constantly. So I am wary.

What you have to say about your American theologian confirms my own impressions here. Americans, hitherto oppressed and with little social standing if they are Catholic, are intoxicated with Americanism and confidence in modern society. While often, the Protestants, if they are not fundamentalists, have more distance and awareness of the cultural decay advancing more or less everywhere.

This society, taken as a whole, with all its somewhat barbaric [*un peu barbares*] excesses, still has a spring in its step and some confidence in its existence, a faith in reality [*garde un ressort, et une confiance dans l'être, une croyance en la réalité*], which has often disappeared in Europe. At the same time, the decadence of the churches that support the minorities, the blacks for example, brings in its wake a cultural decomposition [*entraîne une décomposition culturelle*] that is quite frightening. This is what strikes me most at the moment. Even in France, despite the presence of old remnants of Catholic stability that are popular deep down [*dans le fond populaire*], [we see] the cultural impoverishment of these last few years, the nihilist futility that seems to sweep everything away [*la futilité nihiliste semblent tout emporter*], not in a wave of madness, as in the '60s, but in a kind of general indifference.

Agreed concerning Ratzinger. But I think, even so, that at the heart of the church, it is good that a voice is raised to speak of the formidable crisis that we are living through, instead of the kind of progressivist self-congratulations that we hear everywhere, and of extreme resentment against the church itself, such as one often hears, for example, among the chic Parisian clergy, some of whom openly identify themselves as atheists, more or less. I speak from experience. The good thing about Ratzinger is that from now on we can

---

attend them. He asked about them in two follow-up letters (December 24, 1986; February 4, 1987), but Girard did not react to that. In his letter of January 6, 1988, Girard announced a symposium for autumn 1988 in Stanford on vengeance (October 27–29, 1988, organized by the Program of Interdisciplinary Research at Stanford University). Schwager participated at this symposium, giving a paper ("Vengeance in the Old Testament"), which is available online.

say certain things without being taken for Lefebvrists.[387] Obviously, I never suffered under the repressive and reactionary church before the council. Partly because my father, who had himself suffered from it (under the Jesuits in Avignon), put all his children into a state high school. And my mother had enacted her own personal "little council" around 1925 [*Et ma mère avait fait son petit concile personnel vers 1925*]. Above all, I experienced [*J'ai surtout connu*], after the very real physical terror of the totalitarian right during the war, the intellectual terror of the totalitarian left since the end of the war. And here, in our university circles, even if it's mostly verbal, that's the norm, the real "establishment." Congratulations on your two books,[388] which I am looking forward to trying to read.

With love.
René

JESUITENKOLLEG INNSBRUCK

Innsbruck, May 18, 1986

Dear Friend,

The Day of Pentecost—I hope that you are experiencing a little of this Spirit of God who overcomes violence. I feel more and more that a theory of violence is not enough to overcome evil. The "struggle" never finishes; every day there are new tensions that appear—even in our faculty. But on the whole, I can be content and there is also a little progress. I will tell you about it if you manage to get here in a few months.

---

[387] The Lefebvrists are ultra-conservative Tridentine Rite Catholics of the (anti–Vatican II) Society of St. Pius X, and followers of Archbishop Marcel Lefebvre (1905–91). A later letter (that of June 27, 1988) makes reference to events of 1988 when Lefebvre consecrated four bishops for his movement without Vatican approval and was promptly excommunicated with his new bishops by Pope John Paul II. The suggestion here seems to be that Ratzinger has made conservative Catholicism more mainstream once again (indeed, as Pope Benedict XVI, he lifted the excommunication on the four bishops whom Lefebvre had consecrated).

[388] Schwager, *Der wunderbare Tausch*; Schwager, *Für Gerechtigkeit und Frieden*.

The Stuttgart symposium[389] will not be as imposing as the colloquium in Cerisy[390] or in Provo.[391] But I hope that it will nevertheless be useful. We now have a list of thirty people who want to participate (professors of philosophy, sociology, education, economics, languages, and theology). For the first part of the symposium, in order to have a real dialogue, we don't want more than thirty to forty people.

Would you let me know soon the title of your paper?[392] That will help us with the program—and another question: I've contacted the French Institute in Innsbruck, which is linked to the French Institute in Vienna. There is a person there who likes your books, and who would like to invite you to give a paper in Vienna. Would you accept such an invitation? There are flights between Vienna and Innsbruck. You could—theoretically—give a paper in Vienna on September 30 and be in Innsbruck for October 1. But perhaps this is a little "inhuman"? Everything would go better if you had an extra day at your disposal. Would you let me know what you decide? From when will you be in Europe this summer?

I hope that you are well and I am looking forward to seeing you here.
Sincerely,
    Raymond

JESUITENKOLLEG INNSBRUCK

Innsbruck, August 1, 1986

Dear Friend,

When I got back from Switzerland, from where I telephoned you, I found a letter from your secretary Margaret Tompkins. It made me think about your itinerary Stuttgart–Vienna–Innsbruck.

---

[389] Girard Symposium of the Catholic Academy Stuttgart-Hohenheim, September 25–8, 1986.
[390] Symposium *Colloque René Girard*, Centre Culturel International de Cerisy-la-Salle, June 11–18, 1983. Cf. Girard's letter of August 9, 1981.
[391] Symposium *Myth, Literature, and Bible*, Provo, Utah, November 12–16, 1984.
[392] See the relevant editorial footnote to Girard's letter of April 13, 1984.

My first idea was that you come with us from Stuttgart to Innsbruck (on the afternoon of September 28) and that you leave on the evening of September 29 for Vienna, returning to Innsbruck on the morning of September 30.

Given that you would like to see something of the town of Vienna, my suggestion to you on the telephone was to leave on the morning of September 29 for Vienna and to return on September 30.

Your secretary's letter made me realize that the journey in the car from Stuttgart to Innsbruck would take about four or five hours. Which does not leave much time for us on September 28. Of course, we could talk in the car. But I don't know if you like traveling by car.

Perhaps it would be more enjoyable for you if we follow your first idea, and you fly from Stuttgart to Vienna on September 28 and from Vienna to Innsbruck on September 30.

Given that it is the beginning of the semester, I can't be absent from Innsbruck for too long—because of my role as Dean. And this is why it's going to be difficult for me to come with you to Vienna. After my stay in Stuttgart, I have to take up my duties on the twenty-ninth. Then I will be free for you on September 30 and October 1.

For me, you see, it's more pleasant if you come with us in the car from Stuttgart to Innsbruck, and then leave for Vienna. But perhaps it's the opposite for you. So I would like you to decide yourself which arrangement would suit you best.

In the event that you leave directly for Vienna, I hope that you could come to Innsbruck on the morning of September 30, so that we could have two hours for us together. (There are only *morning* and *evening flights* between Vienna and Innsbruck.)

I am looking forward to seeing you.
With love.
    Raymond

Maria Assad from Buffalo was here two days ago. She has finished the translation of my *Sündenbock*.[393]

---

[393] Schwager, *Brauchen wir einen Sündenbock?*. English translation: Schwager, *Must There Be Scapegoats?*.

PROGRAM OF INTERDISCIPLINARY RESEARCH—Stanford University

August 21, 1986

Dear Raymund,

A word to let you know that I am very pleased to come to Stuttgart and Innsbruck.

That's settled. I will leave Stuttgart for Innsbruck with you and your friends and will travel from there to Vienna. I'm counting on you for the tickets for the twenty-ninth and thirtieth.

I will arrive in Stuttgart by plane from Paris on the evening of the twenty-fifth at 9:55 p.m. I regret that I did not follow your advice and come for the twenty-fifth. Unfortunately I can't change this, as I have a lecture in Paris on the evening of the twenty-fourth, and a dinner after.

I can't wait to see you.

I realize that what I have sent you for the lecture is twice as long as it should be.[394] You can decide what is worth translating as you see fit, but I don't think it is worth the trouble to translate it all.

I hope you will be there to be my interpreter for the question and answer session.

See you soon—with love,
René

To telephone Paris, you now have to put an extra 4 at the beginning. So my number is [...]

Bob Hamerton-Kelly is coming to Stuttgart.[395] Perhaps he will arrive on the same plane as me.

Attached is a copy of my itinerary.

---

[394] Cf. the relevant editorial footnote to Girard's undated letter of January–May 1986.
[395] Girard Symposium of the Catholic Academy Stuttgart-Hohenheim, September 25–8, 1986.

JESUITENKOLLEG INNSBRUCK

Innsbruck, October 12, 1986

Dear Friend,

I hope that you are safely home and that all is well. I have very fond memories of your stay here, and I sincerely thank you for taking the time to come to the German-speaking countries. I hope that this seed will bear fruit sooner or later. For the past few days I've received very positive reactions to your paper (a paper in the same series that followed yours had only fifty people in attendance). The coverage in the press was also quite positive. The text in the *Frankfurter Allgemeine Zeitung* is of some importance, as it is the most important daily newspaper in Germany. The report is well-meaning, but the author seems to have some difficulties with your position in relation to philosophy.[396] Two days ago I had a discussion with one of my students. He was, at first, completely hostile to your thinking, and is now beginning to sense positive aspects, but he has not yet found a link with philosophy, which he thinks is essential. These reactions demonstrate once again that there are things to clarify to reduce the risk of misunderstandings.

I wish you all the best for your work and also for your family, and I will write as soon as I know if the question of "de honoris causa" is progressing.[397]

With love,
Raymond

---

[396] Busche, "Das Ende der Gewalt."
[397] This refers to a process, initiated by Schwager, to have Girard awarded an honorary doctorate by the University of Innsbruck.

Stanford, October 19, 1986

My dear Raymund,

I'm back from my second round of travels (!), this time to Chapel Hill and Johns Hopkins, and now, here I am once again, home for a while. I don't need to tell you that the best of these journeys was that to Innsbruck, with the great comfort that your presence and friendship brings me. I am happy that you work in such a good place for you, so conducive to thought [*méditation*]! My stay in Innsbruck and Austria was truly marvelous; above all, perhaps, the walk in the mountains and the conversations with you. I am really very pleased to have come to Germany and Austria.

Now I am making an effort to finish my Shakespeare[398] as fast as possible, in order then to apply myself to a book more focused on the religious and cultural problems of our times, and that will be entitled "Ce que je crois" [What I believe][399] if it comes out with Grasset.[400] I am not going to let myself be distracted by anything whatsoever.

Thanks to all those around you who contributed to making my visit so enjoyable. During the return trip, I read Poliakov with even greater interest than at Innsbruck; this is really a man whose striving for justice and impartiality is altogether remarkable. Every day, I also force myself to read a little Schwager on the Fathers of the Church,[401] and I'm getting better and better at it. I am starting to forget the problems of language, to grasp the strength of the approach and its continuity from one author to another. You must apply yourself to getting back to writing very quickly. Also thank all the Fathers from your college whom I met.

With love.
René

---

[398] Girard, *A Theater of Envy*. The friends refer throughout to "your Shakespeare" and "my Shakespeare."
[399] Cf. Girard's letter of August 1, 1979.
[400] A book of this title was never published. His next book was: Girard, *Je vois Satan tomber comme l'éclair*. It is very possible that preparatory work done for the project "Ce que je crois" became part of that book.
[401] Schwager, *Der wunderbare Tausch*.

JESUITENKOLLEG INNSBRUCK

Innsbruck, December 24, 1986

Dear Friend,

Christmas is coming, the time of peace. I am happy that I can forget for a few days both the faculty and the university. The last weeks have been pretty exhausting. A Jesuit has left the order and the priesthood. The predicament is quite difficult to resolve, because of our special status.[402] The matter [*chose*] concerns the community, the faculty, the Father Provincial, the bishop and the Ministry of Science. But this whole procedure helps to make clear somewhat the spiritual atmosphere of the faculty [*aide à clarifier un peu le milieu spirituel à la faculté*]. There are parallels here with the question of "Ehrendoktorat Girard" [Girard's honorary doctorate]. It raises a lot of dust [*Ça soulève de la poussière*]. Almost everybody said at the start: I don't know Girard well enough to say "yes." There was a mute kind of resistance that came, on the one hand, from an underlying rivalry and, on the other, from an unease with the question of violence. All that made me a little angry. For the moment we have agreed to form a working group that will look further into the question.

So it's too late for '87, but I hope we will have some success for '88. I am doing this for you, but at the same time it is a means to deal with something [*remuer quelque chose*] in our own house, and at the faculty.

And you? I hope that you are able to have some days of peace with your wife and children during this Christmas time. I think of you in my prayers and I wish you much courage and confidence for '87. Is your work on Shakespeare[403] progressing as you would like? And what are your projects for the summer? Is Dupuy's symposium[404] going ahead?

In issue 43 of *Time* magazine (October 27, 1986) there is a photo of the

---

[402] The reference here is to the Concordat between the Republic of Austria and the Holy See. See http://wissenschaft.bmwfw.gv.at/fileadmin/user_upload/wissenschaft/naric/english/austria_holysee_conc-protocoll.pdf (accessed April 25, 2016).
[403] Girard, *A Theater of Envy*.
[404] Schwager probably refers to the Stanford symposium, September 13–16, 1987. Its results were published: Varela and Dupuy, eds., *Understanding Origins*.

Nobel laureate Wiesel.[405] In it we can see a part of his library, and the only title that is decipherable is: René Girard, *Le bouc émissaire*. Have you seen this photo?

The influence of your thinking is slowly gaining ground in this part of the world. A seminar was held on you and on my book in a Swiss faculty[406] (nearly all the professors participated), and they invited me for the last session. Likewise, I have just received a letter from Denmark, where they inform me of a similar seminar in Århus.

The countryside here in Innsbruck is at the moment very different from what you saw three months ago. For some days we've had lots of snow. It creates an atmosphere of peace.

I wish you true peace. With all my best wishes—also for your wife.
Sincerely,
Raymond

January 2, 1987

Very dear Raymund,

Thank you for your New Year greetings, and Martha joins me in sending ours to you. Don't worry if this *honoris causa* doctorate doesn't come off [*ne peut pas se faire*]; don't waste too much time on it. Your time is too precious. It will be good if it happens, but in the event that it doesn't, that will be fine, too.

All is well here. My Shakespeare[407] is coming along more slowly than I would have liked, perhaps because of the English, perhaps because the subject is too literary for me at this stage of my life. Anyway, I'm going to try to finish the thing [*la chose*] as quickly as possible.

Lately, I have been rereading philosophy and French criticism, in particular Derrida, but also on the side a little Heidegger, and I am struck, with Derrida

---

[405] Elie Wiesel; the photo is on p. 30.
[406] This seminar, attended by professors and students, at the *Theologische Hochschule Chur* in the winter semester of 1986-7, took place every Friday. It focused on: Schwager, *Der wunderbare Tausch*.
[407] Girard, *A Theater of Envy*.

in particular, by his powerful analysis of textual mechanisms, which are actually *sacrificial mechanisms.*

I would like to do something on this, but I am not yet really ready.

I would like to demonstrate that philosophy is a direct extension of the structures of the sacred, and that its defense of the absolute (being, nature, the subject, man), can never guard itself from the internal disintegration of its own concepts [*la désagrégation interne de ses propres concepts*], except by the exclusion of all that threatens these systems from within.

With Derrida, there is always an effort to show that the philosophy of being, and then the philosophy of the subject, beginning with Descartes, is tied to a valorization of the living *word*, or fullness of *speech*, as opposed to *writing*; and *writing* is the obligation to pass through the *substitution* of a sign, a sort of scapegoat victim that we always strive to expel, but that we can't do without, in the same way we can't do without *ritual*.

And all this is bound to a ritual economy and logic, which, in the final analysis, is that of the sacred that he [Derrida] discovers in the texts *behind* the official allegiance of the philosopher or the writer; with this, he critiques the traditional logic of identity and the excluded middle [*du tiers exclu*].

Suddenly, I find this kind of analysis illuminating, and it has become exciting for me. Basically, it is these people, Derrida and Foucault in particular, who demonstrate the secret failure (less and less secret) of idolatrous humanism. That is the best in them. It would be better not to talk of what is the worst in them. [*Dans ce qu'ils ont de meilleur. Il vaut mieux ne pas parler de ce qu'ils ont de pire.*]

I think, today, given the prestige and influence that this Franco-German nihilism enjoys (behind it, there is always Heidegger–Nietzsche, and beyond them Hegel and Kant), it's worth addressing the question. But I don't have any illusions about the chances of a wide dissemination of our ideas at the present time. To the extent to which my ideas become better known here, I sense that an intellectual mistrust with respect to myself is gathering strength in the majority of my colleagues.

Finally, it is perhaps not bad to be in literature, as there, in principle, the bizarre is tolerated and even exalted.

Le bouc émissaire has just come out in English.[408] *Des choses cachées*[409] and *La route antique*[410] are coming out too, as well as a book that charts an encounter with Walter Burkert, an ethnologist from Zürich, and Jonathan Smith from Chicago, (entitled) *Violent Origins*.

I am thinking a great deal about Innsbruck under the snow. I am thinking of the problems of your beautiful house—of its past, of its present. I see clearly what you mean by "mute resistance," but I am sure that you apply lots of diplomacy, and above all charity, to these matters.

With love.
René

JESUITENKOLLEG INNSBRUCK

Innsbruck, February 4, 1987

Dear Friend,

Thank you very much for your last letter. I see that you have developed a taste for philosophy. Given that I don't know much about Derrida, I can't quite grasp the details of your analysis; but that will be a subject for discussion at a future meeting.

The honorary doctorate has finally gone through in our faculty—after a delay of three months and quite a lot of trouble. Now the bishop[411] has to give his "placet"[412] and, before granting it, he must seek the advice of Rome. If all goes well, as I hope, it will finally be the senate of the university that has the last word. All this takes time and it's definitely too late for '87; the next date is *June 1988*.

The discussions around the doctorate showed me once again that, on the one hand, there is a great deal of appreciation for your work, but on the other,

---

[408] Girard, *The Scapegoat*.
[409] Girard, *Things Hidden*.
[410] Girard, *Job: The Victim of His People*.
[411] Reinhold Stecher.
[412] In Austria, the approval of the local bishop is required for someone to be awarded an honorary doctorate in Catholic theology.

a wariness of the significance of your thinking for theology. All that is not very logical, but that's life, which itself is not always very logical. The mistrust is due to the fact that your thought does not operate within the customary framework of theological thinking [*ta pensée n'entre pas dans les cadres habituels de la pensée théologique*]. Someone or other had also read some negative reviews (Valadier?[413]) without genuinely studying your thought. Last week I was at a theology faculty in Switzerland for a closing seminar on my book, *Der wunderbare Tausch* [The wonderful exchange][414] (eight professors and fifteen students). This discussion revolved almost exclusively around your thought. I felt a great interest, and at the same time the usual objections (monism of violence, the reduction of the religious dimension to an unveiling, lack of a theology of creation, the goodness of creation, etc.). All these reactions demonstrate to me, once again, that a small publication in which you reply to all the objections would be desirable.

And how are things with you? Is the program of the summer symposium[415] fixed? I hope your "Shakespeare"[416] is progressing well!

With love.
Raymund

February 25, 1987

Very dear Raymund,

Thank you for all your efforts, now crowned with success, in approaching your colleagues to let me have [*auprès de tes collèges, pour me faire avoir*[417]]

---

[413] Valadier, "Bouc émissaire."
[414] This seminar, attended by professors and students, at the *Theologische Hochschule Chur* in the winter semester of 1986-7, took place every Friday. It focused on: Schwager, *Der wunderbare Tausch*. Schwager participated at the closing seminar session, on January 30, 1987.
[415] Very likely: symposium in Stanford, September 13–16, 1987. Cf. the respective editorial footnote in Schwager's letter of December 24, 1986.
[416] Girard, *A Theater of Envy*.
[417] The French word "*collèges*," which is the same in English, seems incorrect here, especially when Schwager has referred in the previous letter to difficulties convincing his colleagues on the faculty to approve Girard's award. With the addition of one letter, "u," the word becomes "*collègues*," and

this honorary doctorate. This shows the esteem in which they hold you, much more than they hold me, whom they don't know.

I'm going through a good phase with my work. I have the impression of making progress on the Shakespeare front[418]—which has been around for so long that it seems almost ludicrous to me—but also and above all, on the matter of relationships between the mimetic-victimary hypothesis and Heideggerianism-Derrideanism, which seems to me to be the only branch of contemporary philosophy of interest for us. There is, in particular, a text of Derrida, of great analytic power, on both the incoherence and the coherence of the uses of *pharmakon* and its derivatives [*l'incohérence et la cohérence des usages de* pharmakon *et de ses dérivés*] in Plato's texts.[419] It shows that it [the term *pharmakon*] plays a very ambivalent role with respect to the emergence of the major conceptual pairings characterizing Western metaphysics: essence-appearance, mimesis, etc. [*Il montre que ça joue un rôle génétique très ambivalent par rapport aux grandes paires de concepts de la métaphysique occidentale, essence-apparence, mimésis, etc.*]

It is really the problem of the *passage* from mythology and ritual to philosophy. I'd like to get perfectly straight [*arriver à situer parfaitement*] what this text (and quite a few others less important than this) is doing [*font*], within the framework of our hypothesis. I know that it's feasible, and that it's potentially decisive for the incorporation of philosophy into [*rattachement de la philosophie à*] [our] hypothesis, but this creates lots of problems for me because of my very great philosophical incompetence. As you'll appreciate, it's a matter [*Il s'agit, tu t'en doutes*] of demonstrating that the philosophical writings of Plato (and so on up to our own times—Heidegger and Derrida are already taking it on [*se sont déjà chargés de la suite*]) remain dominated by victimary mechanisms and are thus incapable of seeing how their own logic arises from concepts that we bring to Western thought [*que nous fournit la pensée occidentale*].

Once more, and in short: only one *hypothesis*—one hypothesis not based

---

seems to fit better. The same issue with this word arises in a later letter of Girard, on January 24, 1991, where there can be no doubt. Perhaps it was an error or mis-transcription.

[418] Girard, *A Theater of Envy*.
[419] Derrida, "Plato's Pharmacy."

solely on philosophical texts—is likely to bring this logic to light [*Montrer une fois de + en somme que seule une* hypothèse, *mais une hypothèse qui ne se fonderait pas sûr les seuls textes philosophiques, est susceptible de mettre à jour cette logique*].[420] Of course this hypothesis, or even the idea of its necessity, remains inaccessible outside of the gospel text. Derrida's text is, of course, incomplete, since it leads to the most complete nihilism, but nonetheless operates with extreme precision in relating philosophical logic to the logic of exclusion/expulsion, which can be uncovered on the basis of the word *pharmakon*.

Last week, we went as a family to the southern point of Mexican California with all the children. It was very restful and we were able to swim. We are probably not going to France this spring as Martha does not have the time, and I've hardly got any either. University affairs seem to me more and more boring and exasperating, but it is difficult to absent oneself completely from them. This term I collaborated with R. Hamerton-Kelly in giving a course on the Bible and the gospels.

With love.
René

JESUITENKOLLEG INNSBRUCK

Innsbruck, April 16, 1987

Dear Friend,

I hope that you and your family had a very good Easter. I think of you in my prayers, and I feel increasingly the need for prayer in a world where the forces of evil and violence are very powerful. Thought alone is not enough to counterbalance these destructive mechanisms.

Thank you for your last letter. I was very interested to read your analysis of Derrida and philosophy. I am becoming more and more aware that, for many

---

[420] Here, and in the next letter, the phrase *"mettre à jour"* (bring up to date) is used when *"mettre au jour"* (bring to light—i.e., to the light of day) seems clearly intended.

theologians, your position regarding philosophy presents an obstacle to their accepting your thought. So I'm looking for a formula that explains, on the one hand, all that you say about the violence hidden in philosophy and the Greek logos, and that accepts, on the other hand, the positive contribution of philosophy (e.g., the elaboration of the principle of non-contradiction). All the dialogues of Plato are dominated by this principle, which is one of the bases of modern science and, thus, also of your hypothesis. Philosophy is not only dependent on gospel thinking [*la pensée évangélique*], but also on Greek thought, and I think it is important that we recognize this. But how can we accept this positive side of philosophy, and demonstrate at the same time that the same philosophy does not succeed in shedding any light [*à mettre à jour*][421] on the real foundations? Isn't this problem similar to that of the relationship of the OT to the NT? A topic for future discussions.

And the question of the honorary doctorate! The bishop[422] has given his "placet."[423] I am now convinced that everything will go very well next year. And it finally proved to be a good thing that there were problems in our faculty. The university usually gives two honorary doctorates each year; this year there were five nominations from the different faculties (among them, the former President of the Republic of Austria, and the head of the National Bank). After long resistance, the senate of the university accepted all five candidates. So the field is now free for our faculty for next year. And you won't be drowned in a mass of Doctors![424]

I am sending you a book in a separate package that contains your paper from Innsbruck[425] and an article by Father Bono, which has been published in a review in Indonesia.[426]

I have just read Jean Delumeau's book, *Le péché et la peur* (published by Fayard, 1983).[427] There are an enormous number of things in this book that

---

[421] As in the previous letter, rather than "*mettre à jour*" (bring up to date), the near-identical expression "*mettre au jour*" (bring to light) seems to be what was intended.
[422] Reinhold Stecher.
[423] In Austria, the approval of the local bishop is required for someone to be awarded an honorary doctorate in Catholic theology.
[424] In 1988, Girard was actually the only one to receive an honorary doctorate from the University of Innsbruck.
[425] Girard, "Der tragische Konflikt."
[426] This could be an article that was also published in Europe: Banawiratma, "Religion and Peace."
[427] Delumeau, *Le peché et le peur*.

show the importance of your thinking in clarifying a very dubious tradition. Delumeau says specifically that he is in agreement with you regarding the theology of redemption (p. 335).[428] Do you know this book, which is a help to us?

We probably won't meet this year. But I am already thinking of your stay in Innsbruck next year. The day of granting the "honoris causa" is normally in mid-June.

With love.
Raymond

Innsbruck, December 20, 1987

Dear Friend,

Months have passed since my last letter. This has been a very difficult time for me. We've have had an enormous conflict in our faculty. A professor, who has greatly distanced himself—inwardly [*intérieurement*]—from the Church, but who is very skilful at creating intrigues and conspiracies, has tried to dominate the whole faculty. As Dean, I opposed these attempts. At first, nearly all the professors approved of my way of handling the situation. But from the moment that the conflict came out into the open, a fear spread. Most feared conflict, and so began to reproach me for being too harsh in my reactions. For my part, I also feared the conflict, but regarded it as inevitable. And the reaction of many of my colleagues really annoyed me. Even in prayer, I was not able to find any lasting inner peace. I felt that I was in danger of losing myself in a relationship of [mimetic] doubles. Fortunately, the period of my function as Dean expired at the end of September. I took the decision to step back from the conflict and concentrate on my work. But the other continued to try and manipulate the new Dean;[429] at that moment I contemplated leaving

---

[428] Girard wrote on the text of this letter: "Like this author I believe [...] that Jesus, in his passion, suffered from a 'desacralized' violence, which was imposed upon him by humans, not by God: he came to his own and his own did not receive him." The text after the colon refers to Jn 1:11.
[429] George Vass, SJ.

the faculty. The majority finally decided that the situation was intolerable and Professor X lost his place on two important commissions. He is still on a third, and there the conflict goes on. Given that I am not on that commission, the situation does not touch me directly any more, but it concerns the faculty as a whole. I hope the situation will improve next year. The conflict sapped my strength; consequently I have not had much time for intellectual work.

And you? I hope that your time has been more peaceful [than mine] and that your work on Shakespeare[430] has advanced. I also hope to see you next year.

The date for the "honorary doctorate" ceremony is *June 11 or 18, 1988*. I'll let you know the exact date as soon as the decision has been made.

I have just read the four volumes of *Vengeance* (Verdier Group).[431] Do you know this work? This research was aimed against your ideas, but if you read all the studies closely, you realize that they actually support your thought [*on constate qu'elles apportent plutôt un soutien pour ta pensée*]. I've summarized the issues in a short article.[432]

The German translation of *La violence et le sacré*[433] is quite good; in any case better than that of *Des choses cachées*.[434] I hope that this translation will facilitate the dissemination of your thinking in non-theological circles.

After Christmas I am going to Switzerland for a few days, among other things to see my mother and my brothers and sisters. My mother is still well—despite her age.

I hope that you will have hours of profound peace during these feast days. I will think of you and your family in my prayer and I wish you the grace of God for '88.

In friendship,
Raymond

---

[430] Girard, *A Theater of Envy*.
[431] Verdier and Courtois, eds., *La vengeance*, vols 1–4.
[432] Schwager, "Rache—Gerechtigkeit—Religion."
[433] Girard, *Das Heilige und die Gewalt*.
[434] Girard, *Das Ende der Gewalt*, 1983.

PROGRAM OF INTERDISCIPLINARY RESEARCH—Stanford University

January 6, 1988

My very dear Friend,

I am terribly sorry that your life has been troubled by these mimetic problems that you tell me about. Nothing is more conducive to this kind of thing than university life. Several years ago, I was also more or less directly affected by similar things.

You tell me that the honorary doctorate ceremony will be held on June 11 or 18. Does that mean that my nomination has passed all the tests victoriously, including [that of] Cardinal Ratzinger, who I think you told me in one of your letters is associated with the affair? I don't think I have received any notification on the subject, but I could be wrong. In any event I will be in Innsbruck in June, probably with Martha. Not having any news from you, we initially decided to go to France at the beginning of May, but now I think we will arrive about the twentieth, when I have to go to Israel for a week, then give a paper in Milan, before coming to Innsbruck on the eleventh or eighteenth. If you can let me have the exact date as soon as you have it, I'll sort this out [cela m'arrangerait].

I am pleased that you have finished your time as Dean and that you are able to get back to your work. I hope you always have sympathetic students, as you had when I visited you.

Here, all is well and my Shakespeare,[435] this time, is almost finished, though not without trouble. It was a risky decision to do the book in English, as that has stretched my already slow rhythm to extremely slow, and then to even slower. I can no longer get myself interested in the external world, or even in the dissemination of my work, but I am really engrossed [je me suis vraiment pris] in the new chapters on Shakespeare and I'm going to show [je vais montrer] that one can speak about literary language on the basis of the mimetic problematic.

Last term I gave a course on Heidegger through to [→] Derridean

---

[435] Girard, *A Theater of Envy*.

deconstruction and mimetic deconstruction, which interested me greatly. The correlations between what we are doing and the school of deconstruction are closer than I thought. I regret in *La violence et le sacré* not having set out my relationship with anthropology in a style a little more deconstructionist, which would have perhaps prevented certain misunderstandings.

Now that you are no longer Dean, I hope that you will be able to come to our symposium next October, entitled *Vengeance*.[436]

With love—and I am delighted at the idea of seeing you in spring.
René

There will be people from the Verdier group[437] at the symposium "Vengeance." Send me your article.[438] Your clarifications are always illuminating and to be savored [*savoureuses*].

JESUITENKOLLEG INNSBRUCK

Innsbruck, February 22, 1988

Dear Friend,

The date for the "promotio honoris causa" is now fixed for June 11. I am looking forward to seeing you for a second time in Innsbruck, and hope that all will go well.

The German translation of *La violence et le sacré*[439] is quite good, even if I would have preferred another translation for certain key words (e.g., *sakral* [sacred] in the place of *heilig* [holy] for *sacré*). But the text is comprehensible. For the moment there is not much reaction. Your book is intellectually unfashionable [*va contre la mode intellectuelle*]. "The Mythological"[440] has for

---

[436] Symposium organized by the Program of Interdisciplinary Research at Stanford University, October 27–29, 1988. Cf. the relevant editorial footnote to Girard's undated letter of January–May 1986.
[437] Girard is referring to collaborators of the 4-vol. study, *La vengeance*.
[438] Schwager, "Rache—Gerechtigkeit—Religion."
[439] Girard, *Das Heilige und die Gewalt*.
[440] In the French original, Schwager uses the German term "*das Mythologische*."

some time been preferred to the critique of myth. But this fashion certainly won't last long.

Do you know the book by Karl Miller, *Doubles: Studies in Literary History* (Oxford University Press)?[441] I've bought it, but have not yet had the time to read it.

Michel Corbin in Paris has just published a commentary on St. Anselm's doctrine of salvation[442] that I find extraordinary. Michel demonstrates in a very convincing manner that the deepest spirit of Anselm is anti-sacrificial, and that the theologian uses an *ambiguous language in order to submit it to a "conversion" during the argumentation*. I think that it is the best commentary on Anselm that has ever been written (indebted to [*préparé par*] Karl Barth and H. U. v. Balthasar).

As for me, I am starting to prepare my "sabbatical" ["*Freisemester*"] (October '88—February '89). I intend to write a book (a product of my course on Christology and salvation)[443] and I also intend to spend about two months in the US, among other things to visit several Jesuit universities, to do some study of theological currents in the US. I am very happy that your symposium is at this time. Has the exact date been fixed? Would you let me know as soon as possible so that I can make my plans?

And the theme of the symposium? You mentioned "vengeance" as a subject.[444] Is this theme fixed? In any case, I find this very interesting; there is so much to say about it, beginning with the Old Testament.

In your last letter you mentioned a course on Heidegger and Derridean deconstruction. Deconstruction is not familiar to me but I would like to talk to you about it, to discover the link with the mimetic issue [*problématique mimétique*].

I think of you in my prayers.
Very sincerely,
 Raymund Schwager

---

[441] 1987.
[442] Schwager is referring to: Corbin, ed., *L'œuvre de S. Anselme de Cantorbéry*.
[443] Schwager, *Jesus im Heilsdrama*.
[444] Symposium organized by the Program of Interdisciplinary Research at Stanford University, October 27–29, 1988. Cf. the relevant editorial footnote to Girard's undated letter of January–May 1986.

PROGRAM OF INTERDISCIPLINARY RESEARCH—Stanford University

June 27, 1988

My very dear Friend [*Trés cher*],

Here I am, back home, after that beautiful stay in Innsbruck, which leaves me with many fond memories. The best moments were our walk in the mountains, followed by the evening with your students, who are really interesting.

My last days in Paris went well. I read my paper on Shakespeare at the CREA;[445] the return trip also went well, in an almost empty plane. Now, here I am, harnessed again to my Shakespeare,[446] but this time I believe that the end is in sight and I will be finished this year.

I am following the visit of the Pope[447] to Austria in the *New York Times*, which speaks not only of the Waldheim question and the Jews,[448] but also of his nomination of bishops who are too conservative in the eyes of the Austrian Church.[449]

The decision of Msgr. Lefebvre[450] is very distressing. I have the impression that, each time he has discussions with the Vatican envoys, he is ready to sign an accord, then after that, he finds himself back amongst his associates who, afraid of being reduced to nothing again through an agreement with the church, push in the direction of schism.

I have begun to collect texts for my next work on sacrifice, and the desire to get into it is pushing me to quickly finish the Shakespeare.

We will be very happy to have you here for our symposium on vengeance.[451] I hope that you now have the peace of mind [*liberté d'esprit*] and the time you need to concentrate on your work.

---

[445] Centre de Recherche en Épistémologie Appliquée, École Polytechnique, founded by Jean-Pierre Dupuy.
[446] Girard, *A Theater of Envy*.
[447] John Paul II.
[448] Kurt Waldheim's term as President of Austria (1986–92) was overshadowed by debates about his behavior during the Nazi era, when he was an officer in the German army.
[449] The appointments of Hans Hermann Groër as Archbishop of Vienna (1986) and of Kurt Krenn as his auxiliary bishop (1987) were very controversial.
[450] Girard is referring to Archbishop Marcel Lefebvre's decision to consecrate bishops from the ranks of his (anti-Vatican II) Society of St. Pius X without the Pope's approval. This led to the excommunication of Lefebvre and his bishops. See the letter of January–May 1986 for an earlier reference.
[451] Symposium organized by the Program of Interdisciplinary Research at Stanford University, October 27–29, 1988. Cf. the relevant editorial footnote to Girard's undated letter of January–May 1986.

Thank all your colleagues and associates for their contribution to the happiness of my stay with you, and thanks above all to you; I understand that you had to fight to obtain this honor,[452] and I am very grateful.

With love.
René

JESUITENKOLLEG INNSBRUCK

Innsbruck, July 31, 1988

Dear René,

I thank you very much for your last letter. I am glad that you are home and well.—Here, there is finally a little calm during the holidays—despite the new unrest here, on account of a woman having been elected Dean of our faculty for the years 1990–1.[453] From the very start, I stayed out of this, and now I have peace to work. I hope I can finish the first half of a book[454] before I leave for the US.

I received a letter from Mrs. Tompkins with an invitation to your conference.[455] I thanked her; she asked for the title of my presentation and I provided this: "Vengeance in the Old Testament."[456]

There is already an article about this issue in volume 3 of *Vengeance* (Verdier).[457] But this contribution is utterly insufficient. It does not explain the evolution toward the NT. Verdier himself finds that the teaching of Jesus was contrary to the conventions [*en contradiction avec les normes*] of the vengeance system. So I think it is important to see how religious thought in Israel was preparatory for the teaching of Jesus.

---

[452] Girard is referring to the honorary doctorate he was awarded by the University of Innsbruck.
[453] Herlinde Pissarek-Hudelist was Dean from 1989 to 1993.
[454] Schwager, *Jesus im Heilsdrama*.
[455] Symposium organized by the Program of Interdisciplinary Research at Stanford University, October 27–29, 1988. Cf. the relevant editorial footnote to Girard's undated letter of January–May 1986.
[456] Cf. the relevant editorial footnote to Girard's undated letter of January–May 1986.
[457] Verdier and Courtois, eds, *La vengeance*.

By separate mail I will send you a short article on "Verdier" that I published in our journal.[458]

In my new book[459] I'm trying to integrate the "dramatic" model of Balthasar, slightly improved [*en le corrigeant un peu*], into your thinking; and at the same time I want to show that the questions left open in historical-critical exegesis also find a clear answer [*une certaine réponse*].

I think that ultimately Anselm—in the light of Corbin's interpretation[460]—is very close to this view.

The situation in [historical] critical exegesis is very complicated; therefore, I only proceed very slowly. But I hope I am grasping the main lineaments of it.—We will talk it over in October.

With love.
Raymond

JESUITENKOLLEG INNSBRUCK

Innsbruck, December 25, 1988

Dear Friend,

Christmas Day: I hope that you will receive the gift of some days spent in peace, and with an inner presence—the presence of this new life, which is both very close to us and which, at the same time, extends beyond us. I think of you in my prayers and ask God to bless for you for '89—for your work and your family.

I'm back home after my stay in the US. I was happy to leave New York, where I spent only a few days. I couldn't live in a city like that. I was very happy to come back to my "little Innsbruck," where my feet are all I need to get about. And architecture as well! After having seen all those "buildings" that I

---

[458] Schwager, "Rache—Gerechtigkeit—Religion."
[459] Schwager, *Jesus im Heilsdrama*.
[460] Schwager is referring to Corbin's 3-vol. edition of the writing of St. Anselm: *L'œuvre de S. Anselme de Cantorbéry*.

mostly found ugly, I developed an almost physical need to feel the great forms of classical architecture e.g., our church.[461] Inside there I could breathe with all my soul [*Je pouvais respirer de toute mon âme dans son intérieur*]. I feel, more and more, that romanesque, gothic, and baroque art are important to me. In Boston, the professors of the "department of theology" invited me for a long evening to discuss your work (Boston College). It was intense and at the same time peaceful. I was impressed. It was the only place where I found a serious interest in your thought.

As to the general situation, I formed the impression that theology is not in a good state. In Boston, several people have the same impression: an almost total loss of tradition. Lots of theologians use psychology, sociology, or literary criticism, but without arriving at a coherent theology. I returned to Europe with the impression that your thinking could be of great importance for theologians in the US (and not only them). I hope that they will discover it one day.

The work on my book[462] is not currently moving ahead as well as it did during summer. I always have to protect myself so that I have the time for work. I hope I can nevertheless finish it by the beginning of March, when I begin to teach again.

Thank you for being so welcoming at Stanford.[463] I wish you and your wife well.
In friendship,
Raymond Schwager

---

[461] Schwager is referring to the (baroque-era) Jesuit Church in Innsbruck.
[462] Schwager, *Jesus im Heilsdrama*.
[463] When Schwager traveled to the United States to attend a symposium organized by the Program of Interdisciplinary Research at Stanford University, October 27–9, 1988, he visited the Girards. Cf. the respective editorial footnote to Girard's undated letter of January–May 1986.

JESUITENKOLLEG INNSBRUCK

Innsbruck, December 19, 1989

Dear Friend,

I hope that you had a good Christmas with your family. More and more, I feel how important these hours of inner peace are for a life that resists losing itself in pointless activities [*activités quelconques*].

Deep tensions continue in our house and in the faculty, but thanks to a new Father Provincial[464] I now have the hope that the situation will get better. This situation has greatly hindered intellectual work; nevertheless my new book is coming out in two months.[465] And your "Shakespeare"?[466] I'm waiting for it.

A German professor[467] told me a bit about your paper in Los Angeles ("Job: Victim of His Own People"). And your stay in Israel? Was it fruitful? Things must be sad in that country. It's the opposite around Austria. The changes at the border of our country were overwhelming. A border that was completely closed—and now? Lots of people talk of a "miracle," and, in a certain sense, it is a miracle. Of course, there are now enormous problems in these countries, but also a will to overcome these difficulties.[468]

The situation is different in Russia; people who come from there are rather pessimistic, the economic problems are enormous, and there it is not clear how they can be solved. One hears of twenty to thirty million people out of work; these people are against Gorbachev. It's said that the influence of the "pan-slavists" is growing (people like Solzhenitsyn, who are against communism, but also against ideas that come from the West).

For a long time, I have had an idea that we may one day form an alliance against the army and the Orthodox Church in Russia. This will perhaps give Europe an "enemy" once more. What would Europe do without an "enemy"? And the problem of Germany? The year 1990 could be full of surprises!

---

[464] Gerwin Komma, SJ, was the Austrian Jesuit Provincial from 1989 to 1995.
[465] Schwager, *Jesus im Heilsdrama*.
[466] Girard, *A Theater of Envy*.
[467] This could be the sociologist Konrad Thomas.
[468] Schwager is referring to the fall of the Iron Curtain, culminating in the tearing down of the Berlin Wall from November 9, 1989.

I wish you the grace of God for the coming year and I think of you and your family in my prayers.

In all friendship,
Raymond Schwager

STANFORD UNIVERSITY—Stanford, California

January 24, 1990

Dear Raymond,

That good letter of yours [*Ta bonne lettre*] is here and I want to reply to it, but I'm overwhelmed with work. In the last few months there has been a quantum leap in the number of manuscripts that come to me—authors looking for publishers—and I try not to leave them without a reply, but it's difficult.

You spoke of Christmas. We spent it traveling. Martha and I left for Egypt on December 10 (Cairo and Luxor); on the seventeenth we were in Tel Aviv at a symposium,[469] the nineteenth in Haifa,[470] and from the twentieth to the twenty-fifth in Jerusalem.[471] We went to a very beautiful midnight Mass in a monastery near Jerusalem, then we left for Paris, where we stayed until the thirty-first.

It was a very beautiful trip, very moving, with *La violence et le sacré* first, followed by *Des choses cachées*! It was really the only trip I wanted to do, and this time, it's done. The situation in Israel is difficult, but the people don't seem to be as demoralized as you would expect. The universities are hostile to [Yitzhak] Shamir's policies, of course, and quite rightly so, but I didn't get the impression that the country is about to fall apart [*risquait de se défaire*]. What I found extraordinary is how *everybody* speaks Hebrew.

---

[469] Symposium *Thought and Innovation*, Faculty of Humanities, Tel Aviv University. Girard was talking about innovation and repetition; cf. the published paper, "Innovation and Repetition."
[470] Girard gave a Manes Sperber Memorial Lecture at the University of Haifa: "Collective Violence and Sacrifice in Shakespeare's Julius Caesar."
[471] On December 21 he gave a lecture for the Mishkenot Sha'ananim Scholars Retreat, Jerusalem: "Myth and the Bible."

I imagine that Austria is very directly affected by the events in the East and that it's even more intense than it looks from here [*plus passionnant encore que vu d'ici*].

We have three Danes with us here who have been in contact with you: Jørgen Jørgensen,[472] Jensen,[473] and one of their students.[474] They are really very good and have suggested that we should meet up somewhere in Europe, next year. Perhaps I haven't yet told you that, next year, I will be the Director of the Stanford Program in Paris, so I will spend at least six months in France—from October. I really want to do this. And especially since the earthquake[475] we have lost our building and the comforts of an American university [*le confort universitaire américain*].

I have finally finished my Shakespeare, which will come out in English in December with Oxford University Press[476] and in French in September.[477] I've all sorts of little hurdles to clear before me, and a quite heavy teaching load in spring, but I am much looking forward to writing a short book on the Passion that I have been reflecting on for about a year, and that will just be an enlargement of the paper that I frequently give on this subject.

I am happy to know that your book[478] is coming out, and I hope that the situation in your house will calm down entirely.

With love—and I hope to see you next autumn.
René

---

[472] He joined the symposium on March 1, 1990, at Stanford, later becoming a founding member of the Colloquium on Violence and Religion (COV&R).
[473] This should be Hans Jørgen Jensen, also a founding member of COV&R.
[474] Claus Thomas Nielsen.
[475] Girard is referring to the California earthquake of October 17, 1989.
[476] Girard, *A Theater of Envy*. In the end, this book was published in 1991.
[477] Girard, *Shakespeare*.
[478] Schwager, *Jesus im Heilsdrama*.

Theologische Fakultät der Universität Innsbruck

January 4, 1991[479]

Dear Friend,

I hope that you had a very good Christmas with your family and that you were able to experience some grace at this time. For the year that has just begun, I wish God's blessing for you, your family, and your work. And I hope that we will meet again soon, as I will probably be in Paris from February 10 to 23, 1991.

I am very grateful to have your "Shakespeare."[480] I very much liked what I read. You've succeeded well in describing the history and passion of desire and mimesis—including all the detours.

You also make several comments on the subject of mimesis that I really liked, and that I have not found so far in your books. You say, e.g., of Leontes, that he is attracted first of all to the image of his wife (the statue) and that he finds her real presence only after a conversion:

> If mimetic desire is the devil that discredits and ultimately destroys the real, a genuine renunciation should produce the opposite result. A liberated Leontes should experience *real presence* after all, and indeed he does—with a little delay.[481]

In *To Double Business Bound*, you have written on the subject of mimesis: "This mode of imitation operates with *a quasiosmotic immediacy*" (p. 89, emphasis added).

The quasi-osmotic immediacy is certainly central to your concept of mimesis, and I have often cited the aforementioned phrase in *To Double Business Bound*. Nevertheless, it seems to me, that this phrase is ambiguous. The expression "quasi-osmotic immediacy" can suggest the <u>idea that mimesis</u>

---

[479] This letter must have been quite important to Girard: he underlined several parts of it and hand-wrote a number of remarks on it.
[480] Girard, *A Theater of Envy*.
[481] Girard, *A Theater of Envy*, 336.

encounters all of reality (its Being) [*la mimésis rencontre toute la réalité (son Être)*], and that it attaches itself to the deepest desire of its model.[482] But Leontes shows that this is not true. Even if mimesis "operates with a quasi-osmotic immediacy," it makes a (false) image of its model. It does not encounter the Being of the other.

This distinction is fundamental to making the link between your theology and that of Cardinal de Lubac. In *Surnaturel*,[483] de Lubac strongly underlines that there is "desiderium naturale videndi dei" (a desire of human nature [as creature] to see God [supernaturally]) [*un désir de la nature humaine (comme créature) de voir (surnaturellement) Dieu*]. If this is accurate, the mimesis that tends toward violence cannot attain the "desiderium naturale," to the deepest desire of its model. Despite "the quasi-osmotic immediacy" it only meets an image[484] of its model. It is mistaken about the deepest desire of the other.

This intuition has consequences: the most sublime[485] idolatry precedes the scapegoat mechanism. I am happy that you have mentioned the Adam and Eve story in your "Shakespeare" [*A Theater of Envy*] (pp. 324–5).[486] From this story we learn that the lie (concerning God) precedes violence. The sacred, therefore, is not completely identical to violence. Idolatry (the sacred) begins with mimesis. The scapegoat mechanism does not create the sacred (in a certain way disagreeing with *La violence et le sacré*), but it gives it its *social and public structure* (in agreement with *La violence et le sacré*). Are you in agreement with this conclusion?

A minor question about the statue: In "El burlador de Sevilla y convidado de piedra,"[487] there is also a statue, but it destroys itself. Judith Arias identifies this statue with mimesis, which destroys itself (in: *Hispanic Review* 58 [1990]: 361–77[488]). Was the statue an important literary subject in this era?[489]

---

[482] This underlining and indeed all the underlining in this letter are by Girard, perhaps suggesting its importance to him.
[483] De Lubac, *Surnaturel*.
[484] Here, Girard hand-wrote a comment: "Bad desire is not simply an image. It is connected with honor, which comes from humans." The last sentence resonates with the Gospel of John (Jn 5:41; Jn 5:44).
[485] Girard adds: "the tendency toward idolatry."
[486] Gen. 2:4b–3:24. The page number given in the original letter (395) is incorrect.
[487] This is the first literary source of the Don Juan story.
[488] Arias, "Doubles in Hell."
[489] Here, Girard wrote on Schwager's letter: "I do not know."

Another, more important, question: C. G. Jung wrote a terrible book on Job[490] (albeit fascinating for many), in which he basically says: "The God of the final discourse is a (amoral) god of physical force who feels inferior to Job, which poses a moral question. This (amoral) God crushes the (moral) man through physical prowess." I am not at all in agreement with C. G. Jung's vision of Job. Nevertheless, I have difficulties myself with the final speech of God, and so I focused my attention [*je m'attachais donc*]—with you and following on from you—on the discourse of Job and his friends/enemies. Recently, we discussed this speech in a group, and one of my colleagues drew our attention to Job's final words (after the speech of God):

> I was the one who confuses your wisdom, by proposition devoid of meaning. I spoke of things I did not understand, things too wonderful for me to know. *My ears had heard of you but now my eyes have seen you.* (Job 42:3, 5)

The last phrase immediately reminded me of the "Love by hearsay" in your book on Shakespeare. From this perspective one is obliged to say that the final speech brings—despite appearances to the contrary—something absolutely new. In the dialogues between Job and his friends/enemies, *the god of Job himself*—and not only the god of this enemies—was a god of hearsay. Thus, on the one hand, Job was in the right against his adversaries (which God himself recognized, 42:7), but on the other hand, he himself had "spoken of things he did not understand." In his attacks on the theology of his friends/enemies he was himself dependent upon this theology. Job's soul and spirit were confused because of this, and for the duration of the dialogues he could not find peace. After the final speech of God, everything changes. Job finds peace. The discourse did not give him new understanding, but a new experience of the grandeur and the mystery of God. From this I conclude: the critique of the scapegoat mechanism (in the speeches of Job) is correct, but by itself it does not give a true knowledge of God and a solution to the question posed. It does not give inner peace. For that, a new experience is necessary. Are you thinking the same thing in your "Shakespeare" when you say:

---

[490] Jung, *Antwort auf Hiob*.

But this greater knowledge does not solve their problem, does not rid them of their desire; their greater awareness even aggravates their condition, for a very simple reason: being placed in the service of desire.[491]

The "academy" in Stuttgart is organizing a session on "La route antique des hommes pervers" at the beginning of March. I have been invited to present two papers.[492]

I look forward to seeing you—very warmly,
Raymund

Paris, January 24, 1991

Dear Raymund,

Your letter gave me great pleasure, above all, because it contains some very important things. The first idea is that there is a natural desire for God, and that mimesis does not attach itself to this when it gives itself a model, but to a "false image" of the other; this seems to me to be right, except that the idea of a *false image* appears to me a little restrictive. Does not the natural desire for God immediately deviate toward human models by virtue of original sin? Isn't this related to Jesus' saying [*N'est ce pas à cela que se rapporte la phrase de Jésus*] about men searching for the glory that comes from men, and not that which comes from God?[493]

Isn't original sin based on the fact that the *desiderium naturale* has been around all along and is still misdirected toward men?

The idea that the sacred, idolatry, precedes the scapegoat mechanism, would suit me perfectly, if all the structures of the sacred did not depend on this mechanism. But, would it not be sufficient to say that the tendency toward

---

[491] Girard, *A Theater of Envy*, 85.
[492] The conference *Hiob—und der Gott seiner Verfolger* [Job—and the God of his persecutors], organized by the Academy of the Diocese of Rottenburg-Stuttgart, took place in Weingarten, March 2–3, 1991. Schwager gave two lectures: "Hiob—und der Gott seiner Verfolger" and "Hiob: Ein Weg aus der Gewalt" [Job: A way out of violence].
[493] Cf. Jn 5:44.

... the impetus toward idolatry precedes the mechanism? Mimesis turned toward man is always already oriented toward idolatry.

Of primary importance in the victimage mechanism is its role in human history and the fact that it is, at the same time, *satanic*, from the point of view of the revelation, already revealed, *for us*—but from the viewpoint of pre-Christian systems, it is an imperfect prefiguration of the incarnation and of the passion. Is it possible to affirm such a thing without getting into trouble with your colleagues?

On these two points, anyway, I have no fixed view, and I'll go along with your view, because I don't operate as well with abstract concepts as I do intuitively [*je fonctionne mal sur le plan des concepts trop abstraits par rapport à mes intuitions*].

On the third point: the revelation of the scapegoat mechanism, even total knowledge of the mimetic–victimary system is not a religious experience in itself. I am one hundred percent in agreement. And the phrase of Job, to which your colleague [*collège*][494] drew your attention, "My eyes had heard of you but now my eyes have seen you,"[495] interprets very well the expression of this truth. In which case, you are right. [As for] the divine discourse, completely dismissed in *La route antique* (not only what Jung makes of it, and what I hadn't wanted to make of it—whence my reason for dismissing it) ... in everything, a positive experience of God that is not only intellectual is indispensable.

But, between this experience of God and the intellectual experience, which is largely a "descent into hell," there are close, although not necessarily causal, relationships. To put it another way, one can very well imagine Leontes who, knowing what he knows, knowing himself to be fundamentally guilty, would not have the positive experience of God's forgiveness that the "resurrection of the statue" signifies in my view. Do you agree with that? At the same time, Leontes' descent into hell constitutes, retrospectively, an essential phase of the journey that leads to conversion.

The statue, which destroys itself, is excellent from a Shakespearean

---

[494] Here, again, we find "collège" (college) where "collègue" (colleague) was clearly meant. This was remarked upon in the appropriate footnote to an earlier letter, of February 25, 1987, but here there is no doubt; whereas there it just seemed likely.

[495] Job 42:5 (as the text appears in Schwager's letter of January 4, 1991).

perspective. Apart from Don Juan, I know of nothing analogous, but I'm not a specialist in the period.

I am happy at the idea of seeing you again in Paris in February, and I hope that all will go well also for [your visit to] Stanford.[496] We are paying for part of it, at least for the travel. If there are any problems, let me know. We are all praying that the Gulf War[497] ends quickly.

With love.
René

Theologische Fakultät der Leopold-Franzens-Universität—Innsbruck

October 3, 1991

Dear Friend,

I think that our symposium[498] has convinced several theologians that they should take your thought seriously in theology. But there is still much work to do to dispel the misunderstandings. I will use the volume that we're to publish with the papers from the symposium,[499] to clarify several points, if possible, and I want to revisit a few ideas from the paper I gave in Provo/Utah.[500] I would be very grateful if you could tell me what you think of it—above all of the text on pages 8/9 (in red). I think that my text is in line with your thinking on original sin in Shakespeare,[501] but I would like to hear your reaction. It

---

[496] The conference *Mythology, with Particular Reference to the Hypothesis of René Girard* took place at the Stanford Center for International Security and Arms Control (CISAC), May 16-18, 1991. There, COV&R was officially founded; Schwager, who was there, was elected President. Unofficially, however, COV&R was founded at a meeting on March 1, 1990, in Stanford (cf. Williams, *Girardians*).
[497] This war began in summer 1990 after Iraq had invaded Kuwait. This invasion was repelled by the United States of America and a coalition of Western and Arab states.
[498] Symposium *Dramatische Erlösungslehre im Lichte der Theorie Girards* [Dramatic soteriology in the light of Girard's theory], Innsbruck, September 25-8, 1991.
[499] Niewiadomski and Palaver, eds, *Dramatische Erlösungslehre*.
[500] Symposium *Myth, Literature, and Bible*, Provo, Utah, November 12-16, 1984. Schwager gave a paper on mimesis and freedom. Cf. the relevant editorial footnote to Schwager's letter of September 30, 1984.
[501] Girard, *A Theater of Envy*, 321-6.

seems to me that the majority of the misunderstandings (e.g., the question of the creation) depend on one question: violence as an element of human nature or as a sign of original sin. I am trying not to fall into the traditional theory of original sin, which makes of Adam (or Eve) a scapegoat for all the evils of humanity, and I am struggling to avoid the other trap, which makes evil a fact of nature, and thus makes of nature (or of nature's Creator) a scapegoat.

The semester began two days ago. So I don't have much time for research. But working with the students is important.

Very sincerely,
Raymond

PROGRAM OF INTERDISCIPLINARY RESEARCH—Stanford University

October 30, 1991

Very Dear Friend,

My apologies for replying a bit late. The beginning of the term was very full for me, as I have a big course on Shakespeare with the undergraduates.

This paper from Provo[502] is brilliant from start to finish, and for the first time I really get it [*la force de sa pensée m'atteint*]. The implications with respect to Paul are far-reaching; it amounts to a comprehensive interpretation of Paul's attitude to the Law.

How can I not agree with you? What you are saying is basically about a choice of models in mimesis. Should we not think that the option to choose the divine model in the gospel sense is there from the beginning, but it isn't chosen; therefore, it is nowhere present in what we know of mankind [*Ne faut-il pas penser que la possibilité de choisir le modèle divin au sens évangélique est là dès début mais n'est pas choisie est donc n'est présente nulle part dans ce que nous voyons de l'homme*]? And the fact that this choice was not made, makes

---

[502] Schwager, "Mimesis and Freedom."

the other choice something that *seems* natural and that becomes the *wounded* nature of man [*car le fait que ce choix n'ait pas été fait a fait de l'autre choix quelque chose qui* semble *naturel, qui devient la nature* blessée *de l'homme*]? But only the light of revelation can show that man is wounded, and that he renounces his freedom because he lives with the continuing influence of [*elle reste dans le prolongement de*] animal mimesis, which aggravates the violence?

Am I correctly interpreting what you said?

So there is a possibility of another choice, of which there's no objective trace to be found in a natural and evolutionary analysis, because the continuity with animal nature is all that is visible [*la continuité avec l'animal est seule visible*]. This explains so many things. The ambiguous sentences in *Choses cachées*[503] would thus be in the evolutionary line, a bit like [*un peu dans le sens*] reproaches made against Teilhard de Ch[ardin].

What you say in this text about (Jewish) opposition to Jesus, and to the question of his wanting to be the Son of God [*la question de se vouloir le fils de Dieu*]—in the sense of the God of violence or the God of peace—really struck me a great deal too. Basically it's on the level of *metaphysical* desire, which is always there from the beginning in man, and the origin of which can only be the good revelation, turned from its course by the sin that repudiates it.

What is bad about this, or let's say regrettable, in the analysis in *Choses cachées*, is that it did not realize its incapacity to attain this level, or that it gives the impression that this level itself is only a creation of mimetic violence, which is stronger amongst men than amongst animals, thus engendering metaphysical *idolatry*.

From the theological point of view, there is, of course, nothing but idolatry in the beginning.

You make it possible to reconcile this with a naturalistic analysis[504] and give naturalism its proper place, without giving it everything.

If this is true, and I think you're right, it's just that, for me, the act of faith is perhaps incomplete in *Des choses cachées*, because it's definitely there on the

---

[503] Girard, *Des choses cachées*.

[504] The sentence does not say with what the naturalistic analysis is being reconciled by Schwager. Girard obviously wanted to add that, but then decided against it (the word "avec"—with—had been written there and then erased). It is likely that he meant "reconcile the naturalistic analysis with theology."

apocalyptic side of things, more and more illuminated by the turn that world affairs are taking, but it is not there, or is insufficient, from the perspective of what distinguishes the human from the animal at the beginning. According to the extraordinary Ulrich Horstmann,[505] it's absent on both sides—and in orthodox Christianity it's present on both sides.

Your essay provides elements of an analysis that encourages the act of faith where it's going to be most difficult from now on [*du côté où il est le plus difficile désormais*].

On the whole, my tendency is to begin with divine revelation, not at the origin of the human, but with the revelation to Israel, that is to say, from the moment when there are texts that document something other than a religion of violence and the sacred.

Further, your analysis of the words of Satan during the fall, and of the manner in which he deforms the divine intention, in order to oppose God to man, is very rich, subtle, and luminous at the same time.

Here, we have some serious problems at the university and things are going very badly. It's always this question of the relationship with the government, which thinks that Stanford has extorted money from the American taxpayer. All those who are not protected by tenure are at risk. Margaret[506] is not too worried, because her husband now has a good job. And she will perhaps be protected by the fact that the other professor and I, for whom she is the secretary, have promises in writing that guarantee us a secretary. I don't know if I told you that she has adopted a baby and has been on leave since the beginning of summer. She's coming back, part-time, on November 1.

As Jean-Pierre D[upuy] is now director of our "program,"—that is if we have any money left (and Margaret is paid in part with this money)—I can't say what [*je ne sais pas trop ce que*] the situation will be for other meetings of the type we had last May.[507]

You worked so hard for that meeting in Innsbruck.[508] Jim Williams and

---

[505] Cf. Horstmann, *Das Untier*.
[506] Margaret Tompkins.
[507] Cf. the relevant editorial footnote to Girard's letter of January 24, 1991.
[508] Symposium *Dramatische Erlösungslehre im Lichte der Theorie Girards* [Dramatic soteriology in the light of Girard's theory], Innsbruck, September 25-28, 1991. Cf.: Niewiadomski and Palaver, eds, *Dramatische Erlösungslehre*.

Robert Hamerton-Kelly found that there was a great deal of incomprehension among many of the guests, of even the most elementary aspects of mimetic rivalry.

My life is very calm at the moment, but I am very busy with my classes and the book that I am in the process of writing, the celebrated [*fameux*] "Ce que je crois" [What I believe],[509] which is transforming itself into a new version of all of my theses, rooted [*s'enracine*] in the present world, and which I hope will shed light on certain points that now seem to me to be very deficient in my earlier books.

[Wolfgang] Palaver is here, and we are going to hold a seminar with him, Bob,[510] a French couple, and perhaps several others.[511]

With love.
René

Theologische Fakultät der Leopold-Franzens-Universität—Innsbruck

November 21, 1991

Dear Friend,

My heartfelt thanks for your last letter. It's always a great joy for me to know that we continue to think along the same lines. I am in full agreement with what you have written.

There were several people at our symposium[512] who more or less agreed with my theology, but who criticized your books quite severely (or the little that they had read). I want to utilize the publication of the papers at our symposium to defend you and to dispel—if possible—several misunderstandings in German

---

[509] A book of this title was never published. His next book was: Girard, *Je vois Satan*. It is very possible that preparatory work done for the project "Ce que je crois" became part of this book.
[510] Robert Hamerton-Kelly.
[511] The couple were Pascale and Pierre d'Elbée; among "the others" were Byron Bland, Paul Leslie, and Simon Simonse.
[512] Symposium *Dramatische Erlösungslehre im Lichte der Theorie Girards* [Dramatic soteriology in the light of Girard's theory], Innsbruck, September 25–8, 1991.

circles.[513] Your last letter is a valuable aid to that end. *Would you be amenable to my citing a passage from your letter, as a footnote in my article?*

I now have a new assistant who works for the "Girard documentation project" (half-time). His name is *Dietmar Regensburger*. Up to now he's been occupied primarily with technical issues; but now—just at the moment when he could have begun—our secretary has fallen ill. This makes for another delay—but life's like that. On the subject of the documentation, there are two points that are not clear to me. Is it worth the trouble to document every little report in the newspapers? And what to do with reprints?

Wolfgang Palaver wrote to me that he is happy to take part in your seminar next semester. I'm very pleased as well that he will have more contact with you. I hope you get some good work done.

I wish you all the best, and with love.
Raymund

STANFORD UNIVERSITY—Stanford, California

December 7, 1991

My dear Raymund,

My letter is for you and, naturally, you can cite it as you see fit.[514] I am happy too with our agreement, and am looking forward to reading your essay. Wolfgang Palaver gave a presentation on Carl Schmitt for our little group, which was very interesting. Everybody greatly appreciated it.

For us, the term is coming to an end. I am in the process of grading eighty essays on the highly mimetic Shakespeare [*sur le Shakespeare très mimétique*], which I taught at undergraduate level. They are much more open and fun than the graduates in our department, or most of the theologians.

---

[513] Cf.: Niewiadomski and Palaver, eds., *Dramatische Erlösungslehre*.
[514] Schwager cited it: Niewiadomski and Palaver, eds., *Dramatische Erlösungslehre*, 358–9 n.54.

Christmas will be close when you receive this letter. I hope that it will be very happy for you, and the year 1992 as well! I can't write these numbers without an exclamation mark. At the end of 1992, I will be sixty-nine years old.

With love.
    René

Publications Cited in the Correspondence

This is an alphabetical list of books, articles, essays, and reviews mentioned in the correspondence (in the letters themselves and in the editorial footnotes). Details of subsequent English translations of Schwager's books, along with English and other translations of Girard's books originally in French, are also provided.

Books and articles by René Girard

Girard, René. "'The Ancient Trail Trodden by the Wicked': Job as Scapegoat." *Semeia* 33 (1985): 13–41.

Girard, René. *Critique dans un souterrain*. Lausanne: L'Âge d'homme, 1976. This contains his 1963 monograph on Dostoyevsky, *Dostoïevski: du double a l'unité*, which later appeared in English as *Resurrection from the Underground: Feodor Dostoyevsky* (1963, 1976), ed. James G. Williams. New York: Crossroad, 1997.

Girard, René. *Das Ende der Gewalt: Analyse des Menschheitsverhängnisses*. Freiburg: Herder, 1983. This German translation of *Des choses cachées depuis la fondation du monde* (*Things Hidden since the Foundation of the World*), see below, is only fragmentary. Later a complete and better translation was published with the same title: Freiburg: Herder, 2009.

Girard, René. "Das Evangelium legt die Gewalt bloß. Leicht gekürzte Übersetzung des Diskussionsbeitrags Girards in Esprit 41/429 (1973), 551–558." *Orientierung* 38 (1974): 53–6.

Girard, René. *Das Heilige und die Gewalt*. Zürich: Benziger, 1987. German translation of *La violence et la sacré* (see below).

Girard, René. *Delle cose nascoste sin dalla fondazione del mondo: Ricerche con Jean-Michel Oughourlian e Guy Lefort*. Milano: Adelphi, 1983. Italian translation of *Des choses cachées depuis la fondation du monde* (see below).

Girard, René. *Der Sündenbock*. Zürich: Benziger, 1988. German translation of *The Scapegoat* (see below).

Girard, René. "Der tragische Konflikt." In *Das Tabu der Gewalt*, edited by Hildegard Fässler, 63–76. Innsbruck: self-published, 1987.

Girard, René. *Des choses cachées depuis la fondation du monde*. Paris: Grasset, 1978. This later appeared in English as *Things Hidden since the Foundation of the World* (see below).

Girard, René. "Dionysus versus the Crucified." *Modern Language Notes* 99(4) (1984): 816–35.

Girard, René. "Discussion avec René Girard." *Esprit* 41 (November 1973): 528–63.

Girard, René. *El misterio de nuestro mundo: Claves para una interpretación antropológica. Diálogos con Jean-Michel Oughourlian y Guy Lefort*. Salamanca: Ediciones Sígueme, 1982. Spanish translation of *Des choses cachées depuis la fondation du monde* (see above).

Girard, René. "Generative Scapegoating." In *Violent Origins: Walter Burkert, René Girard, and Jonathan Z. Smith on Ritual Killing and Cultural Formation*, edited by Robert G. Hamerton-Kelly, 76–105. Stanford: Stanford University Press, 1987. This book contains an introduction by Burton Mack and a commentary by Renato Rosaldo.

Girard, René. "Hamlet's Dull Revenge." *Stanford Literature Review* 1 (Fall 1984): 159–200. Also included in *A Theater of Envy* (see below).

Girard, René. *Hiob: Ein Weg aus der Gewalt*. Zürich: Benziger, 1990. German translation of *La route antique des hommes pervers* (see below).

Girard, René. "Innovation and Repetition." *SubStance* 62/63 (1990): 7–20.

Girard, René. *I See Satan Fall Like Lightning*. Maryknoll, NY; Ottawa, and Leominster: Orbis/Novalis/Gracewing, 2001. Translation of *Je vois Satan tomber comme l'eclair* (see next).

Girard, René. *Je vois Satan tomber comme l'éclair*. Paris: Grasset, 1999. This later appeared in English as *I See Satan Fall Like Lightning* (see previous).

Girard, René. "Job et le bouc émissaire." *Bulletin du Centre Protestant d'Études* 35, no. 6 (1983): 9–33.

Girard, René. *Job: The Victim of His People*. Stanford: Stanford University Press, 1987. English translation of *La route antique des hommes pervers* (see below).

Girard, René. "La contingence dans les affaires humaines: 'Débat Castoriadis—René Girard.'" In *L'auto-organisation: De la physique au politique* (*Colloque de Cerisy*), edited by Paul Dumouchel and Jean-Pierre Dupuy, 279–301. Paris: Seuil, 1983.

Girard, René. "La danse de Salomé." In *L'auto-organisation: De la physique au politique* (*Colloque de Cerisy*), edited by Paul Dumouchel and Jean-Pierre Dupuy, 331–52. Paris: Seuil, 1983.

Girard, René. "La meurtre fondateur dans la pensée de Nietzsche." In *Violence et vérité: Autour de René Girard*, edited by Paul Dumouchel, 597–613. Paris: Grasset, 1985.

Girard, René. *La route antique des hommes pervers*. Paris: Grasset, 1985. French original of *Job: The Victim of His People* (see above).

Girard, René. *La violence et le sacré*. Paris: Grasset, 1972. This later appeared in English as *Violence and the Sacred* (see below).

Girard, René. *Le bouc émissaire*. Paris: Grasset, 1982. This later appeared in English as *The Scapegoat* (see below).

Girard, René. *Le sacrifice*. Paris: Bibliothèque nationale de France, 2003. This later appeared in English as *Sacrifice* (see below).

Girard, René. "Les malédictions contre les pharisiens et la révélation évangelique." *Bulletin du Centre Protestant d'Études* 27(3) (1975): 5–29.

Girard, René. *Mensonge romantique et vérité romanesque*. Paris: Grasset, 1961. This later appeared in English as *Deceit, Desire and the Novel: Self and Other in Literary Structure*. Baltimore: Johns Hopkins University Press, 1965.

Girard, René. *Sacrifice*. East Lansing: Michigan State University Press, 2011. Translation of *Le Sacrifice* (see above).

Girard, René. *The Scapegoat*. Baltimore: Johns Hopkins University Press, 1986. Translation of *Le bouc émissaire* (see above).

Girard, René. *Shakespeare: Les feux de l'envie*. Paris: Grasset, 1990. French translation of *A Theater of Envy: William Shakespeare* (see next).

Girard, René. *A Theater of Envy: William Shakespeare*. New York: Oxford University Press, 1991 (see previous entry for a subsequent translation into French).

Girard, René. *Things Hidden since the Foundation of the World*. Stanford: Stanford University Press, 1987. Research undertaken in collaboration with Jean-Michel Oughourlian and Guy Lefort. Translation of *Des choses cachées depuis la fondation du monde* (see above).

Girard, René. *"To Double Business Bound": Essays on Literature, Mimesis, and Anthropology*. Baltimore: Johns Hopkins University Press, 1978.

Girard, René. *Violence and the Sacred*. Baltimore: Johns Hopkins University Press, 1977. Translation of *La violence et le sacré* (see above).

Girard, René. *Yo no hajime kara kakusarete iru koto*. Tokyo: Hosei University Press, 2015. Japanese translation of *Des choses cachées depuis la fondation du monde* (see above). First published in Japanese 1984.

Books and articles by Raymund Schwager

Schwager, Raymund. *Brauchen wir einen Sündenbock? Gewalt und Erlösung in den biblischen Schriften.* Munich: Kösel, 1978. This later appeared in English as *Must There be Scapegoats? Violence and Redemption in the Bible* (see below).

Schwager, Raymund. "Christliche Herausforderung ans moderne Denken: Zum Werk des französischen Literaturwissenschaftlers und Anthropologen René Girard." *Vaterland* (7 January 1984): 35.

Schwager, Raymund. "Christ's Death and the Prophetic Critique of Sacrifice." *Semeia* 33 (1985): 109–23.

Schwager, Raymund. "Das Mysterium der übernatürlichen Natur-Lehre: Zur Erlösungslehre des Maximus Confessor." *Zeitschrift für katholische Theologie* 105 (1983): 32–57.

Schwager, Raymund. "Der fröhliche Wechsel und Streit: Zur Erlösungs- und Rechtfertigungslehre Martin Luthers." *Zeitschrift für katholische Theologie* 106 (1984): 27–66.

Schwager, Raymund. "Der geliebte Sohn und die Rotte der Gewalttäter: Christologie und Erlösungslehre." In *Glaube an Jesus Christus: Neue Beiträge zur Christologie*, edited by Josef Blank and Gotthold Hasenhüttl, 117–33. Düsseldorf: Patmos, 1980.

Schwager, Raymund. "Der Heilige Stuhl und die Abrüstung." *Internationale Katholische Zeitschrift Communio* 7 (1978): 543–53.

Schwager, Raymund. "Der Nachahmer als Sündenbock. Zu René Girards Anthropologie." *Evangelische Kommentare* 17 (1984): 680–3.

Schwager, Raymund. "Der Richter wird gerichtet: Zur Versöhnungslehre von Karl Barth." *Zeitschrift für katholische Theologie* 107 (1985): 101–41.

Schwager, Raymund. "Der Sohn Gottes und die Weltsünde. Zur Erlösungslehre von Hans Urs v. Balthasar." *Zeitschrift für katholische Theologie* 108 (1986): 5–44.

Schwager, Raymund. "Der Tod Christi und die Opferkritik." *Theologie der Gegenwart* 29 (1986): 11–20.

Schwager, Raymund. *Der wunderbare Tausch: Zur Geschichte und Deutung der Erlösungslehre.* Munich: Kösel, 1986.

Schwager, Raymund. *Dogma und dramatische Geschichte: Christologie im Kontext von Judentum, Islam und moderner Marktkultur.* Edited by Józef Niewiadomski and Mathias Moosbrugger. Freiburg: Herder, 2014.

Schwager, Raymund. "Eindrücke von einer Begegnung." In *Gewalt und Gewaltlosigkeit im Alten Testament*, edited by Norbert Lohfink, 214–24. Freiburg: Herder, 1983.

Schwager, Raymund. *Für Gerechtigkeit und Frieden: Der Glaube als Antwort auf die Anliegen der Gegenwart.* Innsbruck: Tyrolia, 1986.

Schwager, Raymund. "Geschichtsphilosophie und Erlösungslehre." *Zeitschrift für katholische Theologie* 102 (1980): 13–23.

Schwager, Raymund. "Gewalt und Opfer." *Orientierung* 38 (1974): 41–4.

Schwager, Raymund. *Glaube, der die Welt verwandelt.* Mainz: Grünewald, 1976.

Schwager, Raymund. "Haine sans raison: La perspective de René Girard." *Christus* 31, no. 121 (1984): 118–26.

Schwager, Raymund. *Jesus im Heilsdrama: Entwurf einer biblischen Erlösungslehre.* Innsbruck: Tyrolia, 1990. This later appeared in English as *Jesus in the Drama of Salvation* (see next).

Schwager, Raymund. *Jesus in the Drama of Salvation: Towards a Biblical Doctrine of Redemption.* New York: Crossroad, 1999. Translation of *Jesus im Heilsdrama* (see previous).

Schwager, Raymund. "La bande des violents dans les psaumes d'Israël." *Modern Language Notes* 94 (1979): 850–9.

Schwager, Raymund. "La mort de Jésus: René Girard et la Théologie." *Recherches de science religieuse* 73 (1985): 481–502.

Schwager, Raymund. "Mimesis and Freedom." *Contagion* 21 (2014): 29–45.

Schwager, Raymund. "Mimesis und Freiheit." *Zeitschrift für katholische Theologie* 107 (1985): 365–76.

Schwager, Raymund. *Must There Be Scapegoats? Violence and Redemption in the Bible.* San Francisco: Harper and Row, 1987. Translation of *Brauchen wir einen Sündenbock?* (see above).

Schwager, Raymund. "Rache—Gerechtigkeit—Religion: Überlegungen zu einer interdisziplinären Forschungsarbeit." *Zeitschrift für katholische Theologie* 110 (1988): 284–99.

Schwager, Raymund. "Religion, Gesellschaft und Gewalt." In *Almanach '80 der österreichischen Forschung,* 148–52. Vienna: Bohmann, 1980.

Schwager, Raymund. "Unfehlbare Gnade gegen göttliche Erziehung: Die Erlösungsproblematik in der pelagianischen Krise." *Zeitschrift für katholische Theologie* 104 (1982): 257–90.

Schwager, Raymund. "Vengeance in the Old Testament (Lecture at Stanford University/CA)." *Innsbrucker Theologischer Leseraum.* www.uibk.ac.at/theol/leseraum/texte/143.html (accessed November 20, 2015).

Schwager, Raymund. "Versöhnung und Sühne: Zur gleichnamigen Studie von Adrian Schenker." *Theologie und Philosophie* 58 (1983): 217–25.

Schwager, Raymund. "Von der biblischen Lehre der Gewaltfreiheit." *Welt in Christus* 148/49 (1980): 61–7.

Other books and articles

Aglietta, Michel, and André Orléan. *La violence de la monnaie*. Paris: Press Universitaires de France, 1982.

Arias, Judith H. "Doubles in Hell: El burlador de Sevilla y convidado de piedra." *Hispanic Review* 58(3) (1990): 361–77.

Augustine. *City of God (Concerning the City of God Against the Pagans)*. Translated by Henry Bettenson. London: Penguin, 1972.

Balthasar, Hans Urs von. "Die neue Theorie von Jesus als Sündenbock." *Internationale Katholische Zeitschrift Communio* 9 (1980): 184–5.

Balthasar, Hans Urs von. *Theodramatik III: Die Handlung*. Einsiedeln: Johannes, 1980.

Banawiratma, Johannes B. *Der Heilige Geist in der Theologie von Heribert Mühlen: Versuch einer Darstellung und Würdigung*. Frankfurt: Peter Lang, 1981.

Banawiratma, Johannes B. "Religion and Peace." *Das Prisma* 42 (1986): 62–73.

Bandera, Cesáreo. *Mimesis conflictiva: Ficción literary y violencia en Cervantes y Calderón*. Madrid: Gredos, 1975.

Barblan, Giovanni, ed. *Dante e la Bibbia: Atti del Convegno internazionale promosso da "Biblia" (Firenze, 26-27-28 settembre 1986)*. Florence: Olschki, 1988.

Buillebaud, Jean-Claude. "Le 'scandale' René Girard." *Le Monde aujourd'hui*, May 27–28, 1979, 14.

Burkert, Walter. *Homo necans: Interpretationen altgriechischer Opferriten und Mythen*. Berlin: De Gruyter, 1972.

Busche, Jürgen. "Das Ende der Gewalt: Die religiöse Anthropologie des Franzosen René Girard." *Frankfurter Allgemeine Zeitung*, October 8, 1986, 33.

Corbin, Michel, ed. *L'œuvre de S. Anselme de Cantorbéry*. 2 vols. Paris: Cerf, 1986.

De Lubac, Henri. *La foi chrétienne: Essai sur la structure du symbole des Apôtres*. Paris: Aubier Montaigne, 1969.

De Lubac, Henri. *Surnaturel: Études historiques*. Paris: Aubier, 1946.

Deguy, Michel, and Jean-Pierre Dupuy, eds. *René Girard et le problème du mal*. Paris: Grasset, 1982.

Delumeau, Jean. *Le peché et le peur: La culpabilisation en Occident (XIIIe-XVIIIe siècles)*. Paris: Fayard, 1983.

Derrida, Jacques. "Plato's Pharmacy." In *Dissemination*, 61–172. London: Athlone, 1981.

Descombes, Vincent. "Une solution de la stratégie atomique: La télépathie." *Critique* 35 (1979): 854–68.

Diéguez, Manuel de. "Une ethnologie charismatique?" *Esprit* 28 (1979): 58–71.

Doucet, Marcel. *Dispute de Maxime le Confesseur avec Pyrrhus: Introduction, texte critique, traduction et notes.* 2 vols. Montreal: Université de Montréal, 1972.

Dumouchel, Paul, ed. *Violence et vérité: Autour de René Girard.* Paris: Grasset, 1985.

Dumouchel, Paul, and Jean-Pierre Dupuy, eds. *L'auto-organisation: De la physique au politique* (*Colloque de Cerisy*). Paris: Seuil, 1983.

Dumouchel, Paul, and Jean-Pierre Dupuy, eds. *L'enfer des choses: René Girard et la logique de l'économie.* Paris: Seuil, 1979.

Esprit (dedicated section): "Sur René Girard: les sciences humaines, le sacré, le terrorisme et les sociétés modernes." *Esprit* 28 (April 1979).

Fages, Jean-Baptiste. *Comprendre Girard.* Toulouse: self-published, 1982.

Frazer, James G. *The Golden Bough: A Study in Magic and Religion.* 12 vols. London: Macmillan, 1907–15.

Gans, Eric. *Essais d'esthétique paradoxale.* Paris: Gallimard, 1977.

Gardeil, Pierre. "Le christianisme est-il une religion du sacrifice?" *Nouvelle Revue Théologique* 100 (1978): 341–58.

Goodhart, Sandor. "Leskas Ephaske: Oedipus' and Laius' Many Murderers." *Diacritics* 8(1) (Spring 1978): 55–71.

Hamerton-Kelly, Robert G., ed. *Violent Origins: Walter Burkert, René Girard, and Jonathan Z. Smith on Ritual Killing and Cultural Formation.* Stanford: Stanford University Press, 1987.

Harari, Josué. *Textual Strategies: Perspectives in Post-Structuralist Criticism.* Ithaca, NY: Cornell University Press, 1979.

Heidegger, Martin. *Holzwege (1935–1946).* Edited by Friedrich-Wilhelm von Hermann. Frankfurt: Vittorio Klostermann, 2003.

Hoffmann, Norbert. *Sühne: Zur Theologie der Stellvertretung.* Einsiedeln: Johannes, 1981.

Horstmann, Ulrich. *Das Untier: Konturen einer Philosophie der Menschenflucht.* Vienna: Medusa, 1983.

Huvet, René. "Autour de René Girard: Mémoire et sacrifice." *Études Théologiques et Religieuses* 55 (1980): 385–97.

Jaeger, Werner. *Paideia: Die Formung des griechischen Menschen.* Berlin: de Gruyter, 1934–47.

Jensen, Adolf E. *Mythos und Kult bei Naturvölkern: Religionswissenschaftliche Betrachtungen.* Wiesbaden: Steiner, 1951.

Jung, Carl Gustav. *Antwort auf Hiob.* Zürich: Rascher, 1952.

Kearney, Richard. "Terrorisme et sacrifice: Le cas de l'Irlande du Nord." *Esprit* 28 (1979): 29–44.

Keel, Othmar. "Wie böse ist Gewalt? Rezension zu Schwager, Brauchen wir einen Sündenbock?" *Orientierung* 41 (1978): 43–6.

Knauer, Peter. Review of *Brauchen wir einen Sündenbock?*, by Raymund Schwager, *Theologie und Philosophie* 53 (1978): 564–6.

Koller, Hermann. *Die Mimesis in der Antike: Nachahmung, Darstellung, Ausdruck.* Bern: Francke Verlag, 1954.

Leenhardt, Maurice. *Do kamo: La personne et le mythe dans le monde mélanésien.* Paris: Gallimard, 1947.

Léon-Dufour, Xavier. *Face à la mort: Jésus et Paul.* Paris: Seuil, 1979.

Léon-Dufour, Xavier, et al. *Mort pour nos péchés: Recherché pluridisciplinaire sur la signification rédemptrice de la mort du Christ.* Brussels: Facultés universitaires Saint-Louis, 1976.

Livingston, Paisley, ed. *Disorder and Order: Proceedings of the Stanford International Symposium (Sept 14–16, 1981).* Saratoga, CA: Anma Libri, 1984.

Livingston, Paisley. *Ingmar Bergman and the Rituals of Art.* Ithaca, NY: Cornell University Press, 1982.

Lohfink, Norbert. "El Dios violento del Antiguo Testamento y la búsqueda de una sociedad no-violenta." *Selecciones de teologia* 24 (1985): 83–91.

Lohfink, Norbert, ed. *Gewalt und Gewaltlosigkeit im Alten Testament.* Freiburg: Herder, 1983.

Lohfink, Norbert. "Il Dio violento dell'Antico Testamento e la ricerca d'una società non-violenta." *La Civiltà Cattolica* 135(2) (1984): 30–48.

Lohfink, Norbert, and Rudolf Pesch. *Weltgestaltung und Gewaltlosigkeit: Ethische Aspekte des Alten und Neuen Testaments in ihrer Einheit und in ihrem Gegensatz.* Düsseldorf: Patmos, 1978.

Miller, Karl. *Doubles: Studies in Literary History.* Oxford: Oxford University Press, 1987.

Muray, Philippe. "'Quand les choses commenceront …' Interview de René Girard." *Tel Quel*, Autumn 1978, 35–57; *Tel Quel*, Spring 1979, 32–9.

Nietzsche, Friedrich. *Die fröhliche Wissenschaft.* Leipzig: C. G. Naumann, 1887.

Nietzsche, Friedrich. *Götzen-Dämmerung oder Wie man mit dem Hammer philosophiert.* Leipzig: C. G. Naumann, 1889.

Niewiadomski, Józef. "Die Juden im Neuen Testament und bei den Kirchenvätern." In *Christen und Juden in Offenbarung und kirchlichen Erklärungen vom Urchristentum bis zur Gegenwart*, edited by Erika Weinzierl, 13–31. Vienna: Geyer, 1988.

Niewiadomski, Józef. "Die Mörder Gottes und die Gegner des christlichen Volkes: Bemerkungen zum Hauptargument des christlichen Antijudaismus." *Die Distel— Zeitschrift für Kultur und aktuelle Fragen* 4 (1986): 18–20.

Niewiadomski, Józef. "Vom dogmatischen Gegner zum verhaßten Feind: Judenpolemik und Erlösungsglaube." *Bibel und Liturgie* 58 (1985): 214–18.

Niewiadomski, Józef, and Wolfgang Palaver, eds. *Dramatische Erlösungslehre: Ein Symposion*. Innsbruck: Tyrolia, 1992.

North, Robert. "Violence and the Bible: The Girard Connection." *Catholic Biblical Quarterly* 47 (1985): 1–27.

Nygren, Anders. *Commentary on Romans*. London: SCM, 1952.

Otto, Rudolf. *Das Heilige: Über das Irrationale in der Idee des Göttlichen und sein Verhältnis zum Rationalen*. Breslau: Trewendt and Granier, 1917.

Oughourlian, Jean-Michel. *Un mime nommé désir: Hystérie, transe, possession, adorcisme*. Paris: Grasset, 1982.

Ratzinger, Joseph. *Entretien sur la foi: Entretien avec Vittorio Messori*. Paris: Fayard, 1985.

Ratzinger, Joseph. *Introduction to Christianity*. London: Burns and Oates, 1968.

Ratzinger, Joseph, and Vittorio Messori. *The Ratzinger Report: An Exclusive Interview on the State of the Church*. San Francisco: Ignatius, 1985.

Richard de Saint-Victor. *De Trinitate*. Edited by Jean Ribaillier. Librairie Philosophique: Textes Philosophiques du Moyen Age VI. Paris: J. Vrin, 1958.

Rosny, Éric de. *Les yeux de ma chèvre: Sur le pas des maîtres de la nuit en pays douala (Cameroun)*. Paris: Plon, 1981.

Ruether, Rosemary Radford. *Faith and Fratricide: The Theological Roots of Anti-Semitism*. New York: Seabury, 1974.

Schenker, Adrian. *Versöhnung und Sühne: Wege gewaltfreier Konfliktlösung im Alten Testament*. Fribourg: Schweizerisches Katholisches Bibelwerk, 1981.

Schroeder, Leopold A. von. *Mysterium und Mimus im Rigveda*. Leipzig: H. Hassel, 1908.

Siebers, Tobin. *The Mirror of Medusa*. Berkeley: University of California Press, 1983.

Singer, Isaac B. *The Slave*. New York: Farrar, Straus and Cudahy, 1962.

Stiker, Henri-Jacques. "Sur le mode de penser de René Girard." *Esprit* 28 (1979): 46–55.

Valadier, Paul. "Bouc émissaire et révélation chrétienne selon René Girard." *Études* 357(7) (1982): 251–60.

Varela, Francisco J., and Jean-Pierre Dupuy, eds. *Understanding Origins: Contemporary Views on the Origin of Life, Mind and Society.* Dordrecht: Kluwer Academic, 1992.

Verdier, Raymond, and Gerard Courtois, eds. *La vengeance.* Vols 1–4. Paris: Cujas, 1980–4.

Wieser, Thomas. "Generative Violence and the Extinction of Social Order." *Salmagundi* 63–4 (Spring–Summer 1984): 204–37.

Williams, James G. *Girardians: The Colloquium on Violence and Religion, 1990–2010.* Vienna: LIT, 2012.

Wohlman, Avital. "René Girard et Saint Augustin: Anthropologie et théologie." *Recherches Augustiniennes et Patristiques* 20 (1985): 257–303.

Zenger, Erich. Review of *Brauchen wir einen Sündenbock?* by Raymund Schwager. *Theologischer Literaturdienst* 4 (1979): 49–50.

Who's Who in the Correspondence

Bandera, Cesáreo (b. 1934), Professor Emeritus of Spanish Literature, University of North Carolina at Chapel Hill; Colloquium on Violence and Religion (COV&R) founding member and former President (1995–9).

Dumouchel, Paul (b. 1951), Professor of Philosophy, Graduate School of Core Ethics and Frontier Sciences, Ritsumeikan University, Kyoto; longtime COV&R member.

Dupuy, Jean-Pierre (b. 1941), Professor of French and Political Science, Stanford University, and Professor Emeritus for Social and Political Philosophy, École Polytechnique, Paris; longtime COV&R member.

Gans, Eric L. (b. 1941), Distinguished Professor of French Emeritus, University of California at Los Angeles; founder of the alternative mimetic theory–based research project, "Generative Anthropology"; former COV&R Honorary Board Member (2002).

Goodhart, Sandor (b. 1946), Girard's first postgraduate student (1977) at the State University of New York at Buffalo; now Professor of English and Jewish Studies, Purdue University, Indiana; former COV&R Executive Secretary (1999–2003) and President (2003–7).

Hamerton-Kelly, Robert (1938–2013), New Testament scholar, former Dean of the Chapel, Stanford University (1973–86); COV&R founding member and former Honorary Board Member (2009).

Knauer, Peter, SJ (b. 1935), Professor Emeritus of Dogmatic Theology and Fundamental Theology, Sankt Georgen Graduate School of Philosophy and Theology, Frankfurt am Main; important dialogue partner for Schwager, especially when he wrote *Brauchen wir einen Sündenbock?* (1978) (*Must There Be Scapegoats?* 1987).

Lohfink, Norbert, SJ (b. 1928), Professor Emeritus of Old Testament Exegesis, Sankt Georgen Graduate School of Philosophy and Theology, Frankfurt am Main; important dialogue partner for Schwager in all biblical matters, especially when he wrote *Brauchen wir einen Sündenbock?* (1978) (*Must There Be Scapegoats?* 1987).

Niewiadomski, Józef (b. 1951), Schwager's first graduate student (1981); now Professor of Dogmatic Theology, University of Innsbruck; Schwager's successor as Dean of the School of Catholic Theology in Innsbruck (2004–13); longtime

COV&R member, former coeditor of the *COV&R Bulletin* (1991–8) and member of the COV&R Advisory Board (1999–2004).

Palaver, Wolfgang (b. 1959), Schwager's and Girard's student; Professor of Catholic Social Teaching, University of Innsbruck; Dean of the School of Catholic Theology in Innsbruck (since 2013); former editor of the *COV&R Bulletin* (1991–9), COV&R Executive Secretary (2003–7), and President (2007–11).

Pesch, Rudolf (1936–2011), former Professor of Biblical Studies, University of Frankfurt am Main (1970–80) and Professor of New Testament and Literature, University of Freiburg im Breisgau (1980–4); gave up his professorship to live with the *Katholische Integrierte Gemeinde* (Catholic Integrated Community) in Munich; important dialogue partner for Schwager, especially when he wrote *Brauchen wir einen Sündenbock?* (1978) (*Must There Be Scapegoats?* 1987).

Regensburger, Dietmar (b. 1963), Schwager's student; Assistant Professor, Department of Systematic Theology, University of Innsbruck; supervisor of the Mimesis Database; COV&R Treasurer (Europe) since 1997.

Thomas, Konrad (1930–2010), former Professor at the Sociological Seminary of the University of Göttingen (1972–95).

Williams, James G. (b. 1936), Professor Emeritus of Religion, Syracuse University, New York; specialized in Old and New Testament Studies; COV&R founding member and former Executive Secretary (1990–8).

Index

For life and work dates for Girard and Schwager, see pp. 10–12.
For biographical notes on persons mentioned in the correspondence, see specific names below and "Who's Who in the Correspondence," pp. 199–200.
Titles of selected works are shortened.
"G" signifies Girard; "S" signifies Schwager.
All works and translations are listed and cross-referenced in "Publications Cited in the Correspondence," pp. 189–98.

About Love / Über die Liebe (Pieper) ix
absolute, the 97
accusation and truth 93
Acts of the Apostles 131
  universalization in 32, 35, 36–7, 51
Adam and Eve 177
  sin and 182
Aglietta, Michel and André Orléan: *La violence de la monnaie* 117
American and European societies 149
ancient societies and Old Testament 40
"Ancient Trail Trodden by the Wicked, The" (G) 123 n.281, 128, 129, 131, 140
animal behavior 21
  "dominance patterns" 27–8
  human behavior and 22
  rivalry and mimesis 25, 27–8
animal nature and human nature 183, 184
Anselm, St. 168, 171
anti-Semitism 85, 133
Antwort auf Hiob (Jung) 178
apocalyptic texts 54
Aquinas, St. Thomas 143
Arias, Judith: "Doubles in Hell" 177
Aristotelian thought 146
Assad, Maria 125, 152
Athanasius, St. 92
Auf dem Weg zur Neubewertung der Tradition (S) 3 n.4
Augustine, St. 113
  City of God 108
  doctrine of grace 108
  Pelagius and 104, 108
  Romans (letter) and 113
  on sacrifice 108
Austrian Broadcasting 102 n.186
auto-organization 141
"Autour de René Girard" (Huvet) 44

Balthasar, Hans Urs von 77, 98, 112, 141, 147, 168, 171
  on *Brauchen wir einen Sündenbock?* (S) 71
  on *Des choses cachées* (G) 75
  "Die neue Theorie von Jesus als Sündenbock" 90
  on Girard's ideas 103–4
  Theodramatik III 75, 102
Banawiratma, Johannes 104, 105, 107, 113
  Der Heilige Geist 87 n.152
  "Religion and Peace" 163
Bandera, Cesáreo 121
  Mimesis conflictiva 88
Bann, Steven 102
Barblan, Giovanni: *Dante e la Bibbia* 147 n.381
Barth, Karl 127, 134, 168
  predestination and 138
Basoff, Bruce 88
being and violence 21
Beiträge zur Schöpfungslehre, Erbsündenlehre und zur Pneumatologie (S) 3 n.6

Benedict XVI 150 n.387 *see also* Ratzinger, Joseph
Benziger (publisher) 141 n.359
Bergson, Henri, *élan vital* 35, 36
Berlin Wall 173
Berz, August 116
Bible and mythology 135–6
Bland, Byron 185
Boissonat, Jean 66
Boros, Ladislaus 111, 112
Boston College 172
"Bouc émissaire" (Valadier) 118, 119, 133, 160
Brauchen wir einen Sündenbock? (S) 3 n.5, 48, 117
   the cross in 53
   Des choses cachées (G) and 60, 84
   English translation 3 n.5, 125, 152
   French translation 63 n.96, 86, 89
   manuscript 83
   publication 40, 42, 44, 45
   reactions 35–6, 38–9, 44, 55, 57, 64, 69, 71, 73, 102, 107
   review by Knauer 39
   review by Zenger 107
   second edition 145
   title 46
   writing 29–30, 32, 35
Briefwechsel mit René Girard (S) 3 n.4
Brixen conference 104
Bryn Mawr College, Avignon 19
Buillebaud, Jean-Claude 74
   "Le 'scandale' René Girard" 74
Bundesministerium für Wissenschaft und Forschung, Vienna 85
Burkert, Walter 123, 143, 159
   Homo necans 118
Busche, Jürgen: "Das Ende der Gewalt" 154

Caillois, Roger 68
Cain and Abel 35
Catholic Academy Stuttgart-Hohenheim 142
Catholicism and Protestantism 143, 147, 149
Catholic thought 148

Centre des intellectuels catholiques [françaises] 72–3
Centre of Girardian Studies 139
Centre Protestant d'Etudes, Geneva 18
Centre Sèvres, Paris 82
"Ce que je crois" (G) 76, 78, 155, 185
Cérisy-la-Salle 116
Cérisy-la-Salle symposium 106, 116, 140
Chalcedon, Council of 105
Chantre, Benoît 2
Christ
   death of 98
   Dionysus and 136
   God, the Father, and 51, 94, 98, 139–40
   the Holy Spirit and 98
   imitation of 74
   law and 25, 29, 66
   passion of 180
   redemption and 28
   sacrifice and 25, 53, 93
   Satan and 66, 68, 91, 96
   scapegoating and 36–7, 66, 68, 76, 94, 96, 97, 98
   as victim 52, 134
Christianity
   ethnology and 16–17
   Judaism and 23, 24, 47, 62
   modernity and 77
   as non-sacrificial 79
   sacrifice and 76
   science and 97
   sociology and 119
   violence and 36
"Christliche Herausforderung" (S) 127
Christology 105
"Christ's Death and the Prophetic Critique of Sacrifice" (S) 134, 138–9, 140, 144
Christus (journal) 132–3
church
   change 62
   decadence/dissolution 147, 149–50
   disunity 47
   instability 169
   rejuvenation 126
   sacrifice and 80, 95, 99
   violence and 81–2

church fathers 66, 91, 155 *see also* particular church fathers; patristic thought
Church of St Germain des Près, Paris 68
City of God (Augustine) 108
clergy 149–50
Collected Works (Raymund Schwager *Gesammelte Schriften*) xiii, 2–3, 4
"Collective Violence and Sacrifice in Shakespeare's Julius Caesar" (lecture by G) 174 n.470
Colloque René Girard (symposium) 106, 116, 140
colloquia/conferences/meetings/symposia (formal gatherings italicised)
  Colloque René Girard, Cérisy-la-Salle 106, 116, 140
  Dante e la Bibbia, Florence 147
  Die Gesellschaft der Rivalen, Hofgeismar 135
  Disorder and Order, Stanford 88–9, 102–3, 104, 105, 109, 110
  "Divine in Society, The," Louvain-la-Neuve 34–5
  Dramatische Erlösungslehre, Innsbruck 181, 184–5, 185–6
  Girard symposium, Stuttgart 142, 145–6, 148, 151, 153
  Hiob—und der Gott seiner Verfolger, Weingarten 179
  Myth, Literature, and Bible, Provo, Utah 139 n.349
  Mythology, Stanford 181 n.496
  Religion and Ritual, Pajaro Dunes, CA 118, 123
  Thought and Innovation, Tel Aviv 174
  Understanding Origins, Stanford 156
  Vengeance, Stanford 149 n.386, 167, 170, 172
  "Violence and Nonviolence in the Bible," Munich 48
  Violence and Nonviolence in the OT, Brixen 104
  "Violence and the Sacred and the OT," Frankfurt 39
Colloquium on Violence and Religion (COV&R) 84 n.144, 181 n.496
Comédie française, Paris 45 n.68
Commentary on Romans (Nygren) 131
Comprendre Girard (Fages) 118
computers 125
conferences *see* colloquia/conferences/meetings/symposia
conservatism 147, 150 n.387
conversion 180
Corbin, Michel 82, 84, 112, 113
  L'œuvre de S. Anselme de Cantorbéry 168, 171
Corinthians, second letter to the 52
Council of Chalcedon 105
Courtois, Gerard and Raymond Verdier: *La vengeance* 165, 167
covenant 26–7
creation 182
crisis
  law and 28
  sacrificial 24
Critique (journal) 87
Critique dans un souterrain (G) 30, 31
cross, the
  meaning 8
  sacrifice and 99
  Satan and 66, 91
  source of knowledge/source of life xi, 51, 52, 53, 56, 59
  suppression of 95
cultural malaise 149, 184

Daim, Wilfried 102 n.186
Dante e la Bibbia (Barblan) 147 n.381
Dante e la Bibbia (conference) 147
"Das Ende der Gewalt" (Busche) 154
Das Ende der Gewalt (G) 73 n.114, 78, 90 n.165, 106, 114 n.232, 122, 126–7, 132, 137, 165 *see also Des choses cachées* (G)
"Das Evangelium legt die Gewalt bloß" (G) 16, 17
Das Heilige (Otto) 118
Das Heilige und die Gewalt (G) 165 *see also La violence et la sacré* (G)
"Das Mysterium der übernatürlichen Natur-Lehre" (S) 113
Das Untier (Horstmann) 184

death and law 26–7
Deceit, Desire, and the Novel (G) 30 n.25
  see also *Mensonge romantique et vérité romanesque* (G)
deconstruction 166–7, 168
Deguy, Michel 88
Deguy, Michel and Jean-Pierre Dupuy: *René Girard et le problème du mal* 88, 116, 118
De Keukelaere, Simon 2
d'Elbée, Pascale and Pierre 185
Delle cose nascoste sin dalla fondazione del mondo (G) 121 see also *Des choses cachées* (G)
Delumeau, Jean: *Le péché et la peur* 163–4
demons 58
  of Gerasa 101, 102
demythologization 50
"Der fröhliche Wechsel und Streit" (S) 124
"Der geliebte Sohn und die Rotte der Gewalttäter" (S) 60
Der Heilige Geist (Banawiratma) 87 n.152
"Der Heilige Stuhl und die Abrüstung" (S) 108 n.214
"Der Nachahmer als Sündenbock" (S) 127
"Der Richter wird gerichtet" (S) 127 n.301, 134, 138
Derrida, Jacques 157–8, 159, 162, 166–7
  "Plato's Pharmacy" 161, 162
"Der Sohn Gottes und die Weltsünde" (S) 141
Der Sündenbock (G) 145 n.374
  see also *Scapegoat, The* (G)
"Der Tod Christi und die Opferkritik" (S) 140
"Der tragische Konflikt" (G) 148 n.385, 163
Der wunderbare Tausch (S) 3 n.5, 141, 155, 157, 160
Descartes, René 158
Des choses cachées (G) 117, 183
  Brauchen wir einen Sündenbock? (S) and 84
  English translation 72, 102, 126, 127, 159
  French publication 46–7
  German translation 73, 90, 106, 111, 112, 114, 116, 132, 165
  Italian translation 67, 121
  Japanese translation 67
  Le bouc émissaire (G) and 106
  mimetic theory articulated x
  negative reactions 60, 62, 64, 116, 119, 134–5
  planning 16
  positive reactions 50, 58, 69, 72, 75, 76, 82, 90
  sacrifice in 61
  Spanish translation 67
  success 67, 68, 71, 72
  transcendence-over in 55
  writing 34, 42, 43
  see also *Das Ende der Gewalt* (G)
Descombes, Vincent: "Une solution de la stratégie atomique" 86–7
desiderium naturale videndi dei 177, 179
desire 179
  for God 177, 179
  metaphysical xi, 183
  original sin and 179
  prohibitions and 20
  triangular 25–6, 40
  violence and 21
De Trinitate (Richard of St. Victor) 87, 89
Die fröhliche Wissenschaft (Nietzsche) 136
Die Gesellschaft der Rivalen meeting 135
Diéguez, Manuel de: "Une ethnologie charismatique?" 74
"Die Juden im Neuen Testament" (Niewiadomski) 133 n.328
Die Mimesis in der Antike (Koller) 92
"Die Mörder Gottes und die Gegner des christlichen Volkes" (Niewiadomski) 133 n.328
"Die neue Theorie von Jesus als Sündenbock" (Balthasar) 90
Die Rehabilitierung des Opfers (Moosbrugger) 9 n.7
difference
  hypostatic 21–2
  law and 24
  violence and 21
Dionysian festivals 92
Dionysus and Christ 136
"Dionysus versus the Crucified" (G) 137

disarmament 108–9, 110
"Discussion avec René Girard" (G) 15, 21
Disorder and Order (Livingstone) 89 n.159
Disorder and Order symposium 88–9, 102–3, 104, 105, 109, 110
Dispute de Maxime le Confesseur avec Pyrrhus (Doucet) 148
"Divine in Society, The" conference 34–5
divine wrath 32, 54
divinity and violence 52
Dogma und dramatische Geschichte (S) 2, 105 n.200
Do kamo (Leenhardt) 50
"dominance patterns" in animals 27–8
Don Juan story 177 n.487, 181
Doran, Robert xiii n.9
Dostoevsky, Fyodor 31
Doubles (Miller) 168
"Doubles in Hell" (Arias) 177
doubling 139, 164–5
Doucet, Marcel: *Dispute de Maxime le Confesseur avec Pyrrhus* 148
dramatic theology ix, 171
  research group 2
Dramatische Erlösungslehre (Niewiadomski and Palaver) 181, 185–6
Dramatische Erlösungslehre symposium 181, 184–5, 185–6
Dumouchel, Paul 88, 139
  Violence et vérité 106 n.206
Dumouchel, Paul and Jean-Pierre Dupuy
  L'auto-organisation 103 n.194
  L'enfer des choses 86–7, 103
Dupuy, Jean-Pierre 146, 170 n.445, 184
Dupuy, Jean-Pierre and Francisco Varela:
  Understanding Origins 156 n.404
Dupuy, Jean-Pierre and Michel Geguy:
  René Girard et le problème du mal 88, 116, 118
Dupuy, Jean-Pierre and Paul Dumouchel:
  L'enfer des choses 86–7, 103

Eastern religions 76–7, 79
education and violence 65
"Eindrücke von einer Begegnung" (S) 108

Einführung in das Christentum (Ratzinger) 92
élan vital (Bergson) 36
  founding violence and 35
"El burlador de Sevilla y convidado de piedra" (de Molina) 177
"El Dios violento del Antiguo Testamento" (Lohfink) 134 n.331
El misterio de nuestro mundo (G) 67 see also *Des choses cachées* (G)
emotions and violence 108, 110
Enlightenment 65
Entretien sur la foi (Ratzinger) 147
Espirit (journal) 15, 17, 74, 76
Essais d'esthétique paradoxale (Gans) 88
ethnology and Christianity 16–17
Études (journal) 118
European and American societies 149
evil and nature 182
exclusion 162
existentialism 77
Expansion (journal) 66
expulsion 162
Ezekiel, book of 59

Face à la mort (Léon-Dufour) 82–3
Fages, Jean-Baptiste: *Comprendre Girard* 118
faith 53
  act of 183–4
  freedom and 8
  science and 33, 35, 112, 119
Faith and Fratricide (Ruether) 85
fathers of the church *see* church fathers
Fischer (publisher) 27
Fleming, Chris xiii, 13
  René Girard: Violence and Mimesis xiii
Florence conference 147
Foucault, Michel 158
France Catholique (magazine) 69
Frankfurt conference 39
Frankfurter Allgemeine Zeitung 154
Frazer, James: *Golden Bough, The* 101
Freccero, John 147
freedom
  faith and 8
  love and 23

original sin and 81
revelation and 183
sacrifice and 113, 115
sin and xi–xii, 8
Freud, Sigmund 23, 24, 29
Frühe Hauptwerke (S) 3 n.5
Für Gerechtigkeit und Frieden (S) 144

Gans, Eric: *Essais d'esthétique paradoxale* 88
Gardeil, Pierre 47
 "Le christianisme est-il une religion du sacrifice?" 44
Gay Science, The (Nietzsche) 136
generalization 32–3
"Generative Scapegoating" (G) 125
"Generative Violence" (Wieser) 126
Genesis, book of 35, 56
 on prohibitions and desire 20
Germain des Prés, St., Church of (Paris) 68
"Geschichtsphilosophie und Erlösungslehre" (S) 85, 89
Gewalt und Gewaltlosigkeit im Alten Testament (Lohfink) 104 n.198, 108
"Gewalt und Opfer" (S) 16
"Gewalt und Selbstzerstörung" (lecture by G) 148 n.385
Girard, Martha (née McCullough) 31, 137, 162, 166, 174
Girard, Martin (son of René and Martha) 143
Girard, René
 "Ancient Trail Trodden by the Wicked, The" 123 n.281, 128, 129, 131, 140
 "Ce que je crois" 78, 155, 185
 "Collective Violence and Sacrifice in Shakespeare's Julius Caesar" (lecture) 174 n.470
 Critique dans un souterrain 30, 31
 Das Ende der Gewalt 73 n.114, 78, 90 n.165, 106, 112, 126–7, 132, 137, 165
 "Das Evangelium legt die Gewalt bloß" 16, 17
 Das Heilige und die Gewalt 165, 167–8
 Delle cose nascoste sin dalla fondazione del mondo 67, 121

Der Sündenbock 145 n.374
 "Der tragische Konflikt" 148 n.385, 163
 Des choses cachées see particular entry for *Des choses cachées*
 "Dionysus versus the Crucified" 137
 "Discussion avec René Girard" 15, 21
 El misterio de nuestro mundo 67
 family 129–30, 143, 150, 162
 "Generative Scapegoating" 125
 "Gewalt und Selbstzerstörung" (lecture) 148 n.385
 Glaube, der die Welt verwandelt 27
 "Hamlet's Dull Revenge" 125
 Hiob 141 n.359
 honorary doctorate 154, 156, 157, 159, 160–1, 163, 164, 165, 166, 167, 170
 "Innovation and Repetition" 174 n.469
 Je vois Satan 155 n.400, 185 n.509
 "Job et le bouc émissaire" 122 n.276, 128, 129
 Job: The Victim of His People 159
 "Job: Victim of His Own People" (conf. paper) 173
 "La contingence" 141 n.364
 "La danse de Salomé" 141 n.364
 "La meurtre fondateur dans la pensée de Nietzsche" 121 n.276, 136
 La route antique des hommes pervers 122 n.278, 123 n.281, 140–1, 159, 179, 180
 La violence et la sacré see particular entry for *La violence et la sacré*
 Le bouc émissaire 83 n.140, 93–4, 101, 102, 105–6, 110, 116, 157, 159
 Le sacrifice 77 n.130
 "Les malédictions" 20
 Mensonge romantique et vérité romanesque 30 n.25, 31, 68
 "Mimetic Theory and Theology" xii n.6
 "Myth and the Bible" (lecture) 174 n.471
 One by Whom Scandal Comes, The xii n.6
 reactions to 76, 82–3, 100, 103–4, 107, 112, 113, 118, 120–1, 122, 123, 127,

130, 134–5, 140, 143, 154, 159, 172, 185–6
  rivalry with 33
Scapegoat, The 159
Shakespeare 175
"Sur Job et la philosophie" 121
Theater of Envy, A 83 n.141, 143, 148, 155, 157, 161, 166, 169, 175, 176, 177, 178, 181
Things Hidden 159
To Double Business Bound 67, 80–1, 176–7
"'Tragischer Konflikt'—in Literatur und Bibel" (conf. paper) 148 n.385
"Violence, Difference, Sacrifice" xii
Violence and the Sacred 46
Yo no hajime kara kakusareteiru koto 67
"Girard Documentation Project" 186
Girardians (Williams) 181 n.496
Girard Reader 78
Girard–Schwager collaboration 145, 148
Girard–Schwager correspondence
  date distribution 5–7
  publication history 2–4
  topics 4, 7–9
Girard symposium 142, 145–6, 148, 151, 153
Glaube, der die Welt verwandelt (S) 27
globalization 77
gnosis 96
God
  Christ and the Father 51, 94, 98
  experience of 180
  in Job 178
  Kingdom of 27, 97, 99
  knowledge and 180
  murder of 136
  as non-sacrificial/nonviolent 50, 51, 52, 64–5
  rivalry with 138–9
  violence and 37
  wrath of 131–2
  yearning for xi
Goethe, Johann von 65
Golden Bough, The (Frazer) 101
Goodhart, Sandor: "Leskas Ephaske" 88

Gorbachev, Mikhail 173
gospel/s
  as anti-sacrificial/non-sacrificial 43, 44, 47, 48
  law and 23, 29
  refusal of 37
  salvation and 37
  value of 148
  see also particular gospels
Götzen-Dämmerung (Nietzsche) 136
Grasset (publisher) 49, 67, 78, 90, 115, 116
Groër, Hans Hermann 169 n.449
Guitton, Jean 130
Gulf War 1990–91 181

"Haine sans raison" (S) 132–3
Hamerton-Kelly, Robert 139, 143, 146, 153, 162, 184–5
  Violent Origins 125 n.289, 159
"Hamlet's Dull Revenge" (G) 125
Harari, Josué: *Textual Strategies* 88
Hebrews, letter to the 75
  sacrifice and 8–9, 53, 57, 59, 64, 74, 79–80
Hegel, Georg 28, 158
  "Bewusstein" and "*Selbst*-bewusstein" 26
Heidegger, Martin 157, 161, 166–7
  Holzwege 136
Heilsdrama (S) 3 n.5
Herder (publisher) 2, 73, 111, 141
Herder, Johann 65
Herod Antipas 51
Hiob (G) 141 n.359 *see also* Job, *La route antique des hommes pervers* (G)
"Hiob: Ein Weg aus der Gewalt" (conf. paper by S) 179 n.492
"Hiob—und der Gott seiner Verfolger" (conf. paper by S) 179 n.492
Hiob—und der Gott seiner Verfolger conference 179
historical-critical exegesis 35–6, 40, 171
history and scapegoating 85–6, 99
Hoffmann, Norbert: *Sühne* 113
Hofgeismar meeting 135
Holy Spirit, the 70, 74

Christ and 98
law and 71
violence and 52
see also Paraclete
Holzwege (Heidegger) 136
hominization 28, 50, 103
Homo necans (Burkert) 118
Horstmann, Ulrich: *Das Untier* 184
Huber, Stefan 1
Hug, Josef 19
human behavior and animal behavior 22
humanism 158
human nature
  animal nature and 183, 184
  violence and 182
  wounding of 183
Huvet, René 45, 47, 55, 63, 66, 67
  "Autour de René Girard" 44
hypostatic difference
  law and 21–2
  victim and 24

idealism 121
idolatry 183
  mimesis and 179–80
  scapegoat mechanism and 177, 179–80
"Il Dio violento dell'Antico Testamento" (Lohfink) 134 n.331
Ingmar Bergman and the Rituals of Art (Livingston) 88, 117
"Innovation and Repetition" (G) 174 n.469
Innsbruck 171–2
Innsbruck symposium 181, 184–5, 185–6
intelligence
  murder and 28
  victim and 32
interdisciplinarity 69
interdividuality 58
interpretation 77
  scapegoat effect and 94
Introduction to Christianity (Ratzinger) 92
Iron Curtain 173
Israel 174

Jaeger, Werner: *Paideia* 65, 68

Jensen, Adolf: *Mythos und Kult bei Naturvölkern* 118
Jensen, Hans Jørgen 175
Jesus
  death of 48, 51, 52
  demons and 58
  non-resistance of 139
  opposition to 183
  Pharisees and 58
  Pilate and 58–9
  vengeance and 170
  see also Christ
Jesus im Heilsdrama (S) 168, 170, 172, 173
Jesus in the Drama of Salvation (S) ix n.1, 3 n.5
Jesus of Nazareth (S) 3 n.5
Je vois Satan (G) 155 n.400, 185 n.509
Job, book of 83, 85, 101
  God in 178
  Job in 39, 180
  Servant of YHWH in 39
  see also Hiob
"Job et le bouc émissaire" (G) 122 n.276, 128, 129
Job: The Victim of His People (G) 159 see also *La route antique des hommes pervers* (G)
"Job: Victim of His Own People" (conf. paper of G) 173
John, gospel of 58–9, 80, 91, 93, 95, 101, 115, 124, 164 n.428, 177 n.484, 179
John Paul II 75, 90, 150 n.387, 169
Johns Hopkins University 84
Jørgensen, Jørgen 175
Joseph and his brothers 56
journals/magazines/newspapers
  Christus 132–3
  Critique 87
  Espirit 16, 17, 74, 76
  Études 118
  Expansion 66
  France Catholique 69
  Frankfurter Allgemeine Zeitung 154
  Le Monde 74
  L'Express 68
  MLN 41, 42
  New York Times 169

Nouvelle Revue Théologique 44
Orientierung 16
Paris Match 112
Recherches des Sciences Religieuses 144
Semeia 134, 138, 140
Tel Quel 74
Time 156–7
Judaism 114
   Christianity and 23, 24, 47, 62
Judgment of Solomon 56, 62, 64, 76, 114–15, 139
Jung, Carl 180
   Antwort auf Hiob 178
justice 139

Kant, Immanuel 158
Katholische Akademie, Munich 48
Kearney, Richard: "Terrorisme et sacrifice" 74
Keel, Othmar: "Wie böse ist Gewalt?" 60
Khomeini, Ruhollah 81
Kingdom of God 97, 99
   law and 27
Kings, first book of the 56, 62, 64, 76, 114–15, 139
Kirchliche, politische und theologische Zeitgenossenschaft (S) 3 n.6
Knauer, Peter, review of *Brauchen wir einen Sündenbock?* (S) 39
knowledge 131
   God and 180
Koller, Hermann: *Die Mimesis in der Antike* 92
Komma, Gerwin 173
Krenn, Kurt 169 n.449

"La bande des violents" (S) 41, 42, 43
"La contingence" (G) 141 n.364
"La danse de Salomé" (G) 141 n.364
La foi chrétienne (de Lubac) 126
L'âge d'homme (publisher) 30
"La meurtre fondateur dans la pensée de Nietzsche" (G) 121 n.276, 136
"La mort de Jésus" (S) 140, 144
language and sacrifice 89, 96
"La revelation girardienne" (Oughourlian and Lefort) 40, 41

La route antique des hommes pervers (G) 122 n.278, 123 n.281, 140–1, 159, 179, 180
L'auto-organisation (Dumouchel and Dupuy) 103 n.194
La vengeance (Verdier and Courtois) 165, 167, 170
La violence de la monnaie (Aglietta and Orléan) 117
La violence et la sacré (G) 167, 177
   biblical texts and 38
   compared to *Violence and the Sacred* (G) 46
   distribution 68
   German translation 17, 18, 27, 29, 73, 78, 111, 165, 167–8
   Mensonge romantique et vérité romanesque (G) and 31
   Mort pour nos péchés (Léon-Dufour et al.) and 117
   Mythos und Kult bei Naturvölkern (Jensen) and 118
   reactions xi, 15, 30, 33, 34–5, 36, 39, 42, 46, 48, 49, 57, 58
   writing 17
   see also *Violence and the Sacred* (G)
law
   Christ and 25, 29, 66
   covenant and 26–7
   crisis and 28
   death and 26–7
   difference and 21–2, 24
   gospel/s and 23, 26, 29
   Kingdom of God and 27
   love and 23, 25, 28–9
   misfortune and 24
   precedence of xi
   raison d'être 28
   recognition and 26
   resentment and 24
   sacrifice and 20, 92
   scapegoating and 23
   Spirit and 71
   St. Paul and 25, 28, 182
   transcendence and 24
   victim and 22, 26, 28
   violence and 21–2, 23–4, 26, 58–9

Le bouc émissaire (G) 83 n.140, 157
   English translation 126, 159
   publication 114
   reactions 116
   writing 93–4, 101, 102, 105–6, 110, 114
"Le christianisme est-il une religion du sacrifice?" (Gardeil) 44
Leenhardt, Maurice: *Do kamo* 50
Lefebvre, Marcel 150 n.387, 169
Lefebvrists 150
Lefort, Guy: *Des choses cachées* (G) and 42, 43, 44–5, 114
Lefort, Guy and Jean-Michel Oughourlian: "La révélation girardienne" 40
Lehmann, Karl 71
Le Monde 74
L'enfer des choses (Dumouchel and Dupuy) 86–7, 103
Léon-Dufour, Xavier 72, 82
   on *Brauchen wir einen Sündenbock?* (S) 84, 86
   Face à la mort 82–3
Léon-Dufour, Xavier, et al.
   Mort pour nos péchés 117
Leontes (in Shakespeare) 176, 180
Le péché et la peur (Delumeau) 163–4
Le sacrifice (G) 77 n.130
"Le 'scandale' René Girard" (Buillebaud) 74
"Leskas Ephaske" (Goodhart) 88
Leslie, Paul 185
"Les malédictions" (G) 20
Lessing, Gotthold 65
Les yeux de ma chèvre (Rosny) 112, 115
letter to the Hebrews *see* Hebrews, letter to the
letter to the Romans *see* Romans, letter to the
L'Express 68
life and the cross 52
literature and mimesis 167
Livingston, Paisley 139, 146
   Disorder and Order 89 n.159
   Ingmar Bergman and the Rituals of Art 88, 117

L'œuvre de S. Anselme de Cantorbéry (Corbin) 168, 171
Logos 47, 65
   Johannine vs. Heraclitean 28
Lohfink, Norbert 39, 46 n.72, 118, 124, 138, 139, 141
   Brauchen wir einen Sündenbock? (S) and 35
   "El Dios violento del Antiguo Testamento" 134 n.331
   Gewalt und Gewaltlosigkeit im Alten Testament 104 n.198, 108
   "Il Dio violento dell'Antico Testamento" 134 n.331
   "Violent God of the Old Testament, The" (lecture) 134
Lohfink, Norbert and Rudolf Pesch: *Weltgestaltung und Gewaltlosigkeit* 48 n.76
Louvain-la-Neuve conference 34–5
love 51, 87
   freedom and 23
   law and 23, 25, 28–9
   sacrifice and 94–5
   scapegoating and 98
Lubac, Henri de 130
   desiderium naturale videndi dei xi
   La foi chrétienne 126
   Surnaturel 177
Luke, gospel of 68, 128
Luther, Martin 61, 124
   Romans (letter) and 113
Lyonnet, Stanislaus 138

McCullough, Martha *see* Girard, Martha (née McCullough)
McGill University 139–40
Mack, Burton 118
madness and rivalry 59
Magritte, René 49
Maritain, Jacques 146
Mark, gospel of 101, 102, 115
Marquard, Odo 86
Marxism 16, 49
Mass as sacrifice 99
Matthew, gospel of 58, 83, 115, 128
   law and 25

Maximus the Confessor 113, 148
medieval theology as sacrificial 43
meetings *see* colloquia/conferences/
    meetings/symposia
Mensonge romantique et vérité romanesque
    (G) 30 n.25, 68
    La violence et la sacré (G) and 31
metaphysical desire xi, 183
Metteer, Michael 102 n.184
Miller, Karl: *Doubles* 168
mimesis 65, 68, 92, 108, 176, 177
    desire for God and 179
    idolatry and 179–80
    literature and 166
    models in 182–3
    prayer and 75
    ritual and 92
    violence and 177
"Mimesis and Freedom" (S) xi, 141 n.363,
    181, 182
Mimesis conflictiva (Bandera) 88
"Mimesis und Freiheit" (S) 141 n.363
mimetic crisis/scandal 102, 104
mimeticism 8
mimetic theory x
    acceptance by S 15
"Mimetic Theory and Theology" (G) xii n.6
mimetic triangle and trinitarian love 74
Mirror of Medusa, The (Siebers) 88, 117
misfortune and law 24
MLN (journal) 41, 42
models in mimesis 182–3
modernism 24
modernity 137
    Christianity and 77
Molina, Tirso de: "El burlador de Sevilla y
    convidado de piedra" 177
"mono-causality" 107–8
    mimetic behavior and 109–10
Moosbrugger, Mathias xiii, 1, 2
    Die Rehabilitierung des Opfers 9 n.7
    "René Girard and Raymund Schwager
    on Religion, Violence, and
    Sacrifice" 9 n.7
Morin, Lucien 139
Mort pour nos péchés (Léon-Dufour et
    al.) 117

Munich conference 48
Muray, Philippe: "Quand les choses
    commenceront ..." 74
murder
    intelligence and 28
    rivalry and 25
    sacred 118
Must There Be Scapegoats? (S) 3 n.5, 125,
    152 *see also Brauchen wir einen
    Sündenbock?* (S)
Mysterium und Mimus (Schroeder) 92
myth 32, 50, 167–8
Myth, Literature, and Bible symposium
    139 n.349
"Myth and the Bible" (lecture by G) 174
    n.471
mythological, the 167–8
mythology 83, 93, 161
    Bible and 135–6
Mythology conference 181 n.496
Mythos und Kult bei Naturvölkern
    (Jensen) 118

National Endowment for the Humanities
    (Washington, DC) 85
naturalism and theology 183
nature and evil 182
Nazism 169 n.448
negative and positive behavior 70
neo-Thomism 146–7
newspapers *see* journals/magazines/
    newspapers
New Testament
    as non-sacrificial 44
    Old Testament and 35, 53, 56, 100
    universality of 95
    universalization in 32–3
    see also particular books of the New
    Testament
New York 171–2
New York Times 169
Nielsen, Claus Thomas 175
Nietzsche, Friedrich 23, 24, 29, 158
    Die fröhliche Wissenschaft 136
    Gay Science, The 136
    Götzen-Dämmerung 136
    Twilight of the Idols 136

Wagner–Nietzsche polarity 137
Niewiadomski, József xiii, 1, 2, 60, 133
　"Die Juden im Neuen Testament" 133 n.328
　"Die Mörder Gottes und die Gegner des christlichen Volkes" 133 n.328
　"Vom dogmatischen Gegner zum verhaßten Feind" 133 n.328
Niewiadomski, József and Wolfgang Palaver: *Dramatische Erlösungslehre* 181, 185–6
nihilism 30, 149, 158, 162
non-sacrificial and sacrificial interpretation 89
North, Robert 130
　"Violence and the Bible" 127
Nouvelle Revue Théologique 44
Nygren, Anders: *Commentary on Romans* 131

Old Testament 20
　ancient societies and 40
　"contradictions" within 100
　New Testament and 35, 53, 56, 100
　see also particular books of the Old Testament
One by Whom Scandal Comes, The (G) xii n.6
order and prohibitions 24
Orientierung (journal) 15
original sin
　desire and 179
　freedom and 8, 81
　violence and 182
Orléan, André and Michel Aglietta: *La violence de la monnaie* 117
Otto, Rudolf: *Das Heilige* 118
Oughourlian, Jean-Michel
　contact with G 29, 37, 67
　contact with S 33, 38
　Des choses cachées (G) and 42, 43, 44–5, 114
　Un mime nommé désir 116
Oughourlian, Jean-Michel and Guy Lefort: "La révélation girardienne" 40

Pachet, Pierre 88
paideia 65, 104
Paideia (Jaeger) 65, 68
Pajaro Dunes meeting 118, 123
Palaver, Wolfgang 2, 185, 186
Palaver, Wolfgang and József Niewiadomski: *Dramatische Erlösungslehre* 181, 185–6
Paraclete, the 95
　Satan and 93, 101
　see also Holy Spirit, the
Paradise 35
Paris Match 112
"Parole de Dieu" (series by Seuil, publisher) 84
Pascal's wager 136
passion, the 93, 180
patristic thought 47, 61–2, 91 see also church fathers; particular church fathers
Paul, St.
　on the Holy Spirit 53
　law and 22–3, 25, 28, 182
　on law and desire 20
　on law and Spirit 71
Pelagius and St. Augustine 104, 108
periodicals see journals/magazines/newspapers
persecution 93–4
　texts of 83
Pesch, Rudolf 39, 42, 58
Pesch, Rudolf and Norbert Lohfink: *Weltgestaltung und Gewaltlosigkeit* 48 n.76
Peter, first letter of 139
Peter, Karin xii, 2
Pharisees 58
pharmakon 161, 162
philosophy 9, 95, 148, 154, 158, 161
　theology and 162–3
Pieper, Josef: *Über die Liebe / About Love* ix
Pilate, Pontius 51, 58–9
Pissarek-Hudelist, Herlinde 170 n.453
Plato 65, 163
　on mimesis 92
"Plato's Pharmacy" (Derrida) 161, 162
Poliakov, Leon 155

politics 113
Pontifical Biblical Institute 134–5
popular piety 59
positive and negative behavior 70
prayer 53, 162
   mimesis and 75
   violence and 79–80
preaching 97
priesthood 79
progressivism 147
prohibitions 29
   desire and 20
   order and 24
Prophets, books of the
   universalization in 32
   see also particular books of the Prophets
Protestantism 139
   Catholicism and 143, 147, 149
Protestant Reformation 61
Provo symposium 139 n.349
Psalms, book of 42
   penitential psalms 38
   sacrifice and 79
   Western literature and 43
psychology 58
publishers
   Benziger 141 n.359
   Fischer 27
   Grasset 49, 67, 78, 90, 115, 116
   Herder 2, 73, 111, 141
   Johns Hopkins University Press 84
   L'âge d'homme 30
   Seuil 84, 86, 89
   Suhrkamp 111

"Quand les choses commenceront …" (Muray) 74

"Rache—Gerechtigkeit—Religion" (S) 165, 167, 171
Ratzinger, Joseph 120, 149, 166
   Einführung in das Christentum 92
   Entretien sur la foi 147
   Introduction to Christianity 92
Ratzinger, Joseph and Vittorio Messori: *Ratzinger Report, The* 147

Ravenna 143–4
Raymund Schwager Archive 1
Raymund Schwager Gesammelte Schriften (Collected Works) xiii, 2–3, 4
Recherches des Sciences Religieuses 144
reciprocity 27
recognition 25–6
redemption 28, 65, 91, 104, 141
   theology of 164
Reformation, Protestant 61
Regensburger, Dietmar 186
relativism 77
religion
   university life and 48
   violence and 81
   see also La violence et la sacré (G)
"Religion, Gesellschaft und Gewalt" (S) 86 n.149
"Religion and Peace" (Banawiratma) 163
Religion and Ritual meeting 118, 123
religions, continuity across 56
religiosity 50
religious experience 136, 180
"René Girard and Raymund Schwager on Religion, Violence, and Sacrifice" (Moosbrugger) 9 n.7
René Girard et le problème du mal (Deguy and Dupuy) 88, 116, 118
"René Girard et Saint Augustin" (Wohlman) 143
René Girard: Violence and Mimesis (Fleming) xiii
resentment and law 24
revelation 147, 184
   freedom and 183
   sin and 183
   violence and 32
Richard of St. Victor: *De Trinitate* 87, 89
ritual 158, 161
   mimesis and 92
rivalry
   animal and human rivalry 27–8
   Girard, Schwager, and 33
   with God 138–9
   madness and 59
   murder and 25
   recognition and 26

Romans, letter to the 20, 35, 113
Rosny, Éric de 33
  Les yeux de ma chèvre 112, 115
Rousseau, Jean-Jacques 65
Ruether, Rosemary Radford: *Faith and Fratricide* 85
Rusch, Paulus 40
Russia 173

Saarbrücken, University of 60, 64
sacralization 96
sacraments 75
sacred, the, violence and 177
sacrifice
  Augustine on 108
  Christ and 25, 53
  Christianity and 76
  church and 95, 99
  the cross 99
  forms of 79–80
  freedom and 113, 115
  Hebrews (letter to) and 8–9, 53, 57, 59, 61, 64, 74, 79–80
  language and 89, 96
  law and 20, 92
  love and 94–5
  Mass 99
  meaning/use of term 56, 64–5, 99
  overcoming of 98
  Psalms and 79
  renunciation of 95
  scandal and 95
sacrificial, the, "deconstruction" of 44, 47
sacrificial and non-sacrificial interpretation 89
sacrificial crisis 24
"sacrificialism" 95, 96
Salberg, Jean-François and Pascale Salberg 127
salvation 98
  gospel and 37
Satan 184
  Christ and 66, 68, 91, 96
  the cross and 91
  the Paraclete and 93, 101
satanization 96
scandal 102

sacrifice and 95
Scapegoat, The (G) 159 *see also Le bouc émissaire* (G)
scapegoating
  Christ and 36–7, 66, 68, 76, 94, 96, 97, 98
  history and 85–6, 99
  law and 23
  love and 98
  mechanism 28, 177, 178, 179–80
  principle 36–7
  texts and 94, 97, 99
Schenker, Adrian: *Versöhnung und Sühne* 113
Schmitt, Carl 186
Schönburg palace, Hofgeismar 135
Schroeder, Leopold von: *Mysterium und Mimus* 92
Schwager, Raymund
  archive 1
  Auf dem Weg zur Neubewertung der Tradition 3 n.4
  Beiträge zur Schöpfungslehre, Erbsündenlehre und zur Pneumatologie 3 n.6
  Brauchen wir einen Sündenbock? see particular entry for *Brauchen wir einen Sündenbock?*
  Briefwechsel mit René Girard 3 n.4
  "Christliche Herausforderung" 127
  "Christ's Death and the Prophetic Critique of Sacrifice" 134, 138–9, 140, 144
  Collected Works (*Raymund Schwager Gesammelte Schriften*) xiii, 2–3, 4
  "Das Mysterium der übernatürlichen Natur-Lehre" 113
  "Der fröhliche Wechsel und Streit" 124
  "Der geliebte Sohn und die Rotte der Gewalttäter" 60
  "Der Heilige Stuhl und die Abrüstung" 108 n.214
  "Der Nachahmer als Sündenbock" 127
  "Der Richter wird gerichtet" 127 n.301, 134, 138
  "Der Sohn Gottes und die Weltsünde" 141

"Der Tod Christi und die Opferkritik" 140
Der wunderbare Tausch 3 n.5, 141, 155, 157, 160
Dogma und dramatische Geschichte 2, 105 n.200
"Eindrücke von einer Begegnung" 108
family 129, 132, 165
Frühe Hauptwerke 3 n.5
Für Gerechtigkeit und Frieden 144
"Geschichtsphilosophie und Erlösungslehre" 85, 89
"Gewalt und Opfer" 16
Glaube, der die Welt verwandelt 28
"Haine sans raison" 132–3
Heilsdrama 3 n.5
"Hiob: Ein Weg aus der Gewalt" (conf. paper) 179 n.492
"Hiob—und der Gott seiner Verfolger" (conf. paper) 179 n.492
Jesus im Heilsdrama 168, 170, 172, 173
Jesus in the Drama of Salvation ix n.1, 3 n.5
Jesus of Nazareth 3 n.5
Kirchliche, politische und theologische Zeitgenossenschaft 3 n.6
"La bande des violents" 41, 42
"La mort de Jésus" 140, 144
"Mimesis and Freedom" xi, 141 n.363, 181, 182
"Mimesis und Freiheit" 141 n.363
Must There Be Scapegoats? 3 n.5, 152
"Rache—Gerechtigkeit—Religion" 165, 167, 171
reactions to 71, 82–3, 109, 113, 119, 123, 124, 133, 138, 140, 143, 185
"Religion, Gesellschaft und Gewalt" 86 n.149
rivalry with 33
"Théologie de la colère divine" 121 n.276
"Unfehlbare Gnade gegen göttliche Erziehung" 104 n.199, 108, n.213, 113
"Vengeance in the Old Testament" (conf. paper) 149 n.386, 170

"Versöhnung und Sühne" 113
Violence et le sacré seminar 71
"Von der biblischen Lehre der Gewaltfreiheit" 108 n.214
see also Girard–Schwager correspondence
Schwager Archive 1
Schwager-Girard collaboration 145, 148
science
  Christianity and 97
  faith and 33, 35, 119, 122
Semeia (journal) 134, 138, 140
Seneca 65, 104
Serres, Michel 47, 109
Servant of YHWH and Job 39
Seuil (publisher) 84, 86, 89
Shakespeare (G) 175
  see also *Theater of Envy, A* (G)
Shakespeare, William 83
Shamir, Yitzhak 174
Shestov, Lev 121
Siebers, Tobin: *Mirror of Medusa, The* 88, 117
Simonse, Simon 185
sin 71, 133
  Adam and Eve and 182
  freedom and xi–xii
  revelation and 183
  violence and 35
  see also original sin
Singer, Isaac B.: *Slave, The* 85
skandalon 58
Slave, The (Singer) 85
Smith, Jonathan 118, 159
Society of St. Pius 150 n.387
sociology and Christianity 119
Solomon, King, judgment of 56, 62, 64, 76, 114–15, 139
Solzhenitsyn, Aleksandr 173
Spirit, Holy *see* Holy Spirit, the
Stanford conferences/symposia
  1981 88–9, 102–3, 104, 105, 109, 110
  1987 156
  1988 149 n.386, 167, 170, 172
  1991 181 n.496
Stanford University 115, 146
Stecher, Reinhold 159, 163

Stiker, Henri-Jacques: "Sur le mode de penser de René Girard" 74–5
Stuttgart symposium 142, 145–6, 148, 151, 153
Sühne (Hoffmann) 113
Suhrkamp (publisher) 111
"Sur Job et la philosophie" (G) 121
"Sur le mode de penser de René Girard" (Stiker) 74–5
Surnaturel (de Lubac) 177
"Sur René Girard" (articles in *Espirit*) 74
surrogate victim 28
symbolicity, origin of 28
symposia *see* colloquia/conferences/meetings/symposia

Teilhard de Chardin, Pierre 28, 183
Tel Aviv symposium 174
Tel Quel (magazine) 74
"Terrorisme et sacrifice" (Kearney) 74
texts
  of persecution 50–1
  scapegoating and 94, 97, 99
textual mechanisms 158
Textual Strategies (Harari) 88
Theater of Envy, A (G) 83 n.141, 178, 181
  publication 175
  reactions 176, 177
  writing 143, 148, 155, 157, 161, 166, 169
Theodramatik III (Balthasar) 75, 102
"Théologie de la colère divine" (S) 121 n.276
Theologische Hochschule Chur 157
theology 97, 99, 172, 181–2
  medieval 43
  naturalism and 183
  philosophy and 162–3
  traditional 59, 99
Things Hidden (G) 159 *see also Des choses cachées* (G)
Thomas, Konrad 110, 111, 147–8, 173
Thomas Aquinas, St. 143
Thomism 146–7
Thought and Innovation symposium 174
Time (magazine) 156–7
To Double Business Bound (G) 67, 80–1, 176–7

Tompkins, Margaret 151, 170, 184
totalitarianism 150
"traditional theology" 59, 99
"'Tragischer Konflikt'—in Literatur und Bibel" (conf. paper by G) 148 n.385
transcendence and law 24
transcendence-over 55
triangular desire 25–6, 40, 74
trinitarian love and 87
truth and accusation 93
Turner, Victor 118
tu/vous usage 137
Twilight of the Idols (Nietzsche) 136

Über die Liebe / About Love (Pieper) ix
Understanding Origins (Varela and Dupuy) 156 n.404
Understanding Origins symposium 156
"undifferentiation" and violence 21
"Une ethnologie charismatique?" (Diéguez) 74
"Une solution de la stratégie atomique" (Descombes) 86–7
"Unfehlbare Gnade gegen göttliche Erziehung" (S) 104 n.199, 108 n.213, 113
"union in love" 87
universalization 32–3, 51–2, 74–5
  Acts of the Apostles and 35, 36–7
  New Testament and 32–3
universities
  Johns Hopkins 84
  life in 31, 34, 47, 48, 77, 142, 145, 148, 150, 156, 158, 162, 163, 164–5, 166, 171, 184
  McGill 139–40
  research in 36
  Saarbrücken 60, 64
  Stanford 115, 146
Un mime nommé désir (Oughourlian) 116
US government 105

Valadier, Paul 130
  "Bouc émissaire" 118, 119, 133, 160
Varela, Francisco and Jean-Pierre Dupuy: *Understanding Origins* 156 n.404

Vass, George 164
vengeance 143
  Jesus and 170
  "Vengeance in the Old Testament"
    (lecture by S) 149 n.386, 170
Vengeance symposium 149 n.386, 167,
  170, 172
Verdier, Raymond and Gerard Courtois:
  La vengeance 165, 167, 170
"Versöhnung und Sühne" (S) 113
Versöhnung und Sühne (Schenker) 113
victim
  hypostatic difference and 24
  innocence of 51
  intelligence and 32
  law and 22, 26, 28
  surrogate 28
victimage mechanism 22
violence
  Christianity and 36
  difference and 21
  divinity and 52
  education and 65
  emotions and 108, 110
  founding 35
  God and 37
  the Holy Spirit and 52
  human nature and 182
  law and 21–2, 23–4, 26, 58–9
  mimesis and 177
  original sin and 182
  prayer and 79–80
  recognition and 26
  rehabilitation of 28
  religion and 81
  revelation and 32
  the sacred and 177
  sin and 35
  "undifferentiation" and 21
  the Word and 45
"Violence, Difference, Sacrifice" (G) xii
"Violence and Nonviolence in the Bible"
  conference 48
"Violence and Nonviolence in the OT"
  conference 104
"Violence and the Bible" (North) 127
Violence and the Sacred (G)
  compared to *La violence et la sacré*
    (G) 46
  see also *La violence et la sacré* (G)
"Violence and the Sacred and the OT"
  conference 39
Violence et le sacré (seminar by S) 71
Violence et vérité (Dumouchel) 106 n.206,
  121 n.276
"Violent God of the Old Testament, The"
  (lecture by Lohfink) 134
Violent Origins (Hamerton-Kelly) 118
  n.262, 125 n.289, 159
virtue 65
"Vom dogmatischen Gegner zum
  verhaßten Feind" (Niewiadomski)
  133 n.328
"Von der biblischen Lehre der
  Gewaltfreiheit" (S) 108 n.214

Wagner, Richard 23, 137
Wagner–Nietzsche polarity 137
Waldheim, Kurt 169
Wandinger, Nikolaus xii, 2
Weingarten conference 179
Weltgestaltung und Gewaltlosigkeit
  (Lohfink and Pesch) 48 n.76
Western literature and Psalms 43
"Wie böse ist Gewalt?" (Keel) 60
Wiesel, Elie 157
Wieser, Thomas: "Generative Violence" 126
Williams, James 184–5
  Girardians 181 n.496
Wissenschaftliche Buchgemeinschaft,
  Darmstadt 73
witch trials 93–4
Wohlman, Avital: "René Girard et Saint
  Augustin" 143
Word, the
  violence and 45
word processing 123, 125

Yo no hajime kara kakusareteiru koto (G)
  67 see also *Des choses cachées* (G)

Zedong, Mao 65
Zenger, Erich, review of *Brauchen wir
  einen Sündenbock?* (S) 107

Raymund Schwager (L) and René Girard (R), Wiesbaden, 1994 (Photo courtesy of Herlinde Koelbl)

Lightning Source UK Ltd.
Milton Keynes UK
UKHW01f0024120718
325591UK00005B/161/P